Sharpening Psychology's Concepts

I0131089

A big problem of psychology in the tradition of C.G. Jung is that many concepts and orientations are being used by its adherents that are not really compatible with a true psychology because they have their home ground in other orientations.

It is essential for psychology that its views and concepts are ultimately derived from a rigorous notion of psychology and from the concept of its key metaphor, soul. This book diligently examines a host of diverse psychological stances and concepts using this insight as its compass. Beginning with a thorough elucidation of the unique foundational orientation of Jung's psychology as an additional crucial guidepost and then exploring the lasting significance of James Hillman's achievement in the field of psychology, it goes on to engage with works from psychologists such as Robert Romanyshyn, Mark Saban, and Stanton Marlan. By reviewing the various theses presented, examples being that synchronicity could be a gate to meaning, that one's anxiety could be a guide to psychological understanding, that there are absolutely unassimilable images, the emphasis is always on making the necessary distinctions and thereby training the mind in truly psychological thinking.

This book will be of great interest to the Jungian community, psychotherapists and psychoanalysts training in Jungian theory and practice, and those interested in psychological, theological, and philosophical issues.

Wolfgang Giegerich is a Jungian psychoanalyst, now living in Berlin, who is a regular speaker at conferences, and teacher at institutions globally. He is the author of numerous publications, including over 20 books, with several books and numerous articles translated into Italian, Japanese, Portuguese, and Spanish.

The Collected English Papers of Wolfgang Giegerich

The Collected English Papers of Wolfgang Giegerich makes the work of one of archetypal psychology's most brilliant theorists available in one place. A practicing Jungian analyst and a long-time contributor to the field, Giegerich is renowned for his dedication to the substance of Jungian thought and for his unparalleled ability to think it through with both rigor and speculative strength.

Titles in this series:

For a full list of titles in this series, please visit www.routledge.com/The-Collected-English-Papers-of-Wolfgang-Giegerich/book-series/CEPWG

Sharpening Psychology's Concepts

The Spirit of Jungian Psychology and the Danger of Faulty Thinking

Collected English Papers
Volume Eight

Wolfgang Giegerich

Routledge
Taylor & Francis Group

LONDON AND NEW YORK

Designed cover image: Getty Images

First published 2026
by Routledge
4 Park Square, Milton Park, Abingdon, Oxon OX14 4RN

and by Routledge
605 Third Avenue, New York, NY 10158

Routledge is an imprint of the Taylor & Francis Group, an informa business

© 2026 Wolfgang Giegerich

The right of Wolfgang Giegerich to be identified as author
of this work has been asserted in accordance with sections
77 and 78 of the Copyright, Designs and Patents Act 1988.

All rights reserved. No part of this book may be reprinted
or reproduced or utilised in any form or by any electronic,
mechanical, or other means, now known or hereafter
invented, including photocopying and recording, or in any
information storage or retrieval system, without permission
in writing from the publishers.

Trademark notice: Product or corporate names may be
trademarks or registered trademarks, and are used only for
identification and explanation without intent to infringe.

British Library Cataloguing-in-Publication Data
A catalogue record for this book is available from the British Library

ISBN: 978-1-041-00740-1 (hbk)
ISBN: 978-1-041-00739-5 (pbk)
ISBN: 978-1-003-61141-7 (ebk)

DOI: 10.4324/9781003611417

Typeset in Times New Roman
by Apex CoVantage, LLC

Contents

Acknowledgments

Chapter 1 first appeared as " 'Geist' or: What gives Jungian psychology its absolute uniqueness and is the source of its true life" in Jennifer M. Sandoval and John C. Knapp (Eds.), *Psychology as the Discipline of Interiority: "The Psychological Difference" in the Work of Wolfgang Giegerich*, London (Routledge) 2017, pp. 17–42. Reproduced by permission of Taylor & Francis Group.

Chapter 2, "James Hillman: An assessment" appears here for the first time. However, a Portuguese translation of it appeared under the title, "Um tributo a James Hillman", tradução: Letícia Capriotti e Gustavo Barcellos, in the Brazilian *Cadernos Junguianos* no. 8–2012, pp. 89–108.

Chapter 4, first appeared as "The psychologist as repentance preacher and revivalist: Robert Romanyshyn on the melting of the polar ice" in *Spring Vol. 82 (Symbolic Life 2009)*, Fall 2009, pp. 193–221.

Chapter 5 first appeared as "A serious misunderstanding: Synchronicity and the generation of meaning" in: *Journal of Analytical Psychology* 2012, 57, pp. 500–511.

Chapter 7 was first published as "Two Jungs. Apropos a paper by Mark Saban" in: *Journal of Analytical Psychology*, 2015, 60, 3, pp. 303–315.

Chapter 8 appeared first bilingually in English and in Japanese, translated by Tsuyoshi Inomata, as " 'Katako' and the Japanese Psyche: Reflections After Reading an Article by Megumi Yama" in: *Japanese Journal of Jungian Psychology*, vol. 8, no.1, Sept. 2022, pp. 89–108 (English), 109–129 (Japanese).

Sources and abbreviations

For frequently cited sources, the following abbreviations have been used:

CW: Jung, C.G., *Collected Works.* 20 vols. Eds. Herbert Read, Michael Fordham, Gerhard Adler, and William McGuire. Trans. R. F. C. Hull. Princeton: Princeton University Press, 1957–1979. Cited by volume and, unless otherwise noted, by paragraph number.

GW: Jung, C.G., *Gesammelte Werke.* 20 vols., various editors, Olten and Freiburg im Breisgau: Walter-Verlag, 1971–1983. Cited by volume and, unless otherwise noted, by paragraph number.

Letters: Jung, C.G., *Letters.* 2 vols. Ed. Gerhard Adler. Bollingen Series XCV: 2. Princeton: Princeton University Press, 1975.

Briefe: Jung, C.G., *Briefe.* 3 vols. Ed. Aniela Jaffé, in Zusammenarbeit mit Gerhard Adler. Olten and Freiburg i. Br.: Walter-Verlag, 1972–1973.

MDR: Jung, C.G., *Memories, Dreams. Reflections.* Rev. edn., Ed. Aniela Jaffé. Trans. Richard and Clara Winston. New York: Vintage Books, 1989. Cited by page number.

Erinn.: Erinnerungen, Träume, Gedanken von C.G. Jung. ed. by Aniela Jaffé. Zürich and Stuttgart: Rascher, 1967.

CEP: Giegerich, W., *Collected English Papers.* 6 vols. New Orleans, LA: Spring Journal Books, 2006 ff., now 8 vols. London and New York: Routledge, 2020–.

Transl. modif: Appearing at the end of a citation, this indicates that I modified the particular quotation from the *Collected Works* or *MDR* in order to bring the English translation a bit closer to the wording and spirit of Jung's original German text.

Preface

Psychology is not an objective science. In it, as C.G. Jung recognized, the psyche "uroborically" observes itself. Consequently, psychology is irrevocably subjective-objective and cannot claim to come up with objective knowledge of facts. Its insights have the status of mere interpretations of interpretations. This is psychology's distinction and at the same time its unusual difficulty. I say unusual difficulty because the phenomena it is concerned with can so easily be confused with and taken as events or states that are part of our ordinary—be it everyday, or be it scientific—experience of reality. The mind is susceptible to the temptation to approach soul phenomena with overfamiliar thought patterns, categories, and assumptions appropriate to ego-consciousness and for its understanding of empirical reality.

This is why a training of the mind is essential for anyone who wants to do psychology, a training that turns it into a truly psychological mind in the first place. With the word training I do not refer to the well-established institution of training-analysis for future psychoanalysts, mainly because it is an open question whether a given training-analysis is a truly psychological one, or is rather one conducted in a commonplace personalistic spirit. What I mean is a training of the *mind*, each interested person's own mind, and a training with a view to learning to make the subtle and yet radical distinctions that are constitutive of a truly psychological psychology and to become practiced in using them. The radical distinctions are radical because they are not passive differences, but psychological acts: One's pushing off from all commonsensical thinking and moving across a threshold.

Neither teachers nor books can train the mind. This training can only happen inside, in each person's mind, and must be performed by this mind itself. But teachers and books can nevertheless be helpful. The present book critically examines in its several chapters the general stances as well as individual conceptions of other psychologists, particularly also their mis-understandings or misconstruals of "psychology as the discipline of in-teriority", and, using them as a kind of whetstone, sharpens and refines psychology's concepts and thus "discerns the spirits to see whether they are" truly psychological or not. One can often learn more from errors than from perfect models. Errors or misunderstandings that one finds clearly spelled out in black and white provide a stepping stone for the mind. They both force and help it to grasp existing crucial differences, thus to become more conscious of, and able to explicitly and more precisely articulate, its own position, so that it can come truly home to itself. For me at least this proved true in writing the essays included in this volume. May this also be the experience of the reader.

Chapter 1

"*Geist*", or: What gives Jungian psychology its absolute uniqueness and is the source of its true life[1]

At the end of his chapter on Sigmund Freud in his *Memories, Dreams, Reflections* Jung states:

> It is a widespread error to imagine that I do not see the value of sexuality. On the contrary, it plays a large part in my psychology as an essential—though not the sole—expression of psychic wholeness. But my main concern has been to investigate, over and above its personal significance and biological function, its spiritual aspect and its numinous meaning, and thus to explain what Freud was so fascinated by but was unable to grasp.
>
> (p. 168)

He adds by way of corroboration that the works in which his thoughts on this subject are contained are "The Psychology of the Transference" and the *Mysterium Coniunctionis*, both studies of his late period. A difficulty posed for us by this quote lies in the translation. By saying this I do not refer to the inaccuracies or mistakes it contains, because in this particular case they do not really change the basic meaning that Jung wants to convey. The serious problem is caused by the translation, "*ihre geistige Seite*" as "its spiritual aspect". Although not a mistake ("*geistig*" is really untranslatable), it is nevertheless misleading. We encounter the same problem a few pages earlier in the same chapter where Jung discusses Freud's attitude toward sexuality in more detail. I quote only the following passage:

> Although, for Freud, sexuality was undoubtedly a *numinosum*, his terminology and theory seemed to define it exclusively as a biological

1 Written in 2015.

DOI: 10.4324/9781003611417-1

function. It was only the emotionality with which he spoke of it that re-vealed the deeper elements reverberating within him. Basically, he wanted to teach—or so at least it seemed to me—that, regarded from within, sexuality included spirituality and had an intrinsic meaning. But his con-cretistic terminology was too narrow to express this idea.

(p. 152)

Jung's text reads, ". . . *daß, von innen her betrachtet, Sexualität auch Geis-tigkeit umfasse, oder Sinn enthalte*" (that regarded from within, sexuality also comprehends *Geistigkeit*, or contains meaning). "[It] comprehends *Geistigkeit*" is equivalent to "its *geistig* side" ("side", rather than "aspect") in the first quote. "Spirituality" does not capture the particular meaning of *Geistigkeit*. Both "spiritual" in the former quote and "spirituality" in the lat-ter are a stopgap solution for the rendering of a not really translatable word. This is not merely a translation problem and not only locally relevant for these particular passages about sexuality. What Jung says here illustrates, by way of this one example of sexuality, his general approach and "main concern". The understanding of Jung's entire psychology is at stake.

Difference

Before we turn to the question of what Jung's words *geistig* and *Geistigkeit* mean and what precise aspect of the reality of sexuality is Jung's foremost focus according to his statement, his statement's logical form alone tells us that Jung operates here with a crucial distinction: Between Freud and himself. Already in 1929 he had written about the "opposition" between the two, about "The Freud – Jung Antithesis".[2] We do well to comprehend such conceptions as more than merely descriptive historical accounts. Other than historians, as psychologists we are on principle not interested in facts as such; just as in dreams we do not comprehend the figures in them (e.g., the dreamer's mother or father, his girlfriend, the figure of the family doctor) on the "object level" as the people they are outside the dream, in external so-cial reality, but rather as personifications of the dreamer's or the soul's own different internal tendencies or "voices", so we can also conceive of the

---

2   "Der Gegensatz Freud und Jung", see *GW* 4, pp. 383 ff. In *CW* 4, pp. 333 ff. it is translated a bit more meekly as "Freud and Jung: Contrasts".

figure of "Freud" in Jung's autobiographical narrative as an *internal* other.[3] As much as this text is ostensibly about Freud and Jung and the difference between them, the difference has its ground not simply in Jung's empirical observation of facts "out there".

We are all the more justified in reading the text in this way because Jung himself prefaced his *Memories, Dreams, Reflections* as a whole with the express comment that ". . . I have now undertaken . . . to tell the myth of my life. I can however . . . only 'tell stories.' Whether they are true is not the problem. The only question is whether it is *my* fable, *my* truth" (p. 3, transl. modif.). Jung conceives his autobiographical narrative not as factual historical account, but as the self-display and unfolding, in story form, of the inner logic of his life, *his* life.

By the same token, when Jung ostensibly shows in these passages what "*his* main concern" is, we have to understand that in a deeper sense he describes *psychology*'s "main concern" (as he sees it). By referring to the contrast between "Freud" and "Jung" his topic is of course his deepest needs *as psychologist* (rather than as private personality) and that means the essential *theoretical* needs of psychology itself. The personal names are abbreviations for different conceptions of the ultimate task and purpose of psychology. And the fact that "this main concern" needs to be articulated by means of the "Freud"–"Jung" *antithesis* in our passages has the function of suggesting that psychology's "main concern" can only be described as a fundamental contrast to its (internal) Other. Psychology constitutes itself by pushing off from its one (the "Freud") side, because only in this way can it come truly into its own, to its "main concern". It establishes, and operates with, a fundamental difference. This difference (here exemplified by the Freud–Jung opposition) is indispensable for psychology—for a psychology in the tradition of C.G. Jung, a "psychology *with* soul"—and because it is indispensable (indeed its constitutive principle), we call it *the psychological difference*.

Freud too knew and worked with opposites, e.g., conscious–unconscious, *eros–thanatos*, etc. But for intrinsic reasons his psychology did not need to be set off against Jung's (or any other psychology) in order to push off from it and come home to itself, the way Jung's psychology *within itself* pushed

---

3 With this focus, the focus of a psychological (rather than historical) reading on psychology's needs, we are at the same time freed of the entire question of whether Jung's description of Freud is factually correct and a fair assessment or whether it is not perhaps based on misunderstandings and misconstruals.

off from Freudian psychoanalysis and furthermore from consulting room and personalistic psychology as such. Freud's psychology was not structured by and did not operate with the psychological difference. The opposites just mentioned are pairs on the same level, alternatives, even mutually exclusive. Each side of any of those pairs of opposites is defined as simply being what the other side is not. Of course, Freud had in a certain sense also pushed off from the previous types of psychology that did not work with the concept of the unconscious. He established his mode of dream interpretation clearly in contrast to former traditional ideas about dreams. However, *this* kind of "pushing off" was something very different because the earlier theories remained external to and logically irrelevant for psychoanalysis. The latter did not need them in order to come into its own by pushing off from them as from its own internal other. Similarly, Alfred Adler did not need a "Freud"–"Adler" antithesis for his thought's coming into its own, although literally he, too, had developed his psychology in open contrast to Freud.

The psychological difference that we discover at work in Jung's cited passages is characterized by a completely different form of relation between the opposites and a different form of pushing off. Jung's psychology has within itself the fantasy of being the *negation* of the Freudian position and this fantasy is, so to speak, its foundation myth. We see this logic of negation also in another instance of the psychological difference in Jung, namely in his crucial distinction between the "personal" and the "collective" unconscious. His psychology does not simply reject (what Jung sees as) the Freudian "personal unconscious". In order to be able to believe in the "collective unconscious" and the *Geistigkeit* of sexuality Jung does not deny or simply turn his back on the "biological function" and "personal significance" side of sexuality exclusively seen by (Jung's) "Freud". No, both "Freudian" tenets are fully confirmed and accepted by Jung's psychology and even interiorized into it as referring to an integral part of the complete reality of the human psyche. In other words, there is not a splitting them off and keeping them outside. Jung does not, as Adler did, *replace* Freud's psychology by his own. On the contrary, the Freudian tenets mentioned are precisely integrated into Jung's psychology—but integrated only as *sublated* realities from which to push off to the standpoint of the "collective unconscious" or to that of the "*geistig* side". This means three things:

1. The relation between the opposite sides of the psychological difference is hierarchical or vertical rather than a horizontal relation of alternatives on the same level (the way we speak, for example, of the political left and right). Jung says unambiguously, in the first passage cited, that

his "main concern has been to investigate, *over and above* its [sexuality's] personal significance and biological function, its spiritual aspect and its numinous meaning" (my emphasis). "Over and above"[4] indicates that its personal significance and biological function are still seen and appreciated as valid, but they are reduced to a sublated moment within psychology proper.

2. Psychology's pushing off from, and thus negating and sublating, the one side is not directed at an external, foreign element. It happens fundamentally within *itself*. The "Freud" from whom Jung pushes off is internal to Jung's own thinking. His pushing off from him is a strictly internal relation and internal logical move; what it pushes off from is not cast outside, not exiled. Psychology within itself negates it as *its own* basis; it sublates an integrated and acknowledged element of itself, and *within itself* rises above this basis to its own true home. With another metaphor, this rising above or negating the prevailing initial standpoint, and thus the beginning of true psychology, is in our second quote represented by Jung as a radical shift from an external view to one's "regard[ing] [the phenomenon] *from within*", or, to say it with a phrase from a late letter of Jung's, as our "changing our point of view and looking at it from the *other* side, i.e., not from outside but *from inside*" (*Letters 2*, p. 580, to Earl of Sandwich, 10 August 1960, my italics). Psychology has to be the discipline of interiority. In yet other and more succinct conceptual terms, the psychological difference is the difference between seeing a phenomenon "from the point of view of the ego" versus seeing the same phenomenon "from the point of view of the soul",[5] which shows once more why I speak of the *psychological* difference.

3. *To* what it pushes off and rises up, cannot be obtained without this *negation* of its own internal basis. It comes into being only through this act of pushing off from the other "side" or through the shift to the "from inside" standpoint. The *"geistig* side" and what Jung calls the "collective unconscious" are not always already naturally and factually given, in the same sense that the biological function of sexuality, to stay with this example, is an empirical positive fact. But the *"geistig* side" and along with it true *psychology* not only come about through negation, they are also in themselves in the status of absolute negativity. This means that there simply and honestly *is* nothing to be seen and therefore also nothing to be "grasped" *for* a strictly empiricist, positivistic approach, or "from outside", or "from

---

4 With equal right Jung could have said "under and beneath", which shows that the spatial metaphor is used to express a *logical* and not a spatial difference.

5 *MDR* p. 314, transl. modif.

the point of view of the ego" (even if the investigating psychologist is as intelligent and gifted as Freud and, what is more, even if unconsciously he should be personally deeply fascinated by this "nothing"). Furthermore, the *geistig* side's and psychology's absolute negativity means that they need to be "made": Soul-*making*.[6] *If* there *is* to be psychology, then one has to *rise* to that "over and above" level and by rising to it *create* it for the first time since it is not positively given, not always already "there" and merely waiting to be discovered. This is the predicament *and* distinction of psychology. It is what gives Jungian psychology its uniqueness. (Jung's) "Freud" did not rise to this level, did not regard things *from inside*, did not enter true psychology. We could also say: he did not perform the psychological difference. He stayed on the obvious, naturalistic or positivistic level of the personal and biological, that is to say, the level of "the *psychic*" (in contrast to "the *psychological*") and consequently also did not break through what for Jung was the narrowness of "his concretistic terminology and theory".

"Numinous meaning"

The cold objectivity of substantial contents

If the "*geistig* side" is first created in the act of our rising to it, it seems to be something entirely subjective. But this is contradicted by the fact that the difference between Freud and Jung is primarily described as not merely a subjective one of the psychologists' different perspectives, their different ways of viewing. The way Jung describes it, it is ultimately a difference that goes right through the *reality* which is to be assessed and comprehended, i.e., right through the phenomenon of sexuality itself. According to Jung's presentation here it is sexuality itself that is divided into two halves, as it were; *it* has two "sides": On the one hand, *ihre geistige Seite* and, on the other hand, the "side" of its personal significance and biological function. The difference is objective, it has its ground in the real itself (which is why I pointed out above that I prefer the translation "side" over "aspect", since the latter word inevitably implies a viewing subject and what is seen from its point of view). One might therefore almost feel tempted to say that the

---

6   Whereas soul needs to be made, psyche, as rooted in the human animal, is something natural and positively given.

difference is "ontological". Sexuality, this is obviously Jung's underlying claim, *has* this "side" (just as it also has the other personal-significance and biological-function side). It has both sides the way a 24-hour period consists not only of day but also of night (or vice versa), or the way that a word has a meaning side in addition to its sound side, and the way we all, in addition to our conscious personality, carry a "shadow" within ourselves.

Likewise, when Jung says that sexuality "has an intrinsic meaning" or when he speaks of "its numinous meaning" he does not want to say that sexuality is something *meaningful*, in other words, a source of meaning (for us),[7] because this would make it, the "other side", precisely part of the "first side", the personal significance side. What he suggests is something else, namely that it objectively *contains* a meaning that is one of the essential integral features making up the total reality of the phenomenon of sexuality.[8] This meaning is part of its nature much like vitamins are contained in certain fruits, or nitrogen in the air. Those fruits contain the vitamins regardless of whether we eat them and benefit from those vitamins or not. In the same way, this meaning, according to Jung, is objectively inherent in sexuality, even if it is not seen or felt. A complete description of the make-up or logical constitution of sexuality, this is Jung's thesis, must include, and do justice to, its meaning quality.

However, whereas vitamins are special ingredients or components *in* fruits, separable from other chemical components, and have an important nutritional *function* for us, meaning is, according to this thesis, not really an ingredient, but the logical *character* or *nature* of the phenomenon of sexuality *as a whole*. Sexuality has—for Jung and *if* seen "from within"—an inherent *meaning structure*; it is itself a meaning phenomenon the way words, or paintings, or novels are meaning phenomena, in contrast to stones, trees, sunshine. The latter simply are what they are; they represent themselves as what they are. Not so a word, say, "table". It does not represent *itself*, not represent itself as what it is, namely, a sequence of sounds or letters. A word is not content and satisfied with representing itself. Rather, it is only what it is by pointing away from itself to the idea, image or reality that it *means*.

---

7 On the problem of the meaning of "meaning" in Jungian psychology cf. my "A serious misunderstanding: synchronicity and the generation of meaning", in: *Journal of Analytical Psychology* 2012, 57, pp. 500–511.

8 Needless to say, "sexuality" in Jung's text always refers to the phenomenon of *human* sexuality.

It points to the meaning by negating itself, having, as it were, the internal logic of, "*it* (the meaning) must increase, but *I* (the combination of sounds) must decrease". The meaning structure is essentially an "about structure". A tree is not "about" anything, does not point away from itself. It does not even point to itself: It simply *is*, it presents itself.

But this fact that a word or a novel has a meaning structure obviously does not also mean that it has the function of "providing" Meaning (with a capital M) to us ("meaning" in the subjective, experiential, or "quest of meaning" sense: Making life, human existence as such meaningful). Even if we don't like it, find it boring or quite trivial, it nevertheless is a meaning phenomenon (in the lower-case sense of meaning). It would be ridiculous to try to find Meaning in the word "table", but just as ridiculous to deny that it is truly a meaning phenomenon. We could also say that the meaning we are concerned with here is not *functional* (not of "personal significance" for us), but describes the cold, sober, logical reality of all meaning phenomena.

The psychological difference goes right through the notion of numinosity itself. The psychological difference divides this term's two radically different, indeed even mutually exclusive senses:

- a person's being deeply stirred or even spell-bound by a *numinosum*, his subjective emotionality and fascination, i.e., the *effect* on the ego, on the one hand,
- and, on the other hand, "its [the phenomenon's] numinous meaning", i.e., its involving the *cognition* of a *numen*[9] (to put it into the old religious language), in other words, its *objective* substantial (Jung would say: "Archetypal") *contents*, its psychological subject matter, the *prima materia*, which is in need of professional ("scientific", scholarly, or therapeutic) psychological investigation and explanation.

What now needs to be elucidated is how the "meaning" of sexuality referred to by Jung (its "*geistig* side") can on the one hand be something that must be created by our rising to the "over and above" level and how it can nevertheless, on the other hand, be an objective "side" of this phenomenon itself. Here it becomes indispensable to try to get a clearer idea of what

---

9 *Numen* in contrast to *numinosum* (which refers to how something is subjectively experienced).

geistig, Geistigkeit (and also *Geist*) in the present context mean and why the translation "spiritual(ity)" does not really capture their specific meaning.

One reason why spirituality (German *Spiritualität*), especially as used in present-day psychological circles, is inappropriate in Jung's statements and indeed misleading is that the idea of "spirituality" predominantly refers to or involves a human subject; its experience of or sensitivity and openness to things of the spirit; its deep attachment to religious values; its "spiritual" practices such as in transcendental meditation, yoga, Zen; or also, in a very general sense, its quest for meaning and its longing for transcendence or for "the sacred". But "*geistig*" and "*Geistigkeit*" in Jung's sentences are used in a strictly objective sense. We already know that in one way it of course makes a tremendous difference whether the *geistig* side is seen and adequately appreciated ("grasped") or not, and this is precisely the bone of contention between Jung and Freud. But in Jung's statement (about sexuality's *also* comprehending *Geistigkeit*) this is not the issue, and not implied. With this statement Jung merely makes a simple factual assertion about the reality of sexuality per se. His point is precisely that despite the fact that Freud was not able to *grasp* it this "*geistig* side" nevertheless exists.

"Grasping": The intellectual obligation and the rigorous process of understanding

No doubt, the quest of meaning is one important topic in Jung's psychology. But it is evident that in our two quotes it is not the "quest of meaning" Jung who is speaking. The one who speaks here is the psychologist Jung who considered himself a natural scientist (in his sense of the word); it is the psychological scholar and theoretician who considers it his (his psychology's) "main concern" to "investigate and explain [*zu erforschen und zu erklären*], over and above its personal significance and biological function", the *geistig* side of sexuality. (Of course, we must add, the *geistig* side not only of sexuality, which merely happens to be singled out here in Jung's discussion because it played an essential role in his strife with Freud, but of all psychologically relevant phenomena.) And the fact that, in Jung's eyes, for Freud sexuality was indeed a *numinosum,* and as such possessed very great personal significance, was precisely not enough. "The emotionality with which he [Freud] spoke of it" is, after all, simply that aspect of personal experiential significance *"over and above" which* that domain only begins which psychology is assigned to investigate. Anyone can be *fascinated* by something. This would be a subjective emotion and part of someone's personal psychic life. But psychologically that is neither here nor there. *Fascination and emotionality are just phenomena, "symptoms". They are not yet psychology.* What Jung demands of the psychologist is that he be able to *"grasp"* (i.e., comprehend) and "explain" (i.e., unfold, spell out in detail) the objective content of the reality in question (as Jung himself felt he had done in his late works, "The Psychology of the Transference" and *Mysterium Coniunctionis*). That this reality may in certain persons have given rise to subjective fascination is not relevant. Grasping, explaining, and the question of the right terminology, the right theoretical framework, are what counts when it is a question of the *objective* psyche.

About Freud Jung states, concerning his one-sided view of sexuality: "Perhaps some inner experience of his own might have opened his eyes; but then his intellect would have reduced any such experience to 'mere sexuality' or 'psychosexuality'" (p. 153).[10] Again we see that it all depends on the *intellect*, on the *"terminology* and *theory"* (we could also say: the entire mindset) and not on "some inner experience of his own"! Jung's example of *his* "Freud" shows us clearly that if it is a question of doing justice to the substantial *contents* of the soul's life, what is needed is not subjective emotion, not a state of fascination, not experienced numinosity. What counts is exclusively what the mind makes of it, to what degree and depth it is capable of apperceiving and comprehending it.

This is why we also have to criticize Jung for saying about Freud (at the end of the next sentence, after the one about the crucial importance of the intellect) that "he was a great man, and what is even more, a man touched and taken hold of in his innermost depth [*ein Ergriffener*]" (p. 153, transl. modif.).[11] This "what is even more" does not make sense. Jung contradicts himself. The fact that (Jung's) Freud was not able in any way to grasp and give expression to

10 Jung's idea of a "reduction to 'psychosexuality'" is a beautiful example of the psychological difference at work: *"psycho*sexuality" represents the merely "psychic", but misses out on the truly "psychological".

11 The translation of *MDR* has, "a man in the grip of his daimon". The point of the German word is, however, that it just talks about a person's subjective state without suggesting any agent that caused this state or being interested in who may have caused it. And the choice of "his daimon" as the causing agent is also an inappropriate fiction since what this context refers to is the *Ergriffenheit* by the (not grasped) "numinous meaning" of the real phenomenon of *sexuality*. On p. 168, *MDR* renders the adjective *ergriffen* much better with "deeply stirred".

the real content he had been touched by and taken hold of means that he had not been up to his own task, the very task specifically set for him by the soul. This deficiency so clearly described by Jung is apt to subtract from Freud's greatness—rather than raise him even above it, as Jung here suggests. The *greatness* of an artist or philosopher lies in no way in what he experienced in his private subjectivity and was deeply touched by, not in "the emotionality with which he spoke of it" (Jung about Freud, p. 152). It lies exclusively in the degree of his power to grasp it in its depth and to authoritatively articulate it in a form that makes it accessible to mankind, to the *generality*. The great man is great because he produces a great *work*, gives *objectivity* to subjectively experienced feelings or ideas. To emotionally experience "the numinous" in one's inner is neither a psychological virtue nor a mark of distinction to be proud of, and being *unconsciously* in the grip of it least of all.

"In retrospect I can say that I alone logically pursued the two problems which most interested Freud: the problem of 'archaic vestiges,' and that of sexuality", Jung said in the same chapter (p. 168).[12] What for us is noteworthy in this statement is not only that (according to his own assessment) he, Jung, pursued the questions that Freud was most interested in but for intellectual reasons[13] was unable to pursue, but also the converse: That while Freud was gripped by the numinosity of sexuality (even if unbeknownst to him), *Jung was not.* Sexuality was not a *numinosum* for him. He makes this very clear in the same chapter on Freud when he describes his overall reaction to the spirit of Freudian psychoanalysis.

> To me it was a profound disappointment that all the efforts of the probing mind had apparently succeeded in finding nothing more in the depths of the psyche than the all too familiar and "all-too-human" limitations. I had grown up in the country, among peasants, and what I was unable to learn in the stables I found out from the Rabelaisian wit and the untrammeled fantasies of our peasant folklore. Incest and perversions were

---

12 "I alone": The Jung of *MDR* has a clear awareness of the uniqueness of his psychology. And what makes it unique is not that he added new empirical observations and new insights (new semantic contents), but that he performed the syntactical move from the whole personalistic ("psychic") level to the fundamentally other level of true *psychology* (in Jung's quote referred to by means of the reference to the "collective unconscious" and to [the "*geistig* side" of] sexuality).

13 This must of course not be confused with a claim that Freud was not an "intelligent" man.

no remarkable novelties to me, and did not call for any special explanation. Along with criminality, they formed part of the black lees that
spoiled the taste of life by showing me only too plainly the ugliness and
meaninglessness of human existence. That cabbages thrive in dung was
something I had always taken for granted. In all honesty I could discover
no helpful insight in such knowledge. "It's just that all of those people
are city folks who know nothing about nature and the human stable,"
I thought, sick and tired of these ugly matters.

(p. 166)

Nothing numinous. Nothing remarkable. No fascination or *Ergriffenheit*.
Only the "all too familiar and 'all-too-human'", "the human *stable*" (!), or
even: Only "sick and tired of these ugly matters". So much for the *numinosum* aspect. The other important aspect for us that comes out in this passage
is that we get a clear idea of what Jung thought about the importance for
psychology of the other, non-*geistig* side of the psychological difference,
i.e., the personal significance and biological function side, and that indeed
he decidedly pushed off from it. The experiential and behavioral reality of
sexuality is described as being irrelevant for psychology: Boring ("all too
familiar"), not remarkable (not worthy of closer attention), and not calling
for any special explanation—in contrast to what for Jung absolutely needed
to be investigated and explained and what in fact got his in-depth attention
in his late works: The *Geistigkeit* of the phenomenon.

In this connection it may be helpful to also call attention to a paragraph
in *MDR* (p. 188) concerning Jung's Red Book in which he discusses that
and why "I gave up this estheticizing tendency in good time, in favor of a
rigorous process of *understanding*. . . . For me, reality meant scientific comprehension." This shift is his pushing off to true psychology not from the
"all-too-human", but from his own previous indulging in and celebrating
numinous feelings through this estheticizing tendency, a celebration that in
the following paragraph (unfortunately omitted in the English edition) he
brands as "the tyranny of unconscious presuppositions": "In order to free
oneself from the tyranny of unconscious presuppositions both are needed:
fulfillment of the intellectual as well as the ethical obligation" (*Erinnerungen*, p. 192, my transl.). Freud was merely unconsciously (and thus honestly) gripped. But the early Jung, the Jung of the *Red Book*, consciously
indulged in mainly self-induced numinous feelings and images. But this is
what the mature Jung uncompromisingly distanced himself from—whereas

many Jungians have succumbed again to the desire to indulge in the egoic cult of (mostly simulated[14]) numinous emotionality, *at the cost of* "its [whatever phenomenon's] numinous meaning" as the objective *prima materia* and "*geistig* side" that quite soberly needs to be made the subject of "scientific comprehension", of a "rigorous process of *understanding*" and "the efforts of the probing mind": Intellectual—and hopefully truly intelligent, insightful—*work*, work on the contents of the objective *soul*.

To sum up this discussion about the numinous: By speaking of sexuality's numinous meaning Jung is precisely not referring to its possible fascination *effect upon the ego*. The term "numinous" is in this phrase roughly synonymous with what Jung elsewhere called "archetypal". It simply points to the contents[15] of the so-called "collective unconscious" in contradistinction to the "all too familiar and 'all-too-human'" that is the topic of personalistic psychology. The two phrases, "its *geistig* side" and "its numinous meaning" are also synonymous, but of course with slight difference of emphases.

Although what "*geistig*" means has by no means been sufficiently elucidated and will occupy us further in the next sections, I am ready—after all that we have heard about Jung's emphasis on grasping, intellect, scientific comprehension, rigorous process of understanding, intellectual obligation—to offer a better (even if far from ideal) translation instead of "its spiritual aspect". I suggest the wording, "its noetic side". "Noetic" brings with it the rich association with the Greek *Noys* (or *Nus*). Of course its drawback is that it is not a term of ordinary language the way "*geistig*" in German and "spiritual" in English are. But this word at least avoids the faulty ideas evoked by "spiritual" ("*spirituell*" in German) and points in the right direction. We could perhaps also have considered "intellective" as a possible translation. However, an uninformed reader might understand this (likewise unusual) word in the abstract sense of "intellectual" (as commonly used today), which would be misleading. The rarely used word "noetic" is free of this danger.

---

14 Whereas in (Jung's) Freud the fascination was a symptom (something that shows that the *soul* has been at work), in many Jungians it is a self-stylization, the work of the modern ego lusting after "high" feelings and self-affirmation. Cf. Michael Whan, "Aurum Vulgi: Alchemy in Analysis, a Critique of a Simulated Phenomenon", in: Dale Mathers (ed.), *Alchemy and Psychotherapy*, London and New York: Routledge, 2014, pp. 170–183.

15 In order to fully present and unfold their internal logical complexity, these contents need book-length essays, as in the case of the "*geistig* side" of sexuality Jung's "The Psychology of Transference" and *Mysterium Coniunctionis* show.

"Geistigkeit"

Overcoming the imagination: Its systematic blindness to the mind's syntactical form and to process and performance

The second reason for my critical rejection of "spiritual" and "spirituality" for *geistig* and *Geistigkeit* in Jung's sentences is that the very idea of "spirit" evokes wrong, far too lofty associations and mystifications. If one wants to grasp the specific meaning of German *Geist* in the sense that underlies the terms *geistig* and *Geistigkeit* as used in Jung's quotes (and only this particular sense of *Geist* is of concern here), then "spirit" and "spirituality" must be kept away (as also any sense of *pneuma*, the "pneumatic", and also the again different concept of "mind").

Concerning the term *Geist*, Jungian psychology and particularly archetypal psychology is haunted by views that have been pointedly articulated in James Hillman's (in its own way admirable) construal of the relation between "spirit" and "soul" in his essay, "Peaks and Vales".[16] A critical discussion of this paper will in the following allow us to develop a clearer idea of the very different reality of *Geist*. Without my wishing to repeat Hillman's argument here in detail, I can at least summarize a few of his essential ideas, namely, that he points out that through the decisions of Councils of the Early Church (Nicaea, 787; Constantinople, 869) the idea of human nature "devolved from a tripartite cosmos of spirit, soul, and body, to a dualism of spirit (or mind) and body (or matter)" and that consequently "that third place, the intermediate realm of psyche—which is also the realm of images and the power of imagination—" was exiled by "theological, spiritual men" (p. 54). Long battles between spirit and soul, between abstractions and images, between iconoclasts and idolaters had been fought (p. 55). He claims that "By returning to image, Jung returned to the soul,

---

16 In: James Hillman et al., *Puer Papers*, Irving: Spring Publications, 1979, pp. 54–74 (all further references to Hillman's work in this chapter are taken from this publication). I critiqued some aspects of the "peaks–vales" ("spirit–soul", "thought–image") opposition also in my "Afterword", in: Wolfgang Giegerich, David L. Miller, Greg Mogenson, *Dialectics & Analytical Psychology*, New Orleans, LA: Spring Journal Books, 2005, pp. 107–112. But after what I wrote in the previous section of the present paper, it should be clear that I completely agree with Hillman's general attack in his "Peaks and Vales" paper on spirituality in the sense, for example, of Maslow's "peak experiences".

reversing the historical process that in 787 had depotentiated images and in 869 had reduced soul to rational intellectual spirit. Jung said that his base is in a third place between the opposites spirit and matter: *esse in anima"* (p. 56). Hillman then goes on in a section devoted to the opposition of "Soul and Spirit" to unfold the image of "peaks" as the imaginal place of the spirit and the image of "vales" as the locus of soul and soul-making.

My interest is not to raise the valid objection that the soul by no means disappeared from theology and Western thought. Until way into the 18th century people's and official theology's main religious concern was care for the immortal soul. To mention one example, is Dante's *Divina Commedia* concerned with either one of the only two realms left according to Hillman (with the "rational intellectual spirit", or, conversely, with the "body [or matter]"), and not much rather with soul? Nor do I want to go into the other necessary objection that as a matter of course Jung did not and could not possibly have reversed the historical process and returned something that had been lost (nobody can do that, probably not even God, as Jung full-well knew: "We cannot turn the wheel backwards; we cannot go back to the symbolism that is gone", *CW* 18 § 632). To want to attempt such a thing would be illusionary wishful thinking and nostalgia. I leave such possible objections about questions of fact aside and turn to psychologically more relevant ones.

It is Hillman who sets up and celebrates the dissociation between peaks and vales as being absolutely fundamental. It is he who tears apart (not "spirit" and "matter", but) "spirit" and "soul" and reduces (not soul, but) the *concept* of spirit to the extreme, and extremely emaciated, form of meaning nothing but "abstractions" and "rational intellectual spirit". Spirit is not the problem, but his narrow-minded, reductive concept of it, the interpretation he gives it, the straightjacket into which he forces it. *He* unwittingly practices the very abstractions that he ostensibly fights. What he does (and it is a doing, *his* doing!) contradicts his message. His own mind that is speaking here is a tough abstract intellect and, notwithstanding his *use* of images and his *plea* for the imaginal, is not really a soulful mind. Certainly, "peaks" and "vales" are images; but in Hillman's text they are precisely images *for abstractions*, if not used *as abstractions*. Inasmuch as image is construed in total opposition to thought, his own thinking is not imaginal in style, but an example of abstract thought.

Precisely by trying to "reconstitute" (p. 54) "that third place" as an intermediate realm of psyche in between, he himself solidifies the split because this third in between inevitably functions as a wedge. This is why the recourse to "image" and "imagination" as the cure for "the malnourished root of Western psychological culture" (p. 54) is its own trap and not at all the cure. The restoration of the realm of images is a cop-out because it "solves" the problem detected by Hillman only on the semantic or content level, the level of *what* is imagined,[17] while precisely reiterating and confirming it in the very style of his own thinking, in the syntax or logical form of consciousness. That third place has to stay "in between" and a "spatial" *intermediary*, when the real psychological task to be achieved would be to *actually perform* the *mediation* or the *mysterium coniunctionis*. Subsisting, substantiated realm—or act to be performed? That is here the question. The third *place* and the intermed*iary* are offered only as a remedy "out there", in *what* is imagined, in the "object" or the semantic content of the imagination (the imagination *about* the constitution of the soul). But the structure of the imagining mind itself, its own syntax or logical form, remains unaffected. It is inherent in the form of the imagination that it "*externalizes*", presents what it presents in spatial and temporal and sensuous forms and as objects, entities. It inevitably reifies and personifies. The imaging mind's own *logical constitution*, by contrast, is by definition out of reach for this mind. The imagination cannot reach and reflect and "cure" itself.

This irrevocable limitation of the image-approach promoted by Hillman (I say "irrevocable" because the limitation is rooted in its own logic) is highlighted when he emphasizes that "Images were venerated and adored all through the antique world" (p. 55) and himself advocates the necessity of the notion of Gods (with capital G!) and of psychological polytheism for soul-making and imaginal psychology. That he does not favor "belief" in the Gods in a theological manner but takes them merely metaphorically[18] makes no difference. Whether this way or that, the notion of Gods comes with and confirms the fundamental *logical* structure of *otherness* and *externality*, even if the Gods are *semantically* imagined to be "within" (p. 72). Due to its own otherness structure, the image-approach is systematically blind to the fundamental difference between "*intermediary* in between", on the one hand, and actual "*mediation*" (which mediates between the two extremes), on the other hand, between what is imagined as a quasi-ontic

---

17 We could also say that he merely "acted out" (on the intellectual level, in the imagination), but did not *erinnern*.

18 I say "merely" despite Hillman's protest against any "merely metaphorical" (p. 59).

"realm" in the middle of a "tripartite cosmos" and the real process and performance (actuosity) of mediation, between semantic content and syntactical form of mind.

This difference is ultimately the difference between two world-conditions, two eons of the world, which I will call here the "cosmological" one versus the "psychological" one (where "cosmological" refers to a focus on the "world", i.e., the object or the "what" of thought/imagination, whereas "psychological" refers to an interest in the subject, or "how"[19]). In the former, associated mainly with the ancient and archaic world (which is, however, one that Hillman, as we see here, attempts to revive), the soul innocently *directly* relates to the world and to experience as *what* is to be seen or imagined and explained, without being aware of the involvement of the subject in the experience. It is all "out there", in the cosmos, in what is imaged. The mind, in self-forgetfulness completely given over to what it sees in its imagination, only focuses upon its own contents: The semantic level.

The other world-condition, which fully came into its own five or six centuries ago, is characterized by the fact that this earlier innocence has been lost. The soul has become aware of *itself* and must take itself into account in all its experiences and semantic contents. It can no longer devote itself merely to the "what" but must also self-reflectingly be aware of the "how", the logical form of its experience as its own active, productive contribution to the experience.

The "Gods" in Hillman's theory guarantee the stance of passive receptivity and the innocence of self-forgetfulness, the stance of the *An-sich* (per se, in-itself). The images come and merely have to be carefully observed and attended to. The late Jung, by contrast, realized that, "So long as one simply looks at the pictures one is like the foolish Parsifal, who forgot to ask the vital question, because one does not become aware of *one's own* [the thinking or imagining mind's own] *participation*" (*CW* 14 § 753, transl. modif.).[20]

With his vertical peak-vale, up-down, tripartite versus two-realms fantasy, we see Hillman move within what I called the "cosmological" orientation. It is the ingenuous dedication to the object, to "how it *is*": whether *it*,

---

19 This term "psychological" as the opposite of "cosmological" is therefore completely different from that other one that is, e.g., evoked by "the psychological difference" and refers to the soul aspect in contrast to the "psychic" or "ego" aspect.

20 Cf. *CW* 10 § 498 where Jung, albeit in a completely different context, speaks of "man's intervention, that is, the indispensable participation of the psyche".

the cosmos, is tripartite or dualistic. The image-approach is characterized by *systematic* self-forgetfulness.

However, despite being a form of the "cosmological" approach it is of course nevertheless *itself* a child of the "psychological" age (of the 20th century) and occurs within psychology! This means it comes too late and its message is belied by its own structure of consciousness (which may also explain the appearance of the emotion of hatred). Hillman tries to replay once more those battles of the bygone 8th and 9th centuries and today reverse their outcome, *at a time when* the issues of those Councils have long lost every actual relevance, a circumstance that turns his fight into a kind of shadow-boxing. These issues have lost their relevance because their final decisions have in the course of the centuries been fully integrated into the very structure of the soul and because the true psychological issue and battleground of today is a totally different one: Namely, the "logical" relation between semantic contents and logical form, between *what* is experienced and the *syntax* of the experiencing consciousness.

"Geist": A structure, not a substance. The logic of self-production and self-knowing

This is where *"Geist"* comes in. *Geist*, as it occurs in Jung, is precisely not the extreme dissociated opposite of soul and image. It does not need to be fought with passionate hatred if soul is to have a chance. It is not what is only or predominantly to be found on peaks. It is not to be imaginatively associated with any *location* as such. It is not the tip of a "tripartite cosmos of spirit, soul, and body (or matter)", for, after all, Jung maintains that, "Sexuality is of the greatest importance as the expression of a chthonic spirit [*Geist*]".[21] As above so below; or heaven above, heaven below, alchemy tells us. For Jung the soul in its entirety (from the most sublime theological dogma to chthonic depth) is itself *geistig*. In Jung the place of the "cosmological" difference between peaks and vales is taken by the psychological

---

21 This quote follows our first citation from *MDR* p. 168. I changed "the chthonic" into "a chthonic" according to the German original. The problem with Jung's expression is of course the mythologizing language which might make credulous people think that he posited different personalized spirits in the plural, when what is meant is only the one *Geist* that can also manifest itself in the more natural, sensuous (here by Jung called "chthonic") sphere.

difference between the personal (or biological), on the one hand, and the soul (the *"geistig* side") on the other, which, as a psychological and thus logical (not cosmological, not natural) difference, can potentially be established within any phenomenon regardless of whether on peaks or in vales.

Geistigkeit is the soul's nature; it is, we might say, the soul of soul. What constitutes the soul aspect of phenomena is nothing but their *"geistig* side", which simply refers to the soul's meaning structure, the "about structure". Jung's " 'psychology with soul,'" is "based on the hypothesis of an autonomous *Geist*" (*GW* 8 § 661, my transl.): it is not *based* on image! Image (because it too has this "about structure" and expresses specific meanings in pictorial form) is itself merely one frequent form in which soul as *Geist* appears. *Geist* has no problem at all with or hostile feelings towards image or the imagination. What it finds fault with is the *abstractness* of the image approach, when image is no longer seen as a form of manifestation of thought, but set up in absolute opposition to thought; when the psychological mind becomes identified, in its own structure, with the image approach and consequently also identifies soul with image. We could also say: When "image" is turned into a belief system and declared to be the fundamental *basis* of the very theory of soul.[22]

Geist in this sense is not a mysterious ("mythological") being or agent behind the scenes, nor a special realm, nor a subsisting substance or substrate. No, it is a specific logical *structure*, a structure not in the static, rigid sense (like a building), but living, dynamic, active: That structure that we earlier provisionally characterized as the "about structure" and that we now want to elucidate a little more closely.

When Jung writes, "In myths and fairytales, as in dreams, the soul speaks about itself, and the archetypes reveal themselves in their natural interplay, as 'formation, transformation / the eternal Mind's eternal recreation'" (*CW* 9i § 400, transl. modified), he actually describes the soul's *Geistigkeit* or *Geist*-nature, in the somewhat flowery language of the poet. For *Geist* is that structure or activity/process ("eternal recreation") that has the following moments: It is (1) a speaking or producing or manifesting; it produces

---

22 But unwittingly even imaginal psychology itself admits that image is implicit thought. For it does not merely mutely stare at images and adore them, but it *works* with them, says something about them, interprets them, i.e., it tries to bring out into the open their inherent meaning and this means, *sit venia verbo*, the thought enveloped in them.

meanings in the form of images, dreams, myths, rites, tombs, paintings, poems, philosophical works; but (2) *what* it produces or speaks about is only *itself*, its own truth or reality. In other words, it is a self-production or self-presentation, self-display. And (3) in this speaking about itself, in its revealing itself together with its internal logical complexity (the "interplay" of opposites), and in this giving itself a real and visible presence in the world, it obtains its *self-knowledge*. It comes home to itself.

Wherever this logical structure is at work, we have a *Geist*-phenomenon. The three moments are not three separate phases but in their interrelation make up the internal structure of all those events or phenomena that have *Geist*-character or in which soul in its *Geistigkeit* manifests—in contrast to all phenomena in *nature* with its clear cause-and-effect and temporal-sequence structure.

It is crucial to understand that the "beginning" of this process is not *a spirit who* speaks, not really an "eternal Mind" as an existing subject. No, it "begins" with speaking as such; there is only this activity or performance—without a performing agent. And when I said that *Geist* comes home to itself, I now have to add that only in this home-coming and self-knowing does it *begin* to exist. Self-knowing is precisely not secondary, not a result. It is also what inspires the original speaking; the achieved self-knowledge is in itself productive, creative, a speaking. We could therefore say this movement is uroboric. The only remote analogue in nature to *Geist* is life. Both life and *Geist* are not a substance. Life *is* only where and for as long as something has the power to perform, and in fact performs, the act of living. It is a doing, not an ingredient in an organism. Analogously, *Geist is* only where the process of self-manifestation and self-knowing actually happens. Being a structure it can—as (to some extent) life and like language (which is of course merely an example of *Geist*)—at one and the same time be concretely and powerfully real in a this-worldly sense and yet be fundamentally "over and above" all positivities, all natural, factual existence.

Because soul, due to its *Geistigkeit*, is a doing, it does not have a permanent (thing-like) existence. Dreams, e.g., as written texts or as memories are not *per se* soul. The soul's speaking about itself only takes place when (and for as long as) we are actually performing the act of interpreting and comprehending them. This is why Jung advised us concerning dreams, or rather concerning what dreams say: "[S]ay it again, as best you can". It is only in this saying it again that the dream begins to speak in the first place and that soul comes into existence. The same can be said about religious dogmas, mythic tales, poems, and so on. They certainly are expressions of soul, and yet they are not, not until and unless the soul or *Geist* in a human subject actively appreciates them in their depth. A work of art is not simply empirically given as a work of art, but needs to be re-created afresh by the viewer. And it exists only in this act of re-creation and only as long as it lasts and is maintained, kept alive. In other words, the *"geistig* side" has the character of a doing, a performance, and precisely not of an existing entity: A positivity. *Geist*, we can say in general, has fundamentally act character. As essentially performative and as production it is not tangible, but fleeting. Just like a musician re-creates *on the literal, physical level* a piece of music by playing the notes written on the sheets of music in front of him, so the mind that apperceives a sculpture or painting truly as a work of art performs, *on the no longer physical level* and therefore *subliminally*, the act of re-creating it from the visible sculpture or canvas in front of him using them as clues or instructions for how to push off from them.[23]

By the same token it needed the soul or *Geist* in C.G. Jung to bring to life, through his mentioned late works, sexuality's *"geistig* side" as it had expressed itself in alchemical tracts. But he brought it to life only for himself, not for us. For us it remains just as entombed in his writings as it had for him been entombed in those tracts—until a reader possesses the intellectual power and depth to "say it again, as best he can".

But even if the dream, the work of art, the alchemical tract or Jung's interpretations of those tracts require an appreciating, comprehending human subject to come alive as soul or *Geist*, this *"geistig* side" is not at all anything merely subjective. Rather, *Geist* is the overarching relation between the objectively given text/work/religious symbol/phenomenon as the hard fact in this world that they are *and* the comprehending subject. It is itself

---

23 What for the viewer of a work of art is the visible sculpture or canvas is for the audience of a concert the physically played music. The musicians' playing is *not* as such the re-creation of the musical piece as a work of art. The work of art only comes about in and through the *re-creative* hearing of what is physically played, the hearing of it both in the playing musician and in the members of the audience. The difference between the playing musician and the audience is primarily that for the literally playing musician the creative hearing must *precede* his playing if he is to be really up to the true art character of the work of music, whereas for the audience the physical hearing of the playing logically comes first, and the re-creative production of the piece of music is entirely dependent on the physically playing.

the psychological difference: The opening up of the distinction, and at the same time its overarching the thereby distinguished opposites (e.g., its seeing the "*geistig* side" *in* the concrete empirical phenomenon of sexuality). *Geist* is not hovering above the world. Nothing transcendent, other-worldly. It is a very sober, unemotional and uninflated concept. It does not imply idle fantasizing or "free association". On the contrary, it requires the labor of the concept.

Beyond the personalistic: The dimension of generality

A while ago I used the phrase: "until and unless the soul or *Geist* in a human subject appreciates them [dreams, myths, dogmas, etc.] in their depth". This phrase entails an important point and corrects my formulations in the last paragraph that focused on the human subject. I now have to emphasize that in contrast to the focus on the human subject the soul in its *Geistigkeit* speaks only to *itself*, and it is only the soul or *Geist* in us (and NOT *we*, nor OUR *Geist*, but THE *Geist* as universal[24]) that knows itself through hearing or seeing and understanding what it itself produced. We humans are only the place in which the soul's self-expression and corresponding self-knowledge occurs, if it occurs.

Soul happens for its own sake, its own needs and own fulfillment. It is its own self-contained logical life that uroborically plays itself out. Negatively put: It is not for our benefit, our understanding, our self-knowledge. This is what the late Jung (1945) tries to suggest through the Goethe quote about the Eternal Mind's[25] eternal recreation. But as the place in and through which it can realize itself, *we* are nevertheless needed, even indispensable for it, and if we let *it* find *its* "eternal recreation" and fulfillment, then even *we* may, through our participation in it, also find our deepest satisfaction, because in the deepest sense we exist not as organism, but as soul or *Geist*.[26]

Geist wants to know *itself* and has no other (separate or prior) existence than in the *events* of such actually happening self-knowing. Again, this has

---

24 In the same sense that language is not the private language of each speaker, but conversely, every speaker avails himself of a language that is the property of the generality.

25 "Mind" is again a stopgap. The German is: *des ewigen Sinnes. Sinn* does by no means imply a kind of mythological being or subject. One could interpret it as the meaning level, the logos, the *Geistigkeit* or mindedness dimension of existence.

26 This satisfaction would not be Meaning, but only (only?) the event of meaning, of *Geist*.

the further ramification that soul in its *Geistigkeit* is a *different dimension* from the world of nature, from all natural (sensuously given) things or processes or experiences: Jung's "over and above" dimension. It is the sphere of generality (the fundamental sharedness-character of meanings) and as such also of logical negativity (*absolute* negativity). Jung's misnomer, "the collective unconscious",[27] can now be comprehended as actually intending to give expression to this sphere of generality "over and above" the positive-factual aspect of things, to the sphere of *Geistigkeit*.

Soul events may at times occur in only one single individual, but they are nevertheless not *his*: *a priori* they do not belong to him the way merely psychic events belong to him. This is precisely what distinguishes "the *psychic*" from "the *psychological*". Psychic events, our emotions, perceptions, desires, fears, fantasies, dreams, etc., are clearly contained in the individual as human animal and are in this sense his property. But the psychological is *geistig* and thus logically universal (Jung would have said collective). To the extent that soul events are truly soul events they originate as (and have the logical [not the empirical] character of) sharedness, of generality. They do not belong to anybody. Indeed, although occurring in the natural world, *as themselves* they do not "exist" in the natural world.

When Heraclitus (fr. 45 DK) said, "You would not find out the boundaries of soul, even by traveling along every path: so deep a *logos* does it have", we now have to point out that it is not the *boundaries* of soul that cannot be found anywhere on earth, i.e., in positive-factual reality, but much rather soul as such in the first place: the "*geistig* side" of real phenomena, because only like sees like. The "*geistig* side" is only accessible to *Geist*. Now we can say that the reason why Jung's "Freud" was unable to see this "*geistig* side" of sexuality was that he insisted on approaching phenomena exclusively as empirical ego and did not rise to the standpoint of *Geist*. The ego's "terminology and theory" are by definition "too narrow" and "concretistic". Jung's shift to the "*geistig* side" and his coining the concept of the (unfortunately so-called) "collective unconscious" as the sphere of generality are one and the same move.

27 *Geist* is neither "collective" nor is what Jung means with the collective unconscious "unconscious". The "archetypes of the collective unconscious" played themselves out openly in archaic peoples' mythological or religious knowledge and cults. Even dreams are always conscious, or else they do not exist.

The phrase "Eternal Mind's eternal recreation" also allows us to point to another feature of the dimension that we call soul, a feature intrinsically connected with the soul's absolute negativity and its status of fundamental generality, namely, its total "uselessness" (from an empirical-practical point of view). Particularly those writings in which Jung said he explored the "*geistig* side" of sexuality, *Mysterium coniunctionis* and "The Psychology of Transference", but also all his other works devoted to alchemy, to the transformation symbolism of the Mass, the visions of Zosimos, etc., openly display this utter "uselessness". This is precisely part and parcel of their devotion to soul.

And yet: Soul as the sphere of generality and absolute negativity does express itself in really existing paintings and sculptures, in the words of language that are actually spoken, in texts that are printed, in dreams that occur in an empirical human being. This confirms once more that soul does not hover above the world as transcendent other-worldly reality. It is world-immanent. Now the question arises how these two insights (absolute negativity vs. expression in real phenomena) can be reconciled.

What reconciles them is the psychological difference, that difference that (not literally, empirically, but absolute-negatively) divides one and the same real phenomenon into its two "sides": Sexuality into Freud's biological function and into Jung's invisible "*geistig* side"; a statue by Praxiteles into the positivity of a stone object as perhaps seen by a dog and the not simply empirically given and *vorhanden* ("present to hand") presence of a god as seen by the artist himself; a text as the printed letters in a book and the nowhere literally existing or subsisting, and in this sense logically negative, story or theoretical discourse; and, of course, also man himself as the natural animal that he is (remember Jung's "human stable"?) and the empirically unprovable and yet undoubtedly real soul or *Geist* that he is. The whole of human culture here on earth and the fact of language as such are evidence of man's soul nature.

No transcendence: Only "this valley of the world"

Therefore I fully concur with Hillman when he writes in his essay, ". . . psychological method remains within this valley of the world, through which history passes and leaves its traces, our 'ancestors'" (p. 61). For as we have seen, Jung's "over and above" dimension and his emphasis on *Geistigkeit* really do not refer to the peaks of transcendence, but to the sphere of absolute negativity and generality opened up within the Real (wherever it be). And like life, *Geist* is a this-worldly reality and yet not a positivity.

However, for two reasons I don't believe that what Hillman says is really valid for himself. The first is that a psychologist who settles in the vale (image) side of the peak–vale or thought–image dichotomy and who needs to rage against the peaks of spirit has himself not really arrived in the valley of the world and along with it in modernity. For if he had arrived, the valley would not be anything special, nothing to make a fuss about, and above all: Not just one side of two. Rather, he would know that modern existence is characterized by the fact that it inescapably has its place in this valley of the world, more than that, that this valley of the world is the only place there is. There is no "peak" anymore as in earlier times (which is precisely why some people today crave for peak experiences and spirituality: Emotions, felt experiences as substitutes for the lost "cosmological" peak or heaven). We today are always in the valley. Even literal mountain peaks, indeed even distant galaxies, are part of this valley of the world, as Jung knew only too well (*CW* 9i § 50). The whole "cosmological" dichotomy—heaven *above*, earth and underworld *below*—no longer exists. Today heaven and hell are just as above as below; the whole "cosmological" above–below distinction has become obsolete. Psychology is as a matter of course only concerned with this real world, with the soul of the real. However, in order to be *psychology*, it has to be aware of the soul's essential *Geistigkeit* and the psychologist's task of "saying again".

Above all, are not the (metaphoricized) "Gods" that Hillman's psychology insists on the semanticized and barely concealed form in which the *syntax of otherworldliness* is surreptitiously packaged and slipped into the—today unavoidably prevailing—valley of the world as a kind of fifth column?[28] And is this valley, as the soulless and literal "universe" (in Hillman's view the radical opposite of "cosmos"), for him not ultimately a "fallen world" and as "fallen" viewed from a standpoint *above* this valley of the world?

The second reason for my not believing that Hillman truly means what he says with all its consequences is that a mind that wishes for a reversal of history and a return to or resuscitation (p. 56) of bygone things does not seem to respect history, which is above all characterized by its *irreversibility*. Without this sense of irreversibility history is not history. But Hillman

---

28 Here it is important to remember that the notion of *Geistigkeit* does not in a similar way involve a betrayal of "this valley of the world", just as the claim that words have a meaning does not leave *this* world in favor of the "peaks" of otherworldliness (transcendence).

insists on Gods as timeless structures of consciousness and denies that Gods (as well as the power of "image") can become historically obsolete. How then can he say, "I ride this horse of history until it drops, for I submit that history has become the Great Repressed" (p. 62), if he nevertheless denies irreversibility and obsolescence?[29] We see: It is not really the soul's history itself that intrigues him; he merely *uses* selected past events for *blaming* his discontent with today's situation (the "malnutritioned" Western psychological culture) on certain forefathers (namely, those "theological, spiritual men" of more than a thousand years ago),[30] much like neurotic psychology tries to blame the patients' present-day neuroses on what their parents did to them in early childhood. And he uses the past, conversely, for selectively picking out certain figures (such as Plotinus or Ficino) as good ancestors of archetypal psychology to provide this modern school of thought with a noble lineage. But just as, biologically speaking, our genetic heritage is our genetic heritage, so also, in psychological and *geistig* regards, our ancestors (*all* of them, the "good" and the "bad") are our ancestors, whether we like it or not. They are *ours*, ingrained in *our* historically grown psychological constitution. We are *their* results. No choice.

If more than a thousand years ago "long battles between spirit and soul" were fought in the Councils of the Early Church and "images were deprived of their inherent authenticity", then the *psychologist* who truly rides the horse of history would have the task of comprehending this as a soul-internal process, one induced by the soul for its own purposes, as the soul's *opus contra naturam*. Otherwise he would himself depotentiate and deprive the soul of its all-comprehensiveness, himself exile from it certain of its moves. He would have to comprehend and affirm what exactly the soul's specific necessity and purpose was in depotentiating and depriving image of its authenticity during those long-bygone centuries. What was its telos? What was to be achieved? It will precisely not do to approach

---

29 Hillman immunized his ahistorical aestheticizing stance against historical arguments by denouncing them as being guilty of what he calls the "historical fallacy" and literalism. But he never showed its fallaciousness. This particular view of his is therefore only a dogma.

30 By contrast cf. Jung: "The true cause for a neurosis lies in the Now, for the neurosis exists in the present. It is by no means a hangover from the past, a *caput mortuum*, ... Because the neurotic conflict faces us today, any historical deviation is a detour, if not actually a wrong turning" (*CW* 10 § 363, transl. modif.).

this historical shift dogmatically from an external superior standpoint with moral judgments (good–bad, right–wrong) or emotions (hatred). I submit, these long-ago battles can be understood psychologically as part of the pivotal events through which the soul's stance towards its own experience was slowly heaved from its habitual "cosmological" (the *An-sich*) orientation to the emerging fundamentally new "psychological" one.

Jung, by contrast, when saying, "without history there can be no psychology" (*MDR* p. 205), fully acknowledged the irrevocable historical ruptures and losses. He knew that "our time [is distinguished] from all others" (*CW* 10 §161) and that "we cannot go back to [what] is gone".[31] This awareness of the irreversible processes of history fits to the soul's *Geistigkeit*. In its deepest layer (covered, of course, by incredibly many serendipitous, meaningless, human-all-too-human occurrences, be they disastrous or happy), human history as a whole is the slow process of the soul's speaking about itself and coming home to itself, from the earliest prehistoric times down to medial modernity and in all likelihood also beyond the latter.

Looking back upon the "peaks–vales" distinction we can say that if one bases psychology on the *corresponding* notion of soul, one would establish a *false* psychological difference. "False" here is not my personal judgment. This difference is *intrinsically* false because it is not different enough.[32] Peaks and vales belong to the same (empirical, "geographical") category. Such a difference is six of one and half a dozen of the other. The real psychological difference, as for example expressed in Jung's statements about sexuality that we started with, brings a breakthrough to a totally other dimension, from the world of positivity ("biological function", "personal significance") to absolute negativity ("its *geistig* side"), from the imagery of empirical, sensually given things ("peaks" and "vales") to the thought of

---

31 That in the "quest of meaning" Jung nevertheless entertained the utopian hope that the lost truth would become "true once more" in "a new form" is another story.

32 It would also be possible to describe this situation exactly in the opposite way, namely that this difference is not "same" enough. By imaginally *distributing* the two sides of the difference onto two from the outset empirical-factually different, separate things, the difference stays external and abstract (literal otherness, two alternatives). This being condemned to externalize is the congenital defect of the imaginal approach. The difference does not come home to itself and thus does not become psychological. In fact, it ceases to be a real *difference* and instead turns into a dissociation or split. The psychological difference, by contrast, is opened up within *one and the same* phenomenon.

Geistigkeit, which as thought is not positively given and has no positive existence. This is also why the "rise" to the "over and above" level is not an attempt to leave the valley in favor of some mysterious height after all. This (indeed) spatial metaphor of verticality is here an a priori sublated metaphor and what it refers to is by no means a literal upwards movement in extensional space, but in reality an *"intensional"*, strictly *logical* movement of negation, an "alchemical" evaporation, distillation.

The true psychological difference can be interpreted as the absolute-negative interiorization-into-itself of the external ("cosmological" or imaginal) peaks–vales dichotomy. We already heard that the latter has, as a whole, gone under into the "vale" side of itself, into the all-comprising inescapable "valley of the world". For the former dichotomy this process of the psychologization of "the cosmological" amounted to a coagulation, a toughening, hardening, of its "vale of soul-making" side into positive facticity, on the one hand, and to the distillation of its former "peak" side into *Geistigkeit*, on the other hand. The *"geistig* side" of phenomena is the *psychological* successor to imaginal psychology's still *"cosmological"* "peak".

No ruling dominants: Only "When the time is fulfilled"

In closing I briefly point to one (major) aspect of Jung's psychology which is incompatible with his own awareness of the *Geistigkeit* and historicity of the soul. This is his theory of the archetypes. As long as they are conceived as mere *forms* or *types* or *patterns* by which human thoughts, images, and experiences inevitably have to be molded if they are to appear at all, the idea of archetypes causes no problem, nor would one's seeing them as a kind of reservoir of sunken substantial contents ("meanings"), as the sedimentation of cultural-historical developments that may re-emerge occasionally. The problem I see comes only because they are also asserted to be timeless, ever-present "archetypes in themselves" that are "the dominants which rule human existence throughout the millenniums" (*Letters 2*, p. 540), "factors" in the literal sense of "makers", or even "personal agencies" (*CW* 5 § 388). "The word 'type' is, as we know, derived from τύπος, 'blow' or 'imprint'; thus an archetype presupposes an imprinter" (*CW* 12 § 15).

With this concept we get mysterious agents behind the scenes, after all, and we are back to a thinking in substances rather than only in living processes, in terms of the soul's self-unfolding logical or *geistig* life. At the same time, this valley of the world has also been left. We now have clearly transcendent causes that *"rule* human existence" fundamentally *heterono-mously*. It is, according to this scheme, not the inner logic of a person's as well as society's real nature and situation with its internal and external determinants and contradictions that moves human existence psychologically. No, that existence is governed from outside, by "higher" external forces. The archetypes in their inalienable otherness, if not other-worldliness, are the true effective causes. The real *power* of images in psychic life (that often is experienced as so-called numinosity) comes from them.

I contrast this conception with another one to be found in Jung. He once wrote, "I have often been asked [by analysands seeking help], 'And what do you *do* about it?' I do nothing; there is nothing I can do except wait, with a certain trust in God, until, out of a conflict borne with patience and fortitude, there emerges the solution destined—although I cannot foresee it—for that particular person" (*CW* 12 § 37). It is clear that "trust in God" and "destined" are used only metaphorically. What Jung wants to indicate is of course not that God directly brings about this solution or that the latter is preordained by fate. On the contrary, the result is effected simply by the self-development of the psychic process itself. No dominant. Nothing ruling from outside. Rather, the internal logic of the conflict, provided that it is borne with patience and fortitude (that is, that it is not subdued, dulled, numbed, but kept alive in its unmitigated acuteness), works itself out in an unforeseeable (productive) way. Emergence. The efficacy and the energy behind the change towards a solution come from *time* (and thus from this valley of the world). The solution comes when the time has come, or as the Bible says, when *the time is fulfilled.*[33]

This theory, elaborated a little more in Jung's idea of the "transcendent function", of the formation of "uniting symbols" through the tension of opposites, is clearly incompatible with the theory of archetypal dominants that *rule* psychic life. If the latter were the rulers, they could bring symbols and conflict solutions at any time and would not be dependent on opposites.

If the source of energy and effective power ("numinosity") really resided in the *archetypal images* themselves, then all archetypal images would inevitably always have to take hold of the consciousness of people. A psychotherapist who hears numerous dreams from his patients and may meet quite

33 History! Not the power of timeless images.

a few archetypal images during one day could not help being swamped by their numinous power, pulling him in all sorts of different directions since people may present to him rather different or even contradictory images in the course of his working day. But this awful effect does by no means occur. As a rule, the therapist can calmly listen to and interpret these dreams and stay personally largely unaffected. This is because the power of images or ideas is not inherent in them *as* images or ideas. *In themselves images and ideas are harmless, neutral.* They do not *come* with numinous power, nor are they loaded with that power by mysterious "imprinters" or ruling dominants. The possible "tyranny of unconscious presuppositions" is also not *caused* by archetypes, not even by the "archetypal", "numinous", and thus also *geistig*, character of those presuppositions. No, the possible power of archetypal images and ideas to fascinate (or sometimes even to tyrannize and possess) consciousness is—very much down to earth—*given* to them by the concrete historical situation of the psyche, the particular locus, be it in the soul history of an individual or in the soul history of a whole people or society. Depending on where one stands in one's psychic development, be it personally or collectively, images become powerful, or lose their gripping power (or do not move one from the outset). This is why images that may once upon a time or in foreign cultures have given rise to great passions or even to wars may not touch us anymore. For us, they are merely curiosities of historical, scholarly, psychological, or touristic interest. The same reason explains why gods and symbols die.

There is no good reason why this "transcendent function" way of conceiving the emergence of something new in the soul should be restricted to solutions of seemingly insolvable internal conflict situations in individuals and to the birth of uniting symbols out of the clash of opposites. It should much rather be the general way of conceiving the appearance of new contents (dream images, visions out of the blue, so-called numinous experiences, new ideas in intellectual history, even neurotic, psychosomatic and certain psychotic symptoms), namely as the very natural emergence into consciousness, *when the time is fulfilled,* of those new contents from out of the internal logical or *geistig* life of the soul; as the soul's pushing off to a new status of consciousness; as the unforeseeable creative result of its internal tensions, contradictions; as its reaction to the pressures arising from all that it is confronted with in real life. No need for ruling dominants. No need for the mystification of "images" as originators and "powers".

But this renunciation of the "ruling dominants" does not detract from the *"geistig* side" of psychic phenomena, which is what represents the inalienable "main concern" and unique specialty of Jungian psychology.

Departedness

Reflecting upon this main concern, there is, however, no denying the fact that, *as far as the cultural level is concerned*, it is devoted to a thing of the past, to what belongs to former world conditions in the history of the soul, namely, to the bygone ages of classical metaphysics and religion. Today, in medial modernity, it cannot be a present reality; it can only be a historical presence, a presence in Mnemosyne. In its commitment to soul, psychology in the tradition of C.G. Jung relates to all actual occurrences of soul as being present only *as absent*; it respects their logical status, namely that in themselves and in their presence they are a priori and irrevocably departed. It is precisely their intrinsic departedness (their presence *as* absent) that identifies them as events of *soul*[34] (in contrast to *"psychic"* experiences of the human animal).[35] If and where psychology nevertheless insists on their having to be a present reality or immediate presence—as, for example, in the form of peak experiences, "high"-feelings, the emotion of numinosity, the veneration of "the imaginal", the presence of "the sacred", "the Gods", "Angels", or the discovery of "one's personal myth"—there it would turn into kitsch, and soul into a consumer good for the gratification of the greedy ego.

---

34 In contrast to the belief that "soul is constituted of images". "Image" is an *empirical* criterion (it is set off against other possible empirical criteria, thought, emotion, desire, drive, etc.). "Departedness" is not empirically determinable. It reflects the soul's absolute negativity.

35 From a Jungian point of view (and in contrast to their own self-understanding) we could say that all psychologies that are openly personalistic isolate the moment of "absence" contained in the phrase "present only *as absent*", take it literally, and absolutize it, so that the soul is nothing, simply does not figure in their theories and thinking (Fr. A. Lange: "psychology without soul", 1866). They cannot hold the dialectical contradiction-and-union of presence and absence and therefore have to choose *either* the one *or* the other moment. But since history deprived the decidedly modern world of the possibility of immediate presence, they did not *have* a choice: For an undialectical approach, the second moment is indeed, as Lange correctly realized, the only one left: The stance of positivism.

Chapter 2

James Hillman

An assessment[1]

James Hillman was outstanding among Jungians, and it would be a mistake to think that "outstanding" here merely refers to the fact that he was more famous, more prolific, more talented, imaginative, and intelligent, more learned than others, all of which is of course true. No, from the outset we have to be very clear about the fact that what made him—or should I rather say, what made "the phenomenon Hillman"—outstanding for Jungian psychology, was something else, something that gives to the word "outstanding" a much more radical meaning and catapults him to a fundamentally higher level. He was not *primus inter pares*. The point I want to make is that his achievement belongs to a different order. His favorite animal, he told me once, was the giraffe. Let me use this as an image: Just as a giraffe stands on the same ground as all the other animals of the savanna, but nevertheless reaches up into higher regions which are inaccessible to all those others, so the appearance of "Hillman" on the scene of Analytical Psychology amounted to a kind of breakthrough to a new dimension.[2] I want to show this through a few examples.

---

1 This paper was written in December 2011/January 2012 upon the request of Gustavo Barcellos, editor of *Cadernos Junguianos*, for a memorial section ("Um tributo a James Hillman") of this Brazilian journal. It was published in its issue no. 8, 2012, pp. 89–108, in the Portuguese translation by Letícia Capriotti and Gustavo Barcellos. The original English version appears here for the first time.

2 Apropos of this image of the giraffe, we may remember what has similarly been said about Pythagoras, namely, that he was able to erect himself and crane his neck so that he was able to reach into regions fundamentally closed to ordinary people (which in his case was of course something totally different from what we are here concerned with in the case of Hillman: The detailed memory of his former ten or even twenty lives).

DOI: 10.4324/9781003611417-2

His outstanding achievement

Already very early in his career as a Jungian analyst, long before he founded Archetypal Psychology, namely in 1963, as publisher and editor of Dunquin Press, Hillman published the posthumous book of a publicly unknown young Jungian analyst from Egypt, Evangelos Christou, who had only recently died in a car accident. Both the obscurity of the author and the austere subject matter expressed in the not exactly inviting book title, *The Logos of the Soul*, could not cause a young publisher to believe that this book would be a success, financially or otherwise. That he published it anyway must have been for the idealistic reason that he believed in the book, its message, and its theoretical importance for psychology. In his extensive "Editor's Introduction" he describes what this book tries to achieve, and thus indirectly also tells us what fascinated him about it and motivated him to make it available to the public. I quote only the first few sentences of this introduction.

> THIS MONOGRAPH IS AN ESSAY in clarification. It attempts to think through a fundamental logic for psychotherapy and to separate this logic from that of the natural sciences and from that of philosophy. Psychotherapy has its own legitimate area of activity and its rights are based on the soul which, like the realms of matter and of mind, requires a logic of procedure, a book of words. The failure of psychotherapy to make clear its legitimacy has resulted in psychologies which are bastard sciences and degenerate philosophies.[3]

We see from this quote that what must have happened in young James Hillman (and probably also in his author) was that a *psychological conscience* made itself felt, a reaction to a failure on the part of psychotherapeutic psychology. As a psychologist, Hillman felt and accepted a responsibility for the theoretical constitution of the field of psychology as such (in contrast to all the individual findings, interpretations, and theoretical assertions occurring *within* psychology). The legitimacy and the rights of psychotherapy are at stake. In Hillman, consciousness has obviously taken a *Schritt zurück* (Heidegger, a "step back") so as to fundamentally widen its horizon in such

---

3 James Hillman, "Editor's Introduction" to Evangelos Christou, *The Logos of the Soul*, Vienna: Dunquin Press, 1963, p. i.

a way that consciousness could for the first time become aware of and concerned with *itself*, so to speak with the woods, when all the others have only eyes for, and exclusively busy themselves with, the trees: with diverse psychic disorders, with individual dreams and dream motifs, with myths and symbols, with different psychological mechanisms (like defense and projection), with the development of the personality and the parts of the psyche (the different complexes and the shadow, the anima or the animus, the self), etc. And so we can say that in Hillman psychology became conscious of itself, whereas in "the Jungians" it was merely unconsciously acted out. By this I of course do not want to suggest that "the Jungians" were *personally* unconscious and conducted their therapeutic work completely unconsciously. What I mean is that in them psychology was unconscious. It had not yet awakened, let alone come home to itself. What was called "psychology" was a conglomerate of empirical findings and theoretical assumptions, in other words, of *data* or, to use another formulation, only of *contents* of consciousness, not of consciousness itself. But Hillman has become aware of the fact that therapeutic psychology "*requires* a logic of procedure", *requires* a "clarification" of its own legitimacy and rights, because without having worked out (Hillman explicitly says "thought through"!) its own logic, it is inevitably in the status either of a "*bastard* science" or a "*degenerate* philosophy". It is this awareness of, and sense-of-responsibility for, psychology as the *horizon* of all psychological work that gives Hillman his singular standing.

What should also not go by unnoticed in our quotation is that Hillman, in accordance with Christou's book title, identifies the heart and source of the logic of psychology: The soul. It is the one point from which the whole logic of (therapeutic) psychology can be and needs to be developed and deduced. "The logos of the soul" is the one and only standard and measure of a possible unfolding of the logic of psychology. And this unfolding cannot rely on empirical observation (nor on imagination). Rather, it requires thought, one's truly thinking through the requirements as well as the legitimate rights of a psychology "based on the soul".

My next example is Hillman's short text added as an editorial postscript to the first (1970) issue of the journal *Spring* edited by him: "Why 'Archetypal' Psychology?"[4] Here we see again psychological conscience and a

---

4 James Hillman, "Why 'Archetypal' Psychology?", *Spring* 1, 1970, pp. 212–219.

sense of responsibility for psychology as such at work. The three names by which psychology-in-the-Jungian-tradition had been referred to up to that point in time, "Jungian", "analytical", and "complex psychology", so Hillman states, "were never happy choices nor were they adequate to the psychology they were to designate". The term "adequate" again suggests the legitimacy question. "It seems right [!] to turn to a word that does reflect the characteristic approach of Jung, both to theory and to what actually goes on in practice, and to life in general."[5] The name of this psychology needs to be derived from the heart of what this psychology is really about and from the spirit that in fact informs it. Nobody else, as far as I know, had felt the need to give any thought to the question of an appropriate name for psychology. Those three conventional names were used unthinkingly. They had merely the function of (in themselves rather meaningless) *labels* that helped to identify this psychology in contrast to others (an external demarcation). For Hillman these "labels", and this was his achievement, began to speak, i.e., to become *words*, and thus they had to *reflect* the inner essence of that which they named: the name as an (abbreviated) self-reflection of psychology.

My third and last example is the obvious and major one of *Re-Visioning Psychology*. It does not need much comment because the very title of this book makes explicit a concern for psychology itself as the horizon for all psychological work. The point I am making is that this book does not offer a revision in the sense of an overhaul of the existing psychology, not a modification of it, nor an alternative to it (all of which would remain on the same level). Its specific achievement is much rather that it raises psychology to a fundamentally higher level of itself by trying to make it conscious of itself and adequate to itself (i.e., to its root metaphor, soul). More subjectively expressed, it raised to a higher level the *standpoint* from which the psychologist viewed psychological phenomenology. Hillman tried to design a conception of psychology that was derived—or better, *generated*—from one single center[6]: From what its root metaphor demanded. His attempt

---

5 James Hillman, "Why 'Archetypal' Psychology?", *Spring* 1, 1970, p. 215f.

6 Hillman's "polytheism" (which also expresses itself in his opting for "archetypal psychologies" in the plural) is secondary. Primary is his commitment to a One, the one central heart or root of psychology, soul. His polytheistic tendency is derived from *his* understanding of the reality and necessities of the soul.

in this book, too, was, just as he had written years earlier about Christou's book, "to think through a fundamental logic for" psychology.

Therefore, his psychological work has no peers among the other types of psychology in the Jungian tradition. And it is a fundamental mistake of Andrew Samuel's book, *Jung and the Post-Jungians*, to present Hillman's Archetypal Psychology *side by side* with the British developmental version of Analytical Psychology and with the mainly Zurich-based orthodox tradition of Analytical Psychology—a failure to see the difference between them (I do not mean the morphological difference, which also exists, but the difference of *dimension* and *rank*). To express it with our insufficient and underdetermined image: The difference between a gazelle or gnu on the one hand, and a giraffe on the other. Or, another image, as if these three "schools" were branches off the same tree. It says a lot about the Jungians and about the mental level or caliber of their doings and theorizing in general that for the most part they did/do not realize that Hillman's work amounted to a fundamental further-development and deepening of the discipline as a whole and to an exposure of their failure, but that they rather chose to put it *aside*, brushing it off as eccentric and idiosyncratic, so that they could go on undisturbed in their same old pedestrian ways—as if nothing had happened. But even most of those who followed Hillman merely took over some of his particular ideas and methods, the *results* of his thought, above all his emphasis on images, but failed to see, and to realize in themselves, the radical logical move Hillman had made, the advance to a fundamentally higher level of reflection. What *Re-Visioning Psychology* brought was a reconstitution of psychology. And it brought it by going back to the level of "first principles" (as the early Hillman had worded it in his introduction to Christou).

For psychology, there are, however, not many "first principles", but only one "first principle" or "root metaphor": Soul. Everything else follows or is generated from it, the categories of psychology, its method, even its particular language and its style of perception. Everything has to be in tune with "soul" and be viewed in terms of it. Whereas the ideas of conventional Jungian psychology were more or less haphazardly picked up either from Jung's work or from practical experience in the consulting room as so many separate items and only secondarily, perhaps, incorporated in a theory (this is what gave this type of psychology the status of a conglomeration), re-visioning psychology was an attempt to construe psychology as one integral whole. All the particular ideas of this psychology were rooted in and derived from one center or ground, the notion of soul.

This had drastic consequences which I will exemplify only with one example: "pathologizing as soul-making". Whereas conventional Jungian psychology had viewed psychic phenomenology from the standpoint of the external observer and thus necessarily perceived psychopathology as a *violation* and *distortion* of the (in itself healthy) soul due to external mishaps, to traumas, or to conflicts with the demands on the individual coming from the social environment, etc., Hillman, because he had shifted the psychologist's external standpoint right into the heart and ground of psychology itself, was able to return pathology to the soul as its own property and as one of its authentic modes of self-expression. In general, we can say that this meant that *the negative* (suicide, nightmare, abandonment, schism, betrayal, pornography, paranoia, and so on) was seen as soul-internal.

Limitation of his notion of soul

If with this internalizing move everything has to be seen in terms of soul, and this means from the soul's point of view, all depends on how in turn "soul" itself is perceived. Here I think above all two features characteristic for Hillman need to be mentioned: (a) His privileging one pole in diverse dualistic schemes and (b) what I call his fetishism and mystifying tendency.

(a) Although Hillman clearly advanced in his consciousness to the notion of the *syzygy* (of anima and animus), not always, but on the whole, he tended to identify soul with the anima and its style. The syzygy did not become his own standpoint.[7] Although his own re-visioning work was an attempt to work out the logic of psychology and although he knew full well that, e.g., the anima *is* a (personified) *notion*, he privileged, *within* the opposition of image (personification, imagination) and notion (concept, thought), the image. The imaginal was the ultimate ground of soul for him. Although he saw the danger of a too literal interpretation of monotheism, he privileged polytheism in the poly-/monotheism pair. Although he knew that *puer* and *senex* were inseparable, he nevertheless sided with the *puer* (and not only in his personal life, which would be his private affair, but also in his psychologizing). Although the phenomenology of the soul brings spirit and soul closely together,

---

7 On this topic see the insightful essay by Greg Mogenson, "Hillman and the Syzygy", in: Stanton Marlan (ed.), *Archetypal Psychologies. Reflections in Honor of James Hillman*, New Orleans, LA: Spring Journal Books, 2008, pp. 171–191.

even identifying the dead souls as ghosts or spirits, Hillman set up "soul" in radical opposition to "spirit". As far as the history of the soul is concerned, he saw a fundamental opposition between "North" and "South" as cultural loci (North: northern Europe, the Reformation, the Enlightenment; "South": the Mediterranean, ancient Greece and the Renaissance) and privileged the latter. Accordingly, he selected, as we could say, particular "saints" of Archetypal Psychology: Plato, Plotinus, Ficino, Vico, etc., and cast out Melanchthon, Descartes, Mersenne, Kant and others as psychological "bad guys".

In other words, that internalizing move of all psychological categories and methodological ideas into soul that he performed in the reconstruction of psychology as a whole and that came out so brilliantly in his idea of "pathologizing as soul-making" he did not perform concerning his conception of psychology's root metaphor, the soul itself. The concept of soul itself, the ultimate standard and "measure of psychology", as he himself explicitly stated, continued for him to have an Other outside of itself (an opposite, the *not*-soulful). As much as on the level of psychic *phenomenology* the *negative* could be seen by him as having a true soul value, negative *phenomena* (such as "pathologizing") being appreciated as a mode of veritable soul-making, *negation* itself was not allowed into, and not integrated in, the very "*definition*" of soul. The soul itself was kept free from negation. It stayed virginally untouched, a romantically perceived soul. It could not be seen as the unity of itself and its own negation, the way the uroboros, the tail-eater, "is said to beget, kill, and devour itself" (C.G. Jung, *CW* 16 § 454). And so by and large, Hillman's standpoint in his thinking about the soul remained innocently beneath the level of the superordinate, comprehensive "third of the two" (in the first-mentioned example this third would, for instance, be the syzygy) on the "*positive*" side of the two opposites into which this third diremnts itself. He did not advance to the full (uroboric, dialectical) concept of soul as the unity of itself and its other.

His not advancing to the full concept of soul was later, with his move to "the world" and to "cosmology", complemented by his not unreservedly releasing "soul" into its own, its full autonomy and freedom. Around fifteen years after *Re-Visioning*, feeling the need to critique, as still being "self-centered", his own earlier concept of "soul-making", which had been a central notion of that book, Hillman raised the question, "But what about the world's soul, Michael? What about the *anima mundi* and making that?"[8] To be sure, through this move the

---

8 James Hillman and Michael Ventura, *We've Had a Hundred Years of Psychotherapy— And the World is Getting Worse*, San Francisco: Harper, 1992, p. 51.

soul is now seen as residing in the world and in things and thus removed from having its center in us, in the human personality. Soul-making no longer revolves around *our* development. But nevertheless, WE are here still the subjects of soul-making, WE are the makers, and the world soul remains the *object* of this our human "making *that*", as he put it. WE are called upon to heal the world.

But this means that the concept of the *anima mundi* is unwittingly still kept in the clutches of the ego and thus in a deeper sense remains, *pace* Hillman, "self-centered". For a true psychology, by contrast, it is only the soul itself which can and has to do the healing of psychic ills. It is the soul's job to cure itself and the world (if it feels the need for such a cure). It is not our, not the human ego's, task. From the *psychological* standpoint, we are not called upon to remedy the wrongs of the world. Psychotherapy is not a curative undertaking. But Hillman's theory does not return "soul-making" to the soul itself, in this case to the *anima mundi*, as *its own* uroborically making itself, where we are no more than the recipients, "careful observers" (Jung), and "therapists"[9] of *its* soul-making. Thus in this scheme, the concept of soul is logically not allowed to come home to itself, to be self-sufficient, self-contained, *free*: it does not become *psychological*, being construed as subservient to some Other, an egoic world-improvement desire, in other words, to an ideological, (psycho-)*political* project.[10]

A tendency to mystification

(b) In order to elucidate *the second characteristic feature* of Hillman's understanding of soul, the mystification aspect, I begin with a quotation. In his "Preface: A Memoir from the Author for the 1992 Edition" (of *Re-Visioning Psychology*) Hillman states in the last paragraph, after having raised and commented on the question of "But who did write the book? . . . Who is the subject?"

The question of authorship cannot be answered except by imagining psychology as religion . . . and the book, like a totem object, a fetish

---

9 As Hillman himself pointed out, the therapist is not a healer. *Therapeia* is merely a kind of "waiting on", "attending to", "nursing", an accompanying of the soul's process with deep feeling and insightful comprehension.

10 It is not political in the hard-core sense, but psycho-political, political in a "soft" sense, because it wants to bring about an *aesthetic*, not a political revolution. What, however, makes it political is that it is expressive of a Will, which is always, namely in itself, a Will to Power.

statue kept alive by its readers, who, by picking it up and turning its pages with quiet attention and emotional participation, polish the statue called a "book". Like that statue, a book gives physical form to invisible presences, gives to the angels in words a local habitation and a name. May both the readers and the angels be pleased to linger a while longer.[11]

A book is not really a book, or it is only a "book" in quotation marks, Hillman suggests. In truth it is the physical embodiment of invisible presences, of "the angels in words", and as such "like a totem object, a fetish statue". And just as a fetish statue is polished by repeated rubbing, so also does Hillman invite his readers to such a polishing of his book as a "religious" act. Fetish objects are rubbed in order to thereby transfer magic power from the object to the person (and, conversely, in order to load the object with new power). In the case of his book, what is supposed to be transferred from it to the reader by the latter's "polishing" is probably the angelic power of the invisible presences which are said to have their local habitation in the book. *Re-Visioning Psychology* is thus ultimately presented by its author as a holy book, and as written not really by Hillman himself, but directly by those presences. In advance—his text is a preface—Hillman tries to supply it with an aura of mystery, the hype of something divine. And in speaking in this preface to his readers, Hillman does not address them as intelligent, wakeful, critical minds, does not evoke their mental powers, their faculties of comprehension and insight. What he really wants for his book is their piety (towards "the angels", etc.).

This is obviously kitschy. But it clearly reveals the fact that *deep down* Hillman's conception of soul is unctuous and mystifying. He does not simply let his book go out into the world as it is on the basis of its own strength or weakness and allow it to speak for itself, letting it have its effect upon the reader, *whatever* effect, that it actually will have. His speaking is suggestive and manipulative, not phenomenological. While ostensibly using a descriptive language, he surreptitiously wants to predetermine the reader's frame of mind, prepossess the reader's mind before reading the book in favor of the idea of those powers and *daimones*, to argue for which is the function of this book. There is an ego will at work in Hillman to claim for his book

---

11 James Hillman, "Preface: A Memoir from the Author for the 1992 Edition", *Re-Visioning Psychology*, New York: William Morrow & Company, 1992, p. xiii, p. xiv.

the status of being fundamentally *more than* an ordinary *presentation* of a psychological *theory*. Rather than merely *his* presentation it is supposed to be the *real presence* of "invisible presences" themselves.

Comparing the book with a fetish statue[12] totally misses the particular and logically fundamentally more complex nature of "book". It is an underdetermination. Fetish objects are always one particular physical thing in its singularity, without possibility of copies, fundamentally irreplaceable. Modern books, by contrast, are mass-produced, printed in hundreds or thousands of copies. What they *are* is not really dependent on any one particular physical copy: the reality of "book" lies above the level of the physical copies in which it may circulate. In extreme cases, physical (and even electronic) copies can be dispensed with altogether, just think of the novel and film *Fahrenheit 451*: Existence only in memory, in the mind. In its true reality a book is psychologically not a physical object.

By the same token, "picking the book up and turning its pages with quiet attention and emotional participation" is not what we mean by reading at all. The former has much more similarity to turning Tibetan prayer wheels, which should probably also be done with quiet attention and emotional participation. Pious *but mindless*. For a true reader, the act of reading is not religious, and a book the opposite of a fetish statue. "Totem object" (as well as "sacred book", for that matter) on the one hand and "reading" on the other hand exclude each other. Fetish and totem are intrinsically connected with taboo, not only in Freud's book title, and with awe. Reading, by contrast, requires an emancipated, alert mind, fundamentally freed from both totem and taboo, a mind free to make *its own* sense of the text *on its own responsibility* and to come to its own judgment. And a good reading requires a fine intellect and the *thought* of the heart. The purpose of reading is also not to polish the *book*, but to "polish" (refine, differentiate, and expand) the *reader's* mind, increase his insight.

---

12 The reader might here of course wish to insist that Hillman's comparison of his book with a statue must not be taken literally, but much rather metaphorically. But quite apart from the difficulty of taking "*physical* form of invisible presences" as metaphor, psychologically such a metaphorical understanding of Hillman's statements about the fetish-statue character of his book would not make any difference. Because what psychologically counts is not whether, but *which* metaphors are used and what they tell us about the actually prevailing fantasy.

For a true reader, a book does not give physical form to invisible presences nor is it a local habitation for the angels in words (quite apart from the fact that the smallest units of a book are not words, but sentences! The words as independent items have to have *gone under* in and into each sentence as a logically higher structure *if* there is to be a meaningful statement). And reading does not mean being visited by those presences and receiving them like guests. Reading is something active, the reader's own mental work. If it should turn out that through one's reading the book, invisible presences indeed come into play, then they do not—essentialistically, fundamentalistically—always already *have* their "local habitation" *in* the physical "book", but *receive* a "local habitation" for the first time through the fundamentally productive, indeed creative act of reading, and exclusively *in the comprehending mind* (rather than in the physical form of the book) and, furthermore, in this mind only while and for as long as this comprehension is in fact happening. In many medieval and Renaissance depictions of the Annunciation, the Virgin Mary is shown as reading the Bible. We could say that it is her insightfully reading this book that first, and within itself, *creates* "the angel" together with his Annunciation and *amounts* to her conception ("concept"!) of the Son of God as the Redeemer,[13] rather than the appearance of a factually existing angel coming to her out of the blue and happening to find her reading rather than, for example, being busy in the kitchen. And because a book in its true sense exists only in the individual minds of its readers, it does not possess an unambiguous identity, nor are always the self-same invisible presences induced by an understanding of it: There are as many versions of *Re-Visioning Psychology* as there are readers. "It" exists only as numerous diverse (better or worse, insightful or superficial) understandings (and misunderstandings).

Assessing what we found here we have to come to the conclusion that Hillman believes the psychologically more simple, more primitive, more naive reality ("invisible presences") to be higher than the more differentiated, more culturally developed, more refined and logically complex ("book"). The immediately impressive takes precedence over what, as something inevitably reflected, becomes accessible only through one's own mental work.[14]

---

13   A "conception" could only occur in her if her reading was *not* pious, devotional, but truly intelligent.

14   This plays also a role in his general privileging images over against concepts.

Rumpite libros, ne corda vestra rumpantur, and "beware of the physical in the matter", the alchemists said. But how can you tear books apart if they come as fetish statues, if they are declared to *be* the physical form and actual habitation of actual invisible presences? When once walking with Hillman through some San Francisco streets at the time of the San Francisco IAAP congress I remember his boldly wearing a cap with the inscription, "I am a born-again pagan!" The focus on physical objects as habitation of "presences" is pagan, even "animistic", just as pagan as the relics in the Roman Catholic Church. It is fundamentally beneath the real level of the modern soul and, for that matter, also of Hillman's own book, which after all *argues* his case, presents revolutionary insights, and makes demands on the intelligence of its readers. His (modern, even decidedly subversive and explicitly polemical) project of a "re-visioning" excludes his idea of totem objects and vice versa. Totems and fetishes are relative to preliterate times.

Of course, with this fantasy Hillman only plays primitive, plays animistic. He *is* not. He goes *with consciousness* beneath the level of consciousness he has reached—a stooping, indeed, a veritable *sacrificium*, which is obviously indispensable for simulating a premodern religious mode under the very conditions of modernity. And as in Jung, although in different ways, it is the *modern* psychological idea of soul that serves as the Trojan horse with which the modern mind can be undermined by planting the suspicion in it that it is merely "surface", having totally forgotten that it carries this so-defined soul, and with it the premodern (in Hillman's case: The pagan animistic) mode, in itself as the very ground and deeper truth on which it is in truth always already based. *Syntactically* we have in Hillman a highly developed, highly cultured and *intellectual* modern mind, but his *semantic message* offers us "fetishism" and a call to "polish" his book. The left hand is not supposed to know what the right hand is doing. In much the same way within his book itself he theatrically stages, as its ending, "A Processional Exit" of all the ideas and persons discussed, a procession off "into memory", thereby stylizing these ideas and cited persons as if they had been actual physical *presences* and not much rather from the outset merely *representations* in the mind (the modern mind!) and contents of consciousness, and as if what one has read would not, all by itself and without any formal procession, drift off into memory, if not, which is perhaps even more likely, into forgetfulness. He wants us to take *his own* personifications of these ideas literally, at face value.

As far as the question of authorship is concerned, especially in a preface I would expect an author to take full responsibility *personally* for the psychological theory presented in the book *as his own ideas* and arguments, offered by him to the public for what they may be worth; that he face his readers as an ordinary fellow human being, as an I, in our case as the James Hillman which he is (and as "*only* that!"[15]), leaving it to his readers to decide if what *he* wrote is in addition expressive of a deeper authority than his personal one or not. Goethe said that poems should be such that their idea or content could also be expressed in simple ordinary prose. Not that he wanted to reduce them to that prosaic content and deny their reaching into higher truly poetic spheres. But he wanted them to have their feet on the ground, and our discussion of them to begin from this sober starting point. No inflated enthusiasm. Hillman does the reverse. He starts out from the higher, the auratic. That he attenuates his own authorship sounds like humility, but it is a sign of hyping up because it is done in favor of a higher (or deeper) "authority" and "power" that he claims for his book, a power that in turn is derived, as he says, "from powers other than what can be accounted for by my witness" (see the paragraph preceding the one quoted). This might of course be so. But it is not for him to judge, to anticipate and claim. The real judge of the presence in his book of such a higher authorship and authority cannot even be his contemporary readers (who cannot have the necessary historical distance). It can only be posterity.

A book that advances the *theory* of "the inherence of the angel in the word" and makes out a case for a "psychology with Gods" is not ipso facto itself an event of the presence of the angel or the Gods. No self-predication. To begin with, it is and remains just the presence of an assertion, a human author's worldly, "secular" theory. If you personify ideas, they do not in fact turn into persons.

"Gods" as first principles of psychology

But with the key word "psychology with Gods" I have arrived at the major issue concerning (the second aspect of) Hillman's notion of soul as root metaphor of psychology for which my discussion of the one minor detail of

---

15 Cf. *MDR* p.325: "The greatest limitation for man is the 'self'; it is manifested in the experience: 'I am *only* that!'"

the authorship question was supposed to prepare the ground. "The Gods" are for Hillman, we could say, something like the soul's "first principles". But this is psychologically untenable. For psychology, the soul is psychology's first principle, and what IS the first principle cannot in turn HAVE first principles. By the same token you cannot at the same time demand a "re-visioning [of] psychology from the point of view of soul" AND a "re-vision of psychology in terms of the Gods".[16] Psychology cannot serve two masters, two sets of first principles. It has to choose, or rather precisely not choose, because it has no choice, but stands under a Necessity, *Ananke*: Its name has always already given it its first principle, soul.

The only legitimate formula for a re-visioning of psychology is thus Jung's, "a psychology with soul". On the other hand, a "psychology with Gods" means that the root metaphor "soul" is taken prisoner for a standard and measure that is introduced into it from outside. It amounts to a dogmatic, ideological prejudice with which psychological phenomenology is then approached: Archetypal Psychology, the way it happens to be set up, knows a priori that all psychic phenomena have to be seen through to the Gods, and it even knows by and large who these Gods are, namely basically, although not exclusively, the ones of Greek mythology. So what I indicated in the discussion of the topic of "author" is repeated here: The psychologist does not wait to see what the phenomena in fact display of their own accord as their own depth, their authority and meaning. He anticipates that it must be a God. The psychologist has always already taken the phenomenology prisoner for his dogma of the Gods. Although he admittedly does not know yet specifically "Who? Which God?" is involved, he nevertheless knows THAT, and he knows so to speak the list of all possible candidates. Psychology thus ultimately becomes theosophy, needless to say: *Polytheistic* theosophy in Hillman's case. (As to "-sophy": It is precisely and only because of the focus on Gods that Hillman speaks of his psychology as "a *nonagnostic psychology*".[17])

16 The first quotation is from James Hillman, "Preface: A Memoir from the Author for the 1992 Edition", *Re-Visioning Psychology*, New York: William Morrow & Company, 1992, p. xv and the second from James Hillman, *The Myth of Analysis*, Evanston: Northwestern University Press, 1972, p. 298.
17 James Hillman, *Re-Visioning Psychology*, New York: William Morrow & Company, 1992, p. 167.

A "psychology with Gods" (and with "angels", "daimones", and "presences") is just as illegitimate as modern physics would be if it had axiomatically constituted itself, for example, as a "physics with nature spirits". Physics is exclusively committed to its own one root metaphor, the physicality of nature. This allows me to point out another difference between "psychology with soul" and "psychology with Gods". *What* soul is, is fundamentally unknown to begin with, still completely open. What it is remains to be seen from how it manifests itself in the course of the history of its self-manifestation. But the Gods are, at least to some extent, already known. So a "psychology with Gods" works within a "closed economy".

Hillman would of course argue that a psychology with Gods is psychologically fully justified because of "the soul's intrinsic affinity with, nay, love for the Gods".[18] But this is precisely his dogmatic presupposition. It is true, such a love is borne out by numerous phenomena in the soul's past. But psychology must not axiomatically codify this empirical finding as eternal truth. We have conversely to let the soul speak for itself and allow ourselves to be taught by its self-display, maybe also be surprised by what all it may love or not love at what time. No anticipation. Today, at any rate, there is little that could show *the soul's* intrinsic love for the Gods. Even what we see in Hillman himself is rather *his own* subjective predilection for the Gods, his own need to have Gods—much like Jung was guided in his psychology-making by a strong personal wish or need for meaning, the numinous, and God (in the singular)—wishes that in both cases were given out as the objective soul's needs.

The intrusion of a strong personal element into the design and character of Hillman's psychology shows not only (a) in his privileging, in each case, only one of the soul's own internal pairs of opposites and (b) in his "psychology with Gods". Above all it is also revealed in the fact that his subjective world-rescue or world-improvement hopes gave his psychology to some extent the character of a *program* or *agenda*, which detracted from its fully being able to be a serious discipline solely devoted to insight. Having such an agenda (viz., of ensouling the nonhuman, the world) is both naive and presumptuous. And despite *what* it aims for (in this case: an ensouling), it is, qua agenda, an ego project. As suggested above, from a psychological

---

18   James Hillman, "Preface: A Memoir from the Author for the 1992 Edition", *Re-Visioning Psychology*, New York: William Morrow & Company, 1992, p. xi.

point of view it is the soul's job to ensoul the world, if it happens to be so inclined (as it obviously was inclined during the ages of animism, mythology, and metaphysics). It is not our, the psychologist's, the ego's, job. The psychologist's task is merely to accompany the real movement of the soul with soulful understanding.

But even in the case of the long periods of history that indeed bear out a love on the part of the soul for the gods,[19] a modern psychology, if it is a psychology with soul, has the task of applying its "seeing through" to the gods themselves, rather than seeing phenomena through to the Gods. For a true psychology, the gods are themselves soul *phenomena* and not the lens through which phenomena have to be seen. Hillman took the phenomenal gods at face value. He literalized, hypostatized them, removing them from the *phenomenal* level of the soul's life, raising them high above the sphere of change and particularity as frozen, atemporal, unchangeable and universal first principles. What are actually *products* of soul-making, by the soul's own making, is turned into *principles* of soul-making or *dominants* of the soul's life. This is a fundamental reversal (the germ of which was already inherent in Jung's archetypal theory), which at the same time happens to amount to a case of *psychological fundamentalism* (a characteristic which is of course in no way remedied by one's defining the Gods as metaphors: Their metaphor character merely prevents this fundamentalism from turning into *religious* or *political* fundamentalism). For a true psychology, the gods, both the polytheistic ones *with* all their immortality and the one high God *with* all his eternity, omnipotence, and omniscience, are necessarily products of the soul, phenomenal guises of itself, part of its self-manifestation, forms of its talking about itself *at certain stages* and *under certain real conditions* of its own historical development. "The soul's intrinsic love for the Gods", too, is an historical phenomenon, relative on the one hand to *pre*modern situations and on the other hand to the times *after* the earliest prehistoric hunting and gathering cultures.

So we see that "the phenomenon James Hillman" means on the one hand an invaluably important revolutionary step forward beyond the conventional versions of Jungian psychology that were fundamentally unconscious of themselves, to a psychology that deserved its name because it made the soul its root metaphor and re-visioned psychology as a whole in

---

19 Since here *I* am speaking, I do not capitalize the word.

terms of this root metaphor. But that on the other hand, *within itself* this re-visioned psychology did not go all the way through to the end with its project of re-visioning because the notion of soul was not fully freed from external points of views or subjective, ideological predilections. Its definition remained decidedly one-sided, and certain essential *phenomenal* products of the soul, the gods, were in some way externalized as first principles governing the soul's life.

Hillman, the man

After this brief discussion of the substantial meaning of James Hillman for psychology I want to at least mention a few of the characteristic features of James Hillman, the man.

Very striking and enjoyable were his broad smile and his refreshing laughter coming from the depth of his whole being, but also his likewise uninhibited anger when he met with views that were unacceptable for him. As a personality Hillman possessed a strong presence, which also showed itself in the fact that without needing to push himself into the foreground he was usually quite naturally the center of groups. Remarkable also was his style, both as person and as writer or speaker. It showed an elegance and lightness, a gracefulness and poetic quality, which had the effect that it caused his presentations to reach his audience *subliminally*. As a speaker (and as a writer) he was enchanting. But beyond the intellectual level, this easy and natural contact with people showed itself also with ordinary, even "simple" people. I remember, for example, when we had once returned to his house in Dallas and he saw two neighbors of his, elderly black ladies, probably rather uneducated and certainly completely ignorant of Archetypal Psychology, sitting across the street on the steps to their house, Hillman before entering his house quite characteristically first walked over to them for a lively chat.

The brilliance and richness of his ideas and insights were amazing. Concerning all kinds of subjects from the most diverse areas (including "alchemical blue" or "yellow", the psychology of old age, political power, the reality of war, "character and calling"), he time and again came up with innovative, surprising and truly illumining interpretations, teaching us to see things from entirely unsuspected perspectives. With virtuosity he used material from an astonishingly large repertoire of examples taken from very different fields and from the whole range of Western (and not only Western) cultural memory, often associating seemingly disparate images or ideas in a meaningful and stimulating way. It is needless to say that his insights were *psychologically* enriching.

In addition to this sparkling intelligence I also found the scholarly side of Hillman impressive. One just has to take a look at the long bibliography of his early book on *Emotion* or consider the enormous amount of reading in biographical literature that must have been at the foundation of his book, *The Soul's Code*. On the other hand, as a self-confessed *bricoleur*, it seems that for his associations he sometimes cited and made use of statements by philosophers and other authors without regarding what these statements and the words used therein meant in their authors' own philosophical schemes and in terms of the thinking of the ages from which these quotes were taken. Guided by a sameness of verbal expressions, a sameness or similarity of idea might be suggested by him where it did not always really exist. This was probably helped along by his general emphasis on imaginal likenesses and his decided disinterest in historical time and the differences brought by history. Naturally, an emphasis on imaginal likenesses is more interested in the impression that images or statements *give* than in a careful genetic reconstruction of their meaning from the body of thought that they *come* from. I jokingly call this tendency Hillman's "impressionism". His rejection of the importance of historical time made it easy for him to approach examples from different ages or periods as if they all belonged, side by side (synchronically, paratactically), to an eternal present. I well remember how during the Eranos conference 1978 when Hillman and I talked about a lecture we had just heard by Marie-Louise von Franz on "The Psychological Experience of Time", Hillman, partly in response to my question why he had not wanted to speak that year and partly in reaction to von Franz's talk, stated flatly that Time was psychologically of no interest to him.

The topic of his "impressionism" brings something else to mind. In the Preface to the 1992 edition of *Re-Visioning* he relates the prehistory of this book, how one day William Sloan Coffin called him by phone to invite him to come to Yale and that he, Hillman, "responded by saying I preferred the set piece and formal audience to smaller workshops". This is characteristic. He definitely wanted to present in front of formal audiences and not so much engage in seminars or study groups painstakingly studying texts. Seemingly in contrast to this preference, he wanted panel discussions (in front of a formal audience) not to be serious formal debates, but casual conversations. For example, at the "International Symposium of Archetypal Psychology" in Santa Barbara in September 2000, organized by Pacifica Graduate Institute, he wanted the panel discussion staged as if its members were sitting in a European café chatting with each other. This suggests he wanted the participants of the panel, while discussing things to work out certain issues in front of an audience, nevertheless at the same time to playact that they were not trying to do this at all, but were rather sitting relaxed around a café table, (imaginally) sipping their coffee and casually exchanging ideas. Somehow like actors *on stage*, and yet at the same time not with each participant saying, as in a real theater, his memorized part, but rather participating in a spontaneous discussion. In a way, this kind of panel was supposed to be a simulation of the wonderful memorable evening gatherings of the Hillman crowd during the Eranos conferences at the one or the other *real* sidewalk café on Ascona's promenade. Similarly, the conference at Notre Dame University in 1992 had to be a "*Festival* of Archetypal Psychology" rather than a normal academic conference. The show and display element as well as the casual form were important for and very characteristic of Hillman.

Hillman has mentioned his own *puer* qualities, so I need not go into them. But in connection with the "impressionism" idea I want to mention one interesting reaction of his. At a time when "spraying graffiti" was still unknown in Europe, there all of a sudden appeared in Zurich someone who soon became known as "the Zurich sprayer". In a spontaneous reaction, Hillman with his martial, somewhat youthful anti-authority bent found this great, because the sprayer "put a face on" naked, blank walls. This was for me a very revealing response, because it is antiphenomenological: putting something on a blank surface to *give* it a face versus letting the phenomena show their actual face *or non-face*, here: letting precisely the emptiness and barrenness of a concrete wall speak.

At least twice Hillman in his writing career made use of Berkeley's *esse est percipi* (to be is to be perceived) to describe the special capability of some people to see the particular gift or later genius in youngsters or students when for the ordinary eye these young people as yet looked rather ordinary or even downright incompetent or maybe even pathological. I think Hillman possessed a little of this capability. He not only inspired, but also supported and fostered as a mentor many young people, encouraging them to write an article or maybe even a book about their at first perhaps timidly expressed ideas that he already saw were worthwhile. As editor of *Spring* and as publisher of Spring Publications he even made the products of these efforts publicly available. He was also an unusually conscientious editor, carefully reading and really editing every manuscript to be printed, making lots of suggestions for modifications.

I myself am one of the people who greatly benefitted from his support. And so I remember him with deep gratitude, both for the enormous inspiration I received from his insights through his writings and for the personal support during my early years as a Jungian, in fact from my 2nd year as a student at the Stuttgart Jung Institute onwards, when we had not yet met in person. I treasure especially the memory of those days during the later 1970s and the 1980s when we were, as he put it once, "comrades in arms, companions in drink, friends". But I also stayed internally in intensive close connection with him at those later times when our views began, I use his words, to "diverge" and it was time for us to go "into the fray" with each other. I regret that a *real* fray never came about despite my repeated efforts to bring one about, but am happy that our personal friendship and mutual respect continued all the time, I hope and believe also on his side, despite the pain that my pointed criticism in all likelihood caused him.

Chapter 3

The "black sun" seen through
Marlan's proton pseudos[1]

Stan Marlan's paper, "The absolute that is not absolute: an alchemical reflection on the *caput mortuum*, the dark other of logical light*",
contains much that one might take issue with. But I will here start out
from only one single statement to be found in it and discuss its wider
implications:

> My work began with the recognition that the image of the black sun re-
> sisted conscious assimilation—that it would not yield or be incorporated,
> did not dissolve, go away, go under, get lifted up, but rather remained to
> challenge one's psychological narcissism to the core, [with] experiences
> of brokenness, incision, wound, castration, cut [,] negation, and with an
> ultimate "no" to consciousness.[2]

The discussion that follows is not meant as a response *to Marlan* (which
would be pointless after all that has been said in my previous publications
and in previous exchanges with him), but addresses itself to those interested in psychology as the discipline of interiority. It has the purpose of
a self-clarification of the psychological standpoint in view of the objections presented by Marlan. Errors and misconstruals can be helpful. One
can learn from them.

1 Written December 2016.
2 All references to Marlan's work in this chapter are taken from the following publication:
Stan Marlan, "The absolute that is not absolute: an alchemical reflection on the *caput
mortuum*, the dark other of logical light*." *International Journal of Jungian Studies*, 9(1),
28–41, DOI: 10.1080/19409052.2016.1237372, p. 33.

DOI: 10.4324/9781003611417-3

Psychology based on empirical personal experience and not on generally valid concept

"My work began": Marlan gives us here not only the temporal beginning, but more importantly also the first principle or axiom from which he starts out, the foundational premise of his work as a psychologist. Two things are noteworthy. First, what he says here has the character of a confessional statement: He reports an *experience* he had. An experience is an empirical and as such irrational event, a happening in time, not a rational conclusion from hermeneutic endeavors or deductive reasoning. In mathematics, the empirical fact that to date nobody succeeded in "squaring the circle" does not mean that it cannot be squared. The latter idea becomes a mathematical truth only if and when the explicit mathematical (logical) *proof has been furnished* that this squaring of the circle is indeed on logical grounds impossible. The same applies mutatis mutandis in psychology to the alleged "unassimilable remnant". In myths and fairy tales, there are often doors or gates that open only if the "right time" or the "right person" has come. So if you come to such a gate and it does not open despite numerous persistent attempts, it does not mean that it *cannot* come open. And in the empirical practice of psychotherapy performed by us finite mortal minds it is a frequent experience that whole dreams or particular dream details remain a total riddle: to us, to particular analysts at particular times. But this does not warrant us to claim that they are unassimil*able*, ununderstand*able*.

Marlan calls this existential experience, which came to him as a finished result, a "recognition", but it really counts for him as a *revelation*, in some ways comparable to visionary experiences of mystics or prophets, because it changed and fixed his outlook and functioned for him as an "absolute that indeed *is* absolute" (in Marlan's undialectical sense of the word). And secondly, what this revelation leads to if taken as a basis for his theory is therefore an ideology, a belief system, and ipso facto not psychology. He is not guided by, does not start out from, the question of what the *concept* of psychology requires, if it really is supposed to deserve its name, not with the question of what the soul wants, and he does not methodically proceed from *there*. This also means that Marlan confuses the *phenomenal* or *experiential* level with the *methodological, epistemological, discipline-constituting* level. Contingencies such as empirical subjective experiences cannot be used as bases to build fundamental tenets of a field or discipline on.

His personal experience with which he begins is a kind of "conversion experience" (it "challenge[d] [his] psychological narcissism to the core"!), similar in type (though not in content) to the ones reported by certain Christians. Starting from it as his basis, he now is, at least in his theorizing, totally in the service of this revelation and works as its faithful preacher who turns to philosophers (such as Kant) not to get a deeper philosophical understanding of *their thinking* but to cite them as *witnesses* to confirm his precious belief.

One single image absolutized

This revelation is one that is intrinsic only to one particular item, one single phenomenon: The image (and a rather rare, isolated one at that) of the black sun. But Marlan absolutizes it and gives it *fundamental* importance as a universally valid principle not only for all psychological thinking, but even for philosophy (e.g., the question of the thing-in-itself). It thus becomes his "god-term" (Paul Kugler) or at least, as Jung might have said, his dogma (and we remember here Jung's critiquing Freud for having made, as Jung thought, a dogma out of "sexuality" as something to be "religiously observed"). But there are of course thousands of other images that can be assimilated and relativize this one "recognition" of his. What Marlan does could be compared to a biologist who were to take one single body organ, say the vermiform appendix, and to claim that its function and nature tells us the ultimate truth of the human organism as such. One particular phenomenon must not be given *normative* significance for the whole of phenomenology.

Certainly, we can say that each archetypal image and thus also "the black sun", when and for as long as it is constellated, is a manifestation of the whole truth of the soul. However, it is this whole truth only as it appears from the one particular angle that the respective specific image represents. It is not *the* truth of the soul and *the* principle for psychology as such. Now, because the black sun gives valid expression to the truth of the soul (although its truth only from one particular vantage point), we can even concede that the message or truth of this one particular image may indeed be "an ultimate 'no' to consciousness". But the other side of the same coin is that this ultimate "no" to consciousness is an *image-internal* truth that must not be extracted from this image (and from the experience of the image) and made use of outside of it.[3] We cannot impose it on all phenomena,

3 A particular archetypal image or myth can only be said to be relevant for *psychology as such* if it can be shown that it gives (imaginal) expression to a truth that corresponds to the concept or definition of psychology.

all psychological images as a, nay, as *the* general truth. From this it follows that the ultimate No to consciousness and the unassimilability do not even apply to that very image of the black sun *itself* whose *internal* message, after all, this No to consciousness is, let alone to psychological experience at large. The unassimilability does not even apply to the black sun itself. For as a matter of course this image, too, can indeed—despite its *internal* "No to assimilation"—be assimilated to consciousness, just like any other archetypal image, be it that of the bottle imp, the virgin mother, Dionysos, Hermes, the underworld, Kali Durga, the navel of the earth, Apollo, Helios, Christ, the Grail, or what have you. But the contradiction between this insight on the one hand and Marlan's belief in unassimilability as a fundamental (even philosophical) truth on the other hand leads to our next point, the definition or understanding of "conscious assimilation".

"Conscious assimilation" misunderstood as dissolving, going away

The consciousness with which Marlan from the outset approached his chosen topic of the black sun was obviously informed by and committed to the wish that it should "dissolve, go away, go under, get lifted up". Only this wish or expectation, ultimately the wish "to get out", explains his violent experience of brokenness, incision, wound. (Jung, for example, reacted quite differently: " 'Depression' means, as a rule, 'having to go downwards'" [Letter to an anonymous woman, 9 March 1959, my transl.]. Or Jung's delight at the dream of an analysand in which she was immersed in a hole filled with hot stuff and tried to get out, when Jung came and pushed her deeper into it, saying: "Not out of it, but through it".[4]) I ask: Why in heaven's name should it dissolve? Who expects that in the case of "the black sun" "assimilation to consciousness" would amount to the dissolution and disappearance of the blackness? Indeed, if it were to dissolve, could we then still speak of its "conscious *assimilation*"?

   This wrong criterion for, this naive and egoic understanding of, "assimilation" is Marlan's *proton pseudos*, and it is something absolutely astounding and weird to come from a Jungian analyst. The human, all-too-human (namely, the ego's wish for relief from the darkness) got here the better

---

4 Reported in Aniela Jaffé, *Aus Leben und Werkstatt von C.G. Jung*, Zürich und Stuttgart: Rascher, 1968, p. 111.

of the professional, the psychologist. Furthermore, is it not unbelievable to hear an analyst proclaim "an ultimate 'no' to consciousness"? At any rate, in Jungian psychology we don't approach phenomena with the goal of eliminating them, doing them in.

Rather, instead of dissolution and disappearance of the problematic or hard-to-bear image, "assimilation" implies a two-way process: The blackness, to stay with this example, is assimilated to consciousness only to the extent that *consciousness is conversely assimilated to the blackness.* Making conscious means "*saving* the phenomena", means getting deeper into them, seeing and appreciating their innermost truth (in the case of the black sun: Seeing its truth *as* black sun!, *as* real darkness); it means our allowing ourselves to be initiated into them, be taught by them. Jung (about neurosis): "We do not cure it, it cures us" (*CW* 10 § 361). Applying the psychological understanding of assimilation to the particular image of the black sun that we are concerned with here, we can say: Once this archetypal image has indeed been constellated (so that we are in it and enveloped by it and it has become the whole world for us), it is truly assimilated to consciousness when the latter *becomes fully aware* precisely of the "ultimate 'no' to consciousness".

The "unassimilable remainder", it now appears, is the *petrified* reflection of the ego's misguided and illusionary expectation in the mirror of the objective soul. If the ego in Marlan (the "psychological narcissism", as he calls it) did not insist on something like dissolution, the black sun would not answer in the form of an experience of brokenness, incision, and castration, but simply result in consciousness's growing awareness of what the *utter darkness* of the dark sun entails.

It is Marlan's unpsychological confusion of assimilation to consciousness with overcoming the phenomena and idealizing them (in the sense of whitewashing and lifting them up into lofty heights) that he also imputes both to Hegel and to our psychology. In other words, it is *his own* original aim, his *proton pseudos*, that he now, after his conversion through his study of the black sun, projects on, and fights in, Hegel and us!

The I reserves itself

Now, his having originally been committed to the psychologically naive, "pious" desire *to get rid of* the darkness of the black sun has the unfortunate psychological consequence that he learns the psychologically wrong lesson from his experience: His consciousness did not suffer that very "castration"

(Marlan's term) that, after all, his *own* experience obviously had in store for him and for his "psychological narcissism". The two-way process mentioned does not occur. Instead we find a unidirectional object-orientation. *It*, the object, the blackness of the black sun, should but does not dissolve; *it*, the black sun, *is* challenging, but the challenge does not transform the mind. The I does not enter the process. The subject is not from the outset involved, which means that thinking does here not become in itself reflexive, although reflexivity is indispensable and constitutive for psychology. A "subject-object", it seems, remains outside Marlan's vision. In his theory the I as *observer* or consciousness is merely faced with an unyielding remainder as its external object vis-à-vis itself. Certainly, he sees the challenge, but he holds it at bay. The I's initiation (Lat. *in-ire*) is avoided; the I reserves itself, keeps itself out. In other words, Marlan (unwittingly) *rescued* the "psychological narcissism" from that very challenge that he himself felt to be inherent in his own experience of the black sun. And he managed to bring about this rescue in two ways. Firstly, by means of the defense mechanism of a simple *reversal into the opposite*, by switching sides, namely from his original wish for an assimilation and overcoming of the blackness to his final stance for which the (originally challenging or threatening) unassimilable blackness is now all of a sudden ego-syntonic, indeed, has become his pet idea. Secondly, by means of the device of "*ideology formation*": What should actually be *his* consciousness's "castration" or alchemical mortification and ipso facto *its* being initiated into a *dark seeing* is turned into a universalized theoretical *doctrine* and *dogma about* an (objectively subsisting) "darkness, unassimilable remnant, ashes, *caput mortuum*, incision, wound" as *objects* of consciousness and as theoretical *contents* of a belief-system. Function or process is turned into entity.

Castration means serious loss. But the encounter with the black sun has for Marlan, on the contrary, the result that he comes out of it with a positive new acquisition: With his now being in possession of a remnant as hard fact that is immune to all attempts at psychologizing or soul-making and whose very nature it is to *remain*. Ashes, *caput mortuum*. No transformation anymore! Having seen Marlan's resistance to the challenge that he felt comes from the black sun, we now realize, that his "unassimilable remainder" is nothing but the reification of the ego's *resistance* to its own "castration", to its own initiation into the blackness of the black sun. What is actually a subjective attitude of his is frozen so that in his theory it appears as objective factual reality, something existing "out there". In this remainder, consciousness unwittingly has before its mental eyes the monument and stronghold of its own subjective steadfast resistance to the mind's own going under into the interiority and absolute negativity of the very image that showed itself to him and impressed him so fundamentally.

The black sun: The dark other of "logical light"?

That the black sun has to do with blackness and thus may be the "dark other of" something can be granted. But the dark other of what? This is the question. Marlan believes it to be the other of what he calls "logical light" (p. 29 and others).

This does not make sense. "Logical light" is an unfitting free association brought in from outside. Not only does the image of the black sun itself not contain any (be it affirmative or negative) reference to the sphere of "the logical".[5] Much more important is the realization that something can only be the other of such a thing or dimension that has already been fully reached and is already a prevailing reality. High schools are not the other of universities. But bitcoin could rightly be considered "the other of" conventional currency. "The other of" implies a relation of negation, off pushing off from something given. This is apparently also accepted by Marlan since for him it is the very character of the black sun that it amounts to "incision, wound" and challenges one's psychological narcissism to the core. An event of wounding requires that the thing to be wounded already prevails.

Now this is the point where the idea of the black sun as the dark other of logical light goes wrong. Being itself *imaginal*, this image antedates "the logical". The latter is historically as well as logically an entirely new dimension of consciousness beyond the level of the imaginal. "The logical" is still unimagined and unimaginable for the black sun. "The logical" presupposes, and comes only into being through, the demise of the entire mythological/imaginal mode of being-in-the-world. It is a new status of consciousness. It logically is, and historically was, the successor of the mythological/imaginal as such. And what Marlan calls "logical light" and identifies above all with Hegel's thinking and with psychology (as the discipline of interiority) is precisely also for Marlan personally a still unknown,

---

5 For the moment I address myself only to the first part of Marlan's phrase "logical light", i.e., the logical. In a later section, I will turn to his association of the logical with "light".

unsuspected new continent, because, although he may indeed have looked through the entrance gate to Hegel's philosophy as well as through that to psychology from outside, he never ventured himself forth through the entrances. He never actually exposed himself to and started to swim in their waters on his own. With critical reservation he systematically halted from the outset before the threshold. So he has only knowledge "about" them, that is, has mere opinions that have the character of prejudgments. His own real horizon is and remains to be partly that of Hillman's imaginal psychology, partly that of classical Jungian and partly that of personalistic psychology, and, philosophically, it seems to be that of the old world of naive metaphysics (that he tries to justify with the oxymoron of his pre-Kantian[6] Kant interpretation).

Since the so-called "logical light" lies outside the horizon of the image of the black sun, it cannot possibly be what this image or experience is the "dark other" of. Something imaginal, an image (and be it the image of the blackest dark sun), is simply not a match for "logical light". It cannot challenge it. Just like bloodletting is not a match for bacterial infections and hammer, pliers, and screwdrivers are not a match for programming mistakes in computer software. The logical may at times challenge the imaginal, but not vice versa. It is a fundamental error to treat the black sun and the "logical light" as if the image of the black sun were at least a peer of the logical.

If one nevertheless wants to see this image as "the other of", then one has to say that it is obviously the other of the bright sunlight that shines in the natural world and produces our *day*light, as well as of the sun in the mythological, imaginal world as, e.g., Helios, Apollo. It is the natural light and the mythological/imaginal sun (whose mythology-internal *real* other, by the way, would be the underworld, not Marlan's black sun) that the black sun negates and intends to push off from to something radically new and previously unheard of. The black sun disappoints and "wounds" our natural expectations of the warm, brightly shining sun in a both literal and imaginal sense.

---

6 In the depth and syntactically, Marlan's thinking remains pre-Kantian due to his irreflexive one-sided object orientation (the Kantian revolution of the *Denkungsart* ["mode of thinking"] [!] did not happen in his own thinking; Marlan does his best to rescue the immediate focus on the object). This is so irrespective of his also *semantically* adopting, in his own way, Heideggerian and Derridean positions.

Having mentioned Apollo, I must dispel the possible misconception that this god represented already what Marlan called the "logical light". Mythology as a whole and thus also the brightness of the Delphic Apollo are still fundamentally ignorant of "the logical", untouched by it, still enfolded in the *anima alba*.[7] "The logical" is something wholly other. "The logical", the conceptual, and reflection (i.e., the logical form of reflectedness) belong to a fundamentally different level that comes only into existence through the ruthless wounding, sublation, and overcoming of the mythological/imaginal status of consciousness as such. Mythology and the imaginal in general are precisely defined by their innocence vis-à-vis "the logical". (By saying this I do not mean to imply that mythology were *in itself* illogical, unreasonable, or irrational and that mythological man, on the behavioral level of his mental *operations*, had not been able to think logically. My point is merely that mythology psychologically, *as a status and constitution of consciousness*, antedates "reflection" and "the logical" *as another status of consciousness*. It is, by the way, this confusion between rationality as inner quality of mythology and as the character of people's mental operations on the one hand and rationality as logical *status* of consciousness on the other, that hampered the correct understanding of Lévy-Bruhl's much-disputed thesis of the "prelogical mentality" of the primitives).

If the "black sun" is not the dark other of logical light, what is it the other of?

What does show itself in the black sun? The blackness of the black sun, in which nothing can be seen, is nothing other than the extreme and totally abstract image *of image stripped of* all its concrete imaginal qualities and concrete sensual (naturalistic) content (of color, nuance, shape, object,

---

7 "Anima alba" is a *psychological* notion. It does not mean that the times during which consciousness was contained in the innocence of the anima alba status was *practically*, on the level of *behavior*, innocent and harmless. The anima alba, on the one hand, and behavioral brutality, on the other, can well go together. Just think of sacrificial killings of humans. "The anima", said Jung (*CW* 9i § 60), "believes in the καλὸν κἀγαθόν, the 'beautiful and the good', a primitive conception that antedated the discovery of the conflict between aesthetics and morals. . . . The paradox of this marriage of ideas troubled the ancients as little as it does the primitives."

person or figure, action . . .), in other words, it is the image *of* no-image. The black sun refuses to be *image* in the full sense and to make sense to the imaginal approach, just as it also refuses to be natural sun and to illumine the natural world for the generality; the confrontation with this image brings the ruthless disappointment, indeed the *voiding*, of consciousness's habitual expectation to find something visible and concrete, something image-like. In this sense the black sun is the image of the radical *voiding of image-quality as such*, or more precisely, the voiding of the *status* of "imaginal" consciousness as a whole (image-focused, pictorially thinking, representational consciousness). With the image of the black sun a condition of extreme abstraction is reached, still within the imaginal, to be sure, but totally untypically for the imaginal, which corresponds to the fact that it is such a very rare image. That is to say, with its totally "unimaginal" abstractness this image has moved to the very border, the extreme margin, of the imaginal as such. This "unimaginal" abstractness becomes all the more striking when we compare and contrast the "black sun" with the truly imaginal, truly mythological idea of the underworld.

Now we understand what the "ultimate 'no' to consciousness" is really about. Marlan got it all wrong. It is by no means the "no" to conscious assimilation, but the "no" to *imaginal* consciousness, to image and to sensuality, the "no" to the "imaginal" stance.

Inasmuch as with the black sun the imaginal has reached, and takes consciousness to, the imaginal's own extreme border, it is a veritable boundary image, an image that borders on what is on the other side of image as such (quite in contrast to "the underworld", which has its sure place in the center and as the ground of the mythological world). The black sun is Janus-faced: in the one direction it is still indebted to the old comfortable imaginal mode and confirms the imaginal (even if its particular quality and content is precisely to deconstruct, with imaginal means, image as such). *And* in the other direction it is image pointing forward beyond itself, beyond the imaginal. As Janus-faced image at the margin it also can be seen as a *threshold*. The totally "unimaginal" abstractness of the image of the black sun, that manifests in its voidness (or blackening) of all sensual content, already betrays its closeness, in its own character, to the sphere of the conceptual and logical. The "black sun" is much more an allegorization (pictorial representation) of an abstract concept than a veritable image. More specifically it is really the (pictorial) portrayal of the logic of stark, abstract self-contradiction: the sun, the very source of light, *in itself* as the opposite of *itself* (rather than the dark other of something else!): Utter darkness.[8] It is a *conceptual* self-contradiction, self-negation (not an imaginal or mythological union of opposites, such as, e.g., the image of the snake as both healing and poisoning, the Great Mother as nourishing and devouring). And by flatly contradicting the natural sun and the mythological sun (Helios, for example) it reveals itself as the soul's need to push off from them. Inasmuch as it is this negation of image, indeed, the black-hole-like absorption of all imaginality into itself, the blackness of the black sun is nothing else but the first immediacy of *absolute negativity* and *interiority* as such.

When it happens that the image of the "black sun" impresses itself on consciousness, then this is that one particular moment, from among all the many diverse archetypal moments in the soul's logical life and self-display, when the soul feels the need to negate its own imaginality and propel itself forward to a new form of itself, by *explicitly* revealing itself as absolute negativity (even though in still *imaginal* and thus in partly misleading form). The black sun image is marginal also in the sense of being very rare, exotic. And so it seems that the soul feels this need to take on this "black sun" guise especially when, in post-mythological times, it is confronted with itself in the form of a consciousness that is still in the status of *anima alba*. It is probably particularly the "white soul" in modern times that tends to get fascinated by the image of the "black sun". The two of them (black sun on the one hand and white-soul consciousness on the other) form a pair (much like, for example, *puer* and *senex*, good and evil, etc.). Together they represent the situation in which the condition of extreme abstraction is reached, an absolutely purified opposition: All black on one side, all light and white on the other. Psychologically seen, the fact that the image of the black sun constellated itself in and for Marlan and that he could get hooked seems to suggest that the anima alba prevails over his consciousness. If, as we heard from Jung, depression means, as a rule, "having to go downwards", that is, being psychologically too high, we can, by the same token, assume that the appearance of the sun as blackness in our time

---

8   This shows that the ("post-imaginal") level of reflection has been reached by this image: As self-contradiction, the image of the black sun refers *within itself* to sun as source of light.

psychologically means, as a rule, consciousness's being rather "white" and being urged to get "darkened".

What does the appearance of this image psychologically mean and want from the consciousness struck by it? I think it is fair to assume that its threshold character together with the weight that the black sun gained for Marlan personally amounted to the soul's invitation to him (an invitation coming from within his own process) to leave both the imaginal and the egoic-naturalistic approaches behind, to transcend the exclusive commitment to imaginal and ego-psychology. The black sun's pointing beyond itself as image is that aspect that gives it the character of an offer to Marlan, whereas its still remaining, as to its form, rooted in the imaginal is accountable for the mere "first immediacy" character of that *to which* it invites.[9] In the image of the black sun the soul had presented him, as if on a silver platter, with the opened entrance gate to *itself as how it appears* on a no longer mythological, no longer imaginal, no longer personalistic level of comprehension. All that was needed for the beholder of this image to be really true to it was his going through it.

---

9 We could ask: Why only "first immediacy"? Why not right away in its fully developed true form? The reason is the difference between movement in empirical space or geography and movement in soul country, from one status of consciousness to another. When I take a plane to America and land there, I find myself not in the first immediacy of America but in the already fully real, fully developed America. But when the soul moves to a new continent, that is, new status, of itself, this new status, other than "America" in our example, does not exist all along. (The same is true for "the other side" "on which" the image of the black sun, as I said, "borders". The "border" metaphor must not either be taken literally, spatially. It must not be imagined in the sense of picture thinking.) All that exists to begin with is the old status of consciousness. The journey to the new status has to create and establish this new status *for the first time* if it is supposed to exist at all, and it has to create it *on the ground of* the old status (since there is not anything or anywhere else to go to: each status of consciousness is "the whole world", "the whole soul", "the whole truth" with nothing outside) and *with the old status's means* and *in its forms*. This is why the soul's journey to its new status can only proceed negatively, self-destructively: By negating, putrefying, decomposing, "deconstructing" and "pushing off from" the old status and by thereby *eventually* transforming it, the old status, into the new. So this journey is not a movement from here to there, not one from one archetypal image or myth to another, not a conversion from one religion or philosophy to another. It is not either a simple metamorphosis of the old status (like processes of getting old). Rather, it is the dialectical, "digestive" self-transportation *on the same spot* to a fundamentally deeper (or higher) logical "level" *of the original status*: Absolute-negative interiorization.

Systematic blindness as mistaken loyalty to the blackness of the black sun

What would "going through it" mean in this context? Of course not a literal movement in space from here to there. Rather, it would mean one's "seeing through" it, and in the special case of a veritable boundary-image, the case of an image-deconstructing image, "seeing through" in turn would mean, his seeing through the *imaginal form* as such; it would mean the move from the (imaginally apparent) simple negation of "image" (absolute blackness as image of "no-image") to the negation of the negation of image *as such* and thus the breakthrough to the coldness of logos or "the logical", as that which is on the other side of the still naturalistically or imaginally perceived blackness of the black sun; or it would mean the move from innocent, passive beholding the blackness as object to *thinking* it and letting it come home to itself (and thus also come home to consciousness), that is, the move from perception and imagination to speculative thought; and, further, it would mean, as far as the discipline of psychology itself is concerned, the move to the corresponding methodological principle of absolute-negative interiorization. Only in this way would the offer be accepted psychologically and the threshold of the entrance gate be really crossed.

Just as the image of the black sun turned out not to be the dark other of "logical light", so we now have to realize that with Marlan's theory of the unassimilable remainder, of ashes, and the *caput mortuum*, etc., the psychologically adequate consequences of the experience of this image have by no means been drawn. To think so would be an illusion. To be loyal to this image requires something else. The soul is always concerned with *itself* and not with (literal) Other; it requires the self-application of its images and thus, in our case, also the negation of the negation of "image as such", *if* the special experience of blackness or "no-image" is itself to come home to consciousness and thereby become psychological.

But the offer that the appearance of the black sun represented was refused (which could be considered the *psychological* equivalent to the Biblical "sin against the Spirit". Marlan did not only miss the chance he was given, but deliberately rejected it). Instead of "invitation" or "entrance" and of going through this entrance and, ipso facto, going into *his own* (not the black sun's!) "going under", Marlan chose to *literalize* the black-hole-like blackness as absolutely impenetrable, frozen object—as the immutably lasting "remnant", the *caput mortuum*. Instead of a threshold, opening, or passageway,[10] Marlan preferred to see the black sun as an impasse, as a non-plus-ultra wall (cf. his "ultimate 'no'") that protects and prevents him from (what he thinks is) "logical light" by forcefully holding him back in the imaginal mindset (the idea of a wall reminds us of Jung's idea, with respect to Kant, of a "wall at which human inquisitiveness turns back" [*CW* 18 § 1734]). Marlan does precisely not try actively to "see through" the image of the black sun, all the way through,[11] but merely "stares" in wonder at the black sun, and it is this transfixion of the subject that produces as its counterpart a dead frozen object. He construes the image, so to speak, as an (ordinary) mirror[12] that stops the gaze and merely reflects where he, the I, is mentally standing anyway. This move of his rescued for him the methodological standpoint of positivity (positive facticity), exteriority, and naive realism (and thus what we are used to calling "the ego").

The dear price to be paid for his literalization of the blackness is, however, consciousness's blindness: It sees nothing, only black, only ashes, remainder, *caput mortuum* as so many objectifications of consciousness's own not seeing. Consciousness has itself become identical with the blackness it sees in the image. Jung spoke of consciousness's becoming unconscious.[13] *This*, consciousness's becoming unconscious, is the inner truth that

---

10 One must not be misled by Marlan's speaking of "a gateway back to the beyond, at the root of imagination, wonder, and transformation" (p. 29). It is a gateway *back*, not forward, and a gateway to the *beyond*, i.e., to what psychologically has to be understood as a *projection*, what is by definition out of reach and unassimilable and what ipso facto can only be the distant object of *wonder*, i.e., of the passive admiration/veneration *by him who* stays put, who remains, on the theoretical level, a mere "voyeur". Truly a gateway that is not a gateway. "Peephole" would be nearer to the mark.

11 With the idea of "wonder" the image as object is frozen and not *seen through*, whereas all movement (and the only movement) happens in the subject on the emotional level (it is struck with wonder). At the same time, the subject is also frozen, inasmuch as the subject's emotionally *being* moved and struck with wonder takes the place of the actually required logical movement of seeing all the way *through* the image.

12 *Ordinary* mirror, in contrast to *speculative* mirrors (such as the one in the Snow White fairy tale or in Albertus Magnus's theory, which always show the true Other).

13 Here it is worth noting that these comments about blind, unconscious consciousness and "seeing nothing" must not themselves be literalized. "Consciousness that has become unconscious" does not mean that it has ceased being consciousness altogether. No, it is still conscious, it still sees what it sees, but it sees what it sees as ashes, as unassimilable remnant, as positivity. Its *mode* of seeing is blind, unconscious. It cannot see the soul's life in what it sees.

is, inadvertently and unwittingly to him, expressed in Marlan's theoretical "ultimate 'no' to consciousness" idea and his fundamental "unassimilability to consciousness" dogma. Marlan prefers the blinding of consciousness to the eclipse of the one familiar (namely, the imaginal, passively beholding) *mode* of being conscious. He even makes a theory, indeed, a dogma or creed of it. *Fiat imaginalitas et pereat conscientia.*

However, it *is* possible to see through the image of blackness and to see what is on its other side. "Seeing through" does not only mean to penetrate the initial appearance and to understand more deeply. It also means "seeing through *to . . .*".[14] This in turn means that consciousness *keeps seeing* all the way through, as long as its encounter with the black sun lasts. It means that it maintains *itself as a consciously seeing one* even in cases where it is fundamentally challenged or threatened by *what* it sees (the image of the black sun as the image of seeing nothing). Marlan took the blackness as "seeing nothing" literally, so that (with a kind of "identification with the aggressor") it put an end to his *seeing*, while psychologically it would have required that the *mode* of seeing would have undergone a radical transformation and he (his consciousness) would have come out of it as seeing differently, having entered a fundamentally *new dimension* of seeing. Consciousness can indeed continue to see and to stay conscious if it allows *itself to die* the death of its old imaginal *form* of consciousness and, instead of merely beholding and imagining and feeling struck with wonder, begins to enter the mode of actively *thinking* and thus the sphere of "the logical". Thinking, *speculative* thinking, is the new mode of "darkened", sublated or sublimated *seeing* (cf., we speak of "insights"), a seeing that emerges when consciousness has "seen" all the way "*through*" the blackness of the black sun and come out on its other side; we could also say: When it has "seen through" the *object form* of the black sun (and ipso facto has come home to itself). As such this darkened seeing is the new form of "yes" to consciousness.

And it is not only a *new* form, but psychologically also a higher, more complex mode, inasmuch as *speculative thinking* is that mode in which consciousness is ipso facto conscious of *itself*, that is to say, it is that mode whose internal structure is such that in its performance "one's own participation" (*CW* 14 § 753, transl. modif.), "man's intervention", "the collaboration of the psyche—an indispensable factor" (*CW* 10 § 498; Jung said: "*die*

---

14 For Hillman, seeing through to the Gods.

unerläßliche Mitwirkung der Psyche") are *objectively reflected*, in other words, all those characteristics that according to Jung "foolish Parsifal" forgot and that in "the natural sciences" (we add: And especially also in imaginal psychology and in mythology) with systematic necessity "remain[-] invisible". In Marlan's theory, however, they not only remain invisible, but are deliberately excluded. The *psychological function* of his insistence on the "unassimilable remainder" and the "thing-in-itself" is nothing else but the passionate defense of the relation of "pure, literal object" (object that is fundamentally separate from, vis-à-vis of, and on principle out of reach of the subject, and thus wholly other), on the one hand, and fundamentally immune, innocent subject, on the other hand, *as the general structure of consciousness*. It is a logically (not necessarily empirically) outward-looking, fundamentally "projecting" and precisely not speculatively self-reflexive consciousness.

This is beautifully, even if unintentionally, illustrated in Marlan's own image in his paper of himself lying in bed with his dying literal dog. The logical structure of the relationship between subject and object as two ontologically separate bodies portrayed in this image is the structure of consciousness celebrated by him. His dictum about the "ultimate 'no' to consciousness" functions psychologically as the ultimate guarantee of one's right, in psychology (!), to believe in consciousness's logical innocence. Marlan's effort with his "remainder" is to revoke the crucial psychological insight that the subject is, inevitably, always already in the object and finds *itself* in *it* and that we are surrounded by soul on all sides. *In the last analysis*, his deep-seated need seems to be to promote a psychology-prevention program.

The false idea of "logical *light*"

As promised I will now turn to Marlan's association of the logical with "light". By taking the blackness of the black sun literally, letting it put a stop to his seeing and by decreeing an "ultimate 'no' to consciousness", that is, by psychologically identifying with darkness and hailing it as ashes, unassimilable ramainder, and *caput mortuum, thinking*—as the continued (even if fundamentally reformed and 'blackened') *seeing*—appeared to him as exclusively "light". The dimension of "the logical", that, due to his consciousness's identification with darkness, for Marlan personally is a still unknown, never trodden territory, turns for him into something that allegedly rises up high above the real darkness into pure light. By speaking of "logical *light*", he suggests that the logical means something cleansed of all concreteness and earthly weight and is totally purified, emaciated: The "poisonous state of splendid solar isolation" (p. 34). He does not show where he got this silly idea from. It is superstitious. And as to his weird interpretation of Hegel, we can say that he seems to see Hegel through Heidegger's and Derrida's distorting glasses and with his own unidirectional object fixation, but not in Hegel's own terms and through an unprejudiced direct access. For him absolute-negative interiorization means dissolution of the reality of the objects.

By the same token one could argue that Leonardo da Vinci, by creating a painting of Mona Lisa, dissolved the reality of the real woman Mona Lisa, and that Jung's individuation process, by striving for the Self (a transcendent idea), dissolved the human being as empirical person. If we agreed with Marlan we would have to tell Leonardo that he should not have painted this painting, but that instead he should have concentrated on "the reality of his relationship with" the flesh and blood woman. Mogenson should not have devoted himself to the topic of "the dog that is not a dog", but to a real dog. Christians should forget the risen and the mystical Christ and instead believe in the historical Jesus, the man, the human preacher. The alchemist's answer to Marlan would have been: *Quod natura relinquit imperfectum, ars perficit*. Psychology is an art, an "alchemical" *ars*. According to Jung it is precisely and only the Self that brings out the real truth of the empirical person. And for any person with an appreciation of art Leonardo's painting outshines the real woman of whom it is a portrait.

The image of the "black sun" could rightly be called the dark other of the "light" of Helios or the Delphic Apollo.[15] Because all these images are commensurable. They belong to the same sphere of imaginal or mythological images. But to identify "the logical" (or the Mona Lisa, or the Self) with "light" and "splendid solar isolation" is a category mistake. The opposition of light and darkness simply does not apply to it. Concepts, algorithms, inferences, and computer programs, as well as speculative thought and works of art and "soul made through absolute-negative interiorization", are not "solar", not "light", and they are not "darkness", nor anything in between.

---

15 If we ignore for a moment the above insight that the dark sun is really the depiction of a logical self-contradiction: Within itself the opposite of *itself* (rather than of some other).

And furthermore (a second logical mistake), a *particular* image or experience like that of the dark sun cannot possibly be "the dark other of logical light" because "the logical" is not likewise a particular experience or content (the way, e.g., "the peaks of spirit" are particulars). It is a whole dimension or general form and status of thinking beyond image as such. *Its* other would have to be another whole dimension, such as "the imaginal", "mythological". But this other dimension could not be its "dark" other, simply because dimensions are neither dark nor light.

This means that Marlan interprets a *syntactical* difference (between the imaginal [or, in other cases, the empirically real] and the logical) in terms of a *semantic* opposition ("dark"–"light"). At the same time he revokes the difference between the level of the mystical/transcendental/logical/soul meaning and the level of the empirical-factual, and that between the cooked and the raw, between art and nature, by eliminating the former element in each contrast.

But it is precisely this view of "logical light" that he *projects* on psychology (psychology comprehended as the discipline of interiority). It is the blindedness of his consciousness that projects its own blank "white soul" character (called by Marlan "psychological narcissism", a narcissism that he defended against the inherent message of the black sun by paying for it the high price indicated) into its own other, while believing to represent, and in fact standing up for, "the dark other" of "logical light". What emerges here is that psychology conceived as the discipline of interiority (together with the conception of the soul as logical life) is, in the last analysis, Marlan's *real* black sun, however his real black sun the way it would appear if it were seen through and thus in no longer imaginal *form*. Small wonder that he is driven to attack it while at the same time also being (negatively) fascinated by it.

The soul seen as *logical* life: This is, far from being the "logical *light*", that real "dark seeing" I spoke of earlier. Of course, not "the logical" itself is dark (or light), as pointed out. Rather a consciousness able to see soul as logical life is this "*dark*" seeing because its seeing is not done with the eyes (neither the literal, physical ones, nor those of the imagination). It has gone through the deconstruction or self-decomposition of the imaginal mode, a self-decomposition which tried to express itself for Marlan, in first immediacy, in his image of the black sun; and a self-decomposition that did not destroy one content in favor of another one, but has left behind the whole *level of contents*, the soul's semantics, and dropped (or rose) to the resulting new level of syntactical or logical structure, logical form: This "seeing" is "insight" into, i.e., *comprehension* of, the inner logic of the matter, the logic that "animates" the matter. Therefore, by comparison with mythology and imaginal psychology, one's thinking on the level of the logical is *"dark"* seeing because it has been stripped of the bright colorful and warm contents of the imaginal. But paradoxically this (by comparison) "dark" seeing of speculative thought appears to Marlan as "logical *light*"—probably because what it comprehends does not have the solid and opaque thing-character of the "unassimilable remnant".

Marlan's presenting the black sun as the dark other of *logical light* has the additional advantage for him that he thereby managed to redirect the dangerous attack (that *he* experienced as coming from the black sun) away from his own (or the field's) consciousness as its addressee to something that he was opposed to *anyway* and all along: To alien others, namely to Hegel, Giegerich, and Mogenson (as representatives of this so-called logical light), and ipso facto to change the originally challenging black sun (and "challenge" psychologically always means challenge to oneself, to one's own constitution of consciousness) into his most precious argumentative weapon against those others—and thus paradoxically, *qua* black sun, into *his* theory's bright sun. (This is of course another instance of the reversal into the opposite referred to above.)

Regression to literalism

It is worth noting that Marlan's return to and clinging to the remnant, the *caput mortuum*, and to the thing-in-itself is a betrayal not only of the invitation he received to the insight into the soul's negativity and its character as logical life, but even of "archetypal psychology's" imaginal approach itself, of Hillman's "poetic basis of mind", his notion of "soul-*making*", and his method of "seeing through" (not to mention even Jung's devotion to the arcane, transcendental level of the soul)—a betrayal of all this in favor of literalism, otherness, and soul-external fact. As his narration about his euthanized dog Curtis shows, initiation, i.e., the transformation of the *structure* or *constitution* of consciousness, has in him become regressively replaced by his cultivation of ego sentiments, events of his *having* and *indulging in* emotions. These he declares, n.b. *as psychologist* (!), to be for him decisive—vide his second subjective confessional statement in this paper: "This view [namely, what he thinks is Hegel's view as well as the view of psychology as the discipline of interiority] does not satisfy me, nor account for the reality of my relationship with Curtis" (p. 33). Marlan's emphasis on his lying with his dying dog and accompanying it with his sad feelings into its death could be interpreted as his favoring the behaviorally acting out of, and substitute for, the actually demanded *psychological* "going under".

His move to ego sentiments is already foreshadowed in his viewing the challenge of the black sun reductively, namely merely personalistically, as a challenge to "*one's* psychological narcissism", in other words, as a psychic one, when it should be seen as a psychological, a *theoretical* challenge: A challenge to *his psychology's* methodological stance. Of course, like everybody, Marlan as civilian man and private individual has every right to have his emotional needs and to treasure them and to stand up for them. But the moment he speaks as psychologist and theoretician and publishes in a psychological journal, he has to leave his private feelings—and along with them his whole human-all-too-humanness and also his beloved pet Curtis—at home and argue, so to speak, "officially", as a professional, a representative-on-duty of the *field* of psychology and its constitutive principle, the *objective soul*. The field or discipline of psychology is transpersonal and has logos-nature ("psycho-logy"). It has no relationship with any dog, and no emotional needs. What Marlan, or people in general for that matter, subjectively feel, or what "the reality of their relationship with" their dog (or whatever or whoever) may be, and even their possible psychological narcissism, is totally irrelevant for the basic theoretical questions of psychology, just as irrelevant as the question whether they prefer tennis over football, or the political left over the right, or whether they love or hate their mothers, or are vigorously healthy or plagued by illnesses.

How did Hillman put it? "The proper measure of mankind is man; of psychology, soul."[16] This is the psychological (psychology-constituting) difference.

---

16 James Hillman, *Re-Visioning Psychology*, New York et al.: Harper & Row, 1975, p. 189. We may also think here of the relentless one-sidedness that Hillman professed in his *The Dream and the Underworld*: Talking about the general direction of his approach to dreams (and thus to psychological phenomena in general) he stated:

> . . . But because this *via regia* [to the unconscious, as Freud had called the dream], in most psychotherapy since his [Freud's] time has become a straight one-way street of all morning traffic, moving out of the unconscious towards the ego's city, I have

But Marlan refuses to accept this challenge, this narcissistic insult that the *field* of psychology inflicts on its students as an indispensable precondition for its, psychology's, coming into existence. On the contrary, it is, as we have seen, Marlan's express goal to establish precisely *the civilian man*, the empirical man in his humanness, and *his* subjective emotional needs and *his* feeling-relationship to literal reality as the indispensable standard and measure of *psychology*. But how can he, as a Jungian, expect in the first place that psychology should take note of, let alone be interested in "the reality of *his* (or any *person*'s) relationship with his dog"? By thus clinging to the ego, he acts as a psychological reactionary, wanting to undo again Jung's and Hillman's revolutionary advances toward a true psychology and to bring the field down from the level and concept of "our" psychology (*psychologia nostra*) to those of "people's" psychology (*psychologia vulgi*).[17] Above I suggested that Marlan confuses the phenomenal level with the methodological, epistemological, discipline-constituting level. Now I can specify that he wants the phenomenal (existential-experiential and personalistic) level to be, just like that, of theoretical, methodological relevance for the field of psychology.

Jung had already had to struggle with the same kind of problem reduction, but in the area of theology. Answering a correspondent who had written as a reaction to *Answer to Job*: "The whole situation would be aired and simplified if we could . . . accept the idea that God is Love", Jung wrote sarcastically:

Mineralogy is just stones, zoology simply animals, technology only how things are made to work, and mythology old fables of no consequence at all. . . . To hell with all -logies. Why should anybody fuss with the history of symbols when everything is quite clear and can be summed up in the short formula 'God is Love'?"

(*Letters 2*, p. 556, 7 May 1960, to Anonymous)

---

chosen to face the other way. Hence my title, which is a directional signpost for a different one-way movement, let us say vesperal, into the dark. So at the beginning, I must admit to working this bridge with a certain singleness of intent.

(James Hillman, *The Dream and the* Underworld, New York: Harper and Row, 1979, p. 1)

Hillman opts for psychology's turning, with "singleness of intent", away from the human-all-too-human. And Hillman's "vesperal", underworldly darkness nicely contrasts with Marlan's *abstract* image-concept of the *absolutely* black sun.

17 I am alluding, of course, to the alchemical dictum, *aurum nostrum non est aurum vulgi*.

Zoology is simply animals, and for Marlan psychology is, at least in this one instance, simply "the reality of my relationship with Curtis".

The topic of Marlan's regression to literalism is the appropriate place to substantiate with a few examples my above assertion of his "weird interpretation of Hegel". Commenting on the topic of the " 'fear of error' which Hegel says is the error itself and thus a fear of truth", Marlan states: "Kant's painstaking philosophical critique is reduced to a psychology of fear and an ad hominem, psychological argument" (p. 32). Preposterous! Marlan's statement is not, as it purports to be, about Hegel, but is much rather an unintended self-display of Marlan's own personalistic, psychologistic mindset. He reads the word "fear" literalistically as if it meant in Hegel's text a human, personal emotion. Marlan's horizon here is that of ego-psychology, of what people think or feel, which shows that he simply has not entered the sphere of philosophical discourse (of thought proper) and has no inkling of what Hegel is talking about. "Fear of error" is in the Hegel passage a philosophical analysis and description of an aspect of the inner *objective* logic inherent in the ordinarily prevailing epistemology. It is Marlan who fails to painstakingly try to think Hegel's thought, he who refuses to meet Hegel on his own philosophical level. Instead, by personalistically seeing nothing but an ad hominem argument in Hegel's point it is he himself who reduces this logical analysis and philosophical argument to an ad hominem argument. As if Hegel had needed to resort to the pettiness of such maneuvers and had been unable to meet Kant on the latter's level of philosophical *thought*. As if he had not been just as painstaking in his philosophical work as Kant was, and as if Hegel had not, throughout his life, held Kant in highest esteem (even when he critiqued certain aspects of his position).

It is quite clear that if you do not get such a simple, very introductory point as the one that Hegel makes here, then the door to his philosophy is shut for you. Marlan, instead of seriously entering Hegel's thought, approaches him from a decidedly external position with an agenda of his own, with a fixed doctrinal position: With his dogma of mind-independent object. Let me stress again, on a practical everyday level (or, as far as Kant's philosophy is concerned, merely in the sense of a "boundary concept") the idea of "mind-independent object" is perfectly in place. I am not objecting to that. And I also believe that it is Marlan's right to pursue an agenda that is incompatible with Hegel. People have different needs. Not everyone needs psychology (as the discipline of interiority). What I object to is that Marlan presents his need of an ideology of "mind-independent object" or his preference for certain modern philosophers as if they were an *argument* capable of refuting psychology's *opus contra naturam* as well as Hegel's work. Going in for football does not refute chess, and going in for Derrida does not refute Hegel. To think that it did would be one's confusing philosophy (real *thought*) with people's doctrinal opinions, human sentences. No real philosophy refutes another real philosophy.

When Marlan speaks of the "long path of approximation to absolute knowing" (p. 32) in Hegel, "absolute knowing" is mystified, in a totally un-Hegelian sense, as a distant hard-to-attain if not superhuman *ideal*, just as Marlan's use of the word "absolute" (e.g., in the title of his article: "The absolute that is not an absolute") betrays that he has no understanding of what "absolute" in Hegel's philosophy means. Marlan understands and uses the term in the ordinary commonsensical sense,[18] even when referring to Hegel.

By the same token "Hegel's and Giegerich's distillation process" (p. 32) is for Marlan one of sidestepping, banishing and hierarchically surpassing, which is nonsense. Distillation, sublimation, evaporation, in alchemy as well as in my psychology, are form changes, processes of refining. In moving, to give a simple example, from solid ice to water and from water to steam, nothing is "banished" or "hierarchically surpassed". The same is true also for Hegel's "sublation", which, by the way, is no more and no less a "magic" (Marlan's word, p. 32; another mystification!) than is the *evaporatio* of water. When Marlan calls this process of sublation a "heroic act" (p. 32) and also uses the word "heroic" with reference to my concept of psychology, we see to what extent his own interpreting consciousness is informed by what we call the (heroic) ego. And when he writes, "Giegerich notes that in the face of impasse, the proper act for the psychologist is to leap into it", and refers to my (alleged) suggestion of bypassing "limits by leaping headlong into stone walls" (p. 32),[19] we see the "man in the street" consciousness at work here in Marlan's mindless out-of-context citation— a consciousness that ridicules the idea of "the leap into the solid stone"

---

18 Commonsensical mindset and mystification (of what is beyond the horizon of this mindset) go together.

19 It escapes me how "leaping headlong into stone walls" could be considered a form of *bypassing* limits. The word "limit" in this context would only make sense if what is meant were really an internalized prohibition to move forward, and instead of a "bypassing" there would really be a disobedience to that prohibition.

because it has not *thought* it and thus has not acquired an understanding of what it means. Here I am reminded of a passage in a letter by Jung (*Letters 2*, p. 410, 14 January 1958, to L. Kling):

> An adequate capacity to understand is essential, for without a considerable degree of subtler intelligence they [the things discussed in this letter] will only be misunderstood. Unfortunately one must abandon from the start any attempt to make such things clear to one's scientifically minded [here I add: or commonsensically and personalistically minded] colleagues.

Sad, but true. As to this "leap into the stone", let me add that it is my *description*, by means of a mythological image, of an *objective reality*, of a possible soul event, a possible movement (that happens if it happens, or that does not occur). It is a movement in the soul's logical life and not a human (intellectual or thinking) behavior on the empirical-practical level, on which Marlan seems to stay in his thinking. It is not—ego-psychologically—something WE do nor is it something we "ought" to do. Because we have no say in the matter, just as not in that other matter whether we have the said "considerable degree of *subtler* intelligence"[20] and do understand—or not.

The whole idea of Hegel's and psychology's side-stepping, banishing, dissolving is obviously due to the fact that Marlan's standpoint is and remains that of external reflection and of his unidirectional commitment to "object" (or the relation of ego to object). But this only shows that he has not entered psychology, which needs to be in itself reflexive, for, according to Jung, in contrast to the sciences it does not have an outside (i.e., an external object), but is that discipline whose object is the very subject that produces all science in the first place (*CW* 8 § 429, transl. modif.). Psychology does not *do* anything to the object, neither side-stepping nor banishing or dissolving it: Because qua psychology it is not concerned with what is outside. Psychology "distills" only what is already its own or the soul's property. Similarly Hegel: From the outset he starts out *in* philosophy, *in* thought, and works with thought's own material. *C'est son métier* as a *thinker*, just as working exclusively with its own "prime matters" is

---

20 "Subtler intelligence" is not to be confused with *higher* intelligence, as if those without it were unintelligent (in the conventional sense). It is not a question of the IQ.

psychology's *métier*.[21] The idea of banishing, side-stepping and dissolving when in truth it is a matter of "distilling" is Marlan's way to surreptitiously establish as *irrenunciable* and *unquestionable* the principle of otherness and externality.

Totalitarian overestimation and the anti-mercurial conception of psychology

The positivistic stance has, as strange as it may seem, its kind of equivalent to psychology's negation of the negation: The *positivization* of the negation. The negation of "man" and the human-all-too-human in favor of "soul" that is required in order for psychology to be what it is meant to be is by this stance literalized as if it amounted to a wholesale practical exclusion of the human-all-too-human from life as such and a general devaluation of or even contempt for the human-all-too-human—when in reality it is a *methodological* step necessary for the constitution of the field of psychology and for its *distinction* both from other fields as well as from the sphere of real life itself. Just as a shoemaker who insists on exclusively making state-of-the-art shoes does not thereby want to get rid of the products of tailors, cabinet-makers, masons, doctors, or cooks, so psychology does not want to eliminate and disparage the realm of, and the interest in, the human-all-too-human or, e.g., people's political concerns. It is only that all this is simply not part of its own business. Just as geology is not concerned with music and musicology not with rocks and plate tectonics, so psychology does not study "what goes on inside people", their feelings and opinions, but only the soul's life. The false intimation that (what I call) true psychology deprives life of central areas and accepts only the smallest, most abstract, most lofty and ivory-tower-like segment of it or "*reduces* everything to knowledge" reveals an underlying misconception of psychology

---

21 Here I need to remind the reader, that it is Marlan (like others before him) who juxtaposed Hegel and Giegerich repeatedly in the same sentences. Quite apart from the incommensurability as to stature between the two authors, the fact that there are certain affinities between Hegel and psychology (as the discipline of interiority) does not mean that psychology is a Hegelian enterprise. Hegel is a philosopher. The psychologist is not. And furthermore, Hegel belongs to another epoch. Between him and us lies the Industrial Revolution, which sets the two world conditions, his and ours, fundamentally and irrevocably apart. We can learn from Hegel, but not become Hegelians.

as a *totalitarian* enterprise: Of psychology as competent and responsible for the whole, for the reality of life at large. But psychology's negation of "man" and "real life" in favor of "soul" serves merely the purpose of establishing itself as one conceptually clearly demarcated *specialty*, and the practice of it therefore precisely as merely one single possible activity of real human life executed by people, who in addition to being psychologists are also human-all-too-human "civilian persons" and private individuals with all sorts of additional interests, needs, and activities. By the same token, to have and operate with a rigorous concept of psychology does not imply that the analyst's consulting room would have to be exclusively and totally devoted to psychology in this sense. In reality it is only a question of one's clearly knowing *when* one is doing *what*: When what one is doing is indeed psychology and when it is something else.[22] What is required is discrimination, conceptual clarity, a rigorous notion of psychology, not a psychological totalitarianism.

The whole issue of "remnant" makes sense only if consciousness thinks in terms of totality. For a psychologist it is a non-issue. A practicing psychologist is used to the fact that not all therapies end successfully or with complete success. Not every one of our interpretations of fairy tales or dreams is capable of making sense of every detail, nor can we ever be sure that our interpretations are correct. We can overlook or misunderstand something or even the whole thing. But all this human, all-too-human imperfection does not affect and should not constrict the *concept* of psychology, soul-making, and distillation.

Psychology is not a *Weltanschauung*, not a religion, not a philosophy of life.[23] Being exclusively about "soul-making", it has life, political con-

---

22 Jung in *CW* 16 § 122, in a still rather early paper, lists, e.g., four possible practical purposes or endeavors in the consulting room (confession, enlightenment [transl. modif.; i.e., interpretation in the psychoanalytical sense], education, and transformation), of which, as is easy to see, only the last one falls into the sphere of psychology or soul-work proper. The first three belong to the merely psychic and human, all-too-human sphere (Jung speaks in this regard of the needs of the *Normalmensch*, "normal human being", § 161). By referring to these purposes as "stages" rather than as options side by side, Jung himself is aware of the qualitative difference between them and especially of the fundamental difference between the first three on the one hand and the fourth on the other.

23 Marlan even tries to claim that psychology in my sense is an ontology! But this is his problem, not mine. This idea is again a consequence of his unidirectional orientation towards object and the decidedly irreflexive nature of his approach.

cerns, the human-all-too-human, society, subjective emotional needs, all the other scientific or scholarly disciplines, etc., and even its own practical reality outside of itself and fully respects them as *others*. But: This methodological negation of these other areas does nevertheless not preclude that *phenomena* stemming from them, also possibly stemming from the sphere of the human-all-too-human, may become prime matters to be studied by it.

However, and this is the crucial point, *when* studying such phenomena, the field-constituting psychological difference requires that psychology does precisely not take them in terms of what they mean in these other areas and how they appear to consciousness in them or in ordinary consciousness—the consciousness of civilian man—but views them exclusively as instances of the soul's speaking about itself. As we can say with an alchemical image: Everything that becomes the object of study of psychology has first to have been ruthlessly extricated[24] from the immediacy of the practical life context that it at first comes with and from the ordinary, common-sense understanding of it and placed in the retort, which thereafter will have to be sealed with the seal of Hermes-Mercurius, so that from then on our attention will exclusively go to its absolute interiority.[25] This "practical" act of placing the particular matter to be studied in the retort expresses a fundamental logical shift or cut, a *separatio*—the radical departure from the original way the phenomena were given in their innocent, natural state which the alchemists called *unio naturalis*. This *separatio* is the alchemical equivalent of what on our modern theoretical level is the methodological act suggested by the "psychological difference". The sealed retort makes all the difference. It amounts to the crucial shift of one's standpoint from let us say the "physics" (the behavior and interrelations) of things or bodies in space (be it real or imaginal) to "alchemy", that is, the matter's own *inner* "chemical" constitution and the transformation of this constitution, apart from its (previous) external context.

---

24 If this extrication and the psychological difference may be what gave rise to Marlan's faulty idea of "banishing", then it must be due to the *totalitarian* conception of psychology I criticized. Leaving something behind that does not belong and is not part of one's project from the outset, is not an act of banishing or sidestepping, nor one of "*reducing* something to . . .". It becomes this only in the eyes of him who thinks that psychology has the obligation to include *everything*.

25 As Jung had said: psychology does not have an outside of itself.

But Marlan does not heed alchemy's warning: Beware of the physical in the matter. He has not put, for example, his dog, and his relationship to his dog, in the retort and thereby created the psychological difference between the dog outside as immediately given literal fact and the dog inside the retort as psychological topic (would it have been another too painful narcissistic wound?). Rather, he insists on staying married to his immediate feelings, married not only to his dying dog, but also, through him, (on the theoretical level) to the *caput mortuum*. We see here a concrete example of what early Hegel referred to as the "love for the sake of what is dead" (*Liebe um des Toten willen*).[26]

Marlan's insistence on the thing-in-itself is in this sense really symptomatic. Coming from a psychologist and taking place in his theoretical reflections, it signals his decision, on principle, to cling to the stance of externality: to phenomena as having their substance and truth fundamentally outside themselves in some utterly mysterious, namely unknowable, other. It is the decision to do on principle without "the retort", to be and remain—totally unalchemically—committed to *immediacy*, to the primary "raw" experience of the factual world, to the prime matter precisely in the very form in which it is found "on the street" (cf. the lapis "in via ejectus") *by "the man in the street" consciousness*. The psychologist decidedly *as* empirical human being, civilian man, *as* the ego. It is quite obvious that for his taking his dog Curtis as a reality in itself and for himself, *psychology* is not at all needed: Because that he, Marlan's dog, is (or was) a reality is the self-evident truth of everyday consciousness.

If Marlan, however, insists *as psychologist* on this commonsensical reality, then psychology qua psychology has literally "gone to the dogs". Why still, with Jung, search for the transcendental Self? Why, with the alchemists, for the *vinum ardens*, for the *aurum nostrum*, the arcane substance? When the title of Marlan's paper claims for his paper the character of its being "*alchemical* reflections", we have to note that sure, semantically he does cite or use a few alchemical images. But syntactically, his program and mentality are decidedly anti-hermetic, anti-mercurial. His thinking takes place within, and is bounded by, the horizon of the "physics" of (imaginal or real) entities in space.

26 G.W.F. Hegel, *Frühe Schriften*, Theorie Werkausgabe vol. 1, Frankfurt am Main: Suhrkamp, 1971, p. 245.

Be that as it may, we can make the general statement that psychology has no stake in the theoretical question of the thing-in-itself as mind-independent object, *one way or the other*, just as "reality as such"/"Being"/"the world at large" are not possible topics for it. Psychology is not a philosophy or world view or doctrine of how to live and how to see the world.[27] Epistemology, ontology, the big questions of life, the riddles of the world, the ethics of life, are not its business. It has a different vocation.[28] *However*, even if the question of the thing-in-itself is no topic for psychology and the latter is therefore neither for nor against it, *methodologically* and *practically* the thing-in-itself mode of thinking and all immediacy as well as any toying with the idea of anything *behind* the phenomena are nevertheless simply out of the question *for it*, as is already apparent from such a merely passing but crucial remark by early Jung as the following: "It may not be superflu-

27 When Marlan states that Giegerich's work is "an important contribution to philosophically thinking through . . . Jung's ideas", this is a fundamental misunderstanding that seems to show that for him philosophy and psychology are undifferentiated from each other, just as real life and psychology are for him. They seem to float in the same primordial soup. He has not acquired a rigorous notion of psychology for himself and apparently does not even feel the need for it. To be sure, he is right: I did attempt to *think through* Jung's ideas. But not philosophically! It is a thinking through pure and simple, and, furthermore, a carrying Jung's ideas forward on their own terms to their logical conclusion, and, thirdly, it is also an *immanent* critique guided by the needs of the discipline of veritable psychology and by Jung's own deepest thoughts as its standard and measure. By the same token Marlan also gives the utterly false impression as if I had discussed the difference between Kant and Hegel, although I do not at all speak about these philosophers directly and on my own: Because I am not a philosopher. I had made it expressly clear that what I discussed was *Jung's* Kant (Kant the way Jung saw him) and *Jung's* Hegel (and the problem, *for psychology*, of Jung's passionate rejection of Hegel). Fully inexcusable is Marlan's assertion that Jung's statement about the barrier that Kant erected across the mental world represents also my understanding of Kant, whereas I am quite critical of Jung's Kant interpretation. It has been my opinion that Jung was unable to see Kant's work as *philosophy*, but reduced it to a mere theory of knowledge. Just as inexcusable is this other allegation of Marlan's that with my re-translation I manipulated a relevant Jung quote in order that it "fits with [my] own" view, when in reality what I did was to restore what Jung had actually said and what had got lost or blurred in the official *CW* translation. Marlan does not seem to realize that in the *CW* he reads R.F.C. Hull and not Jung.

28 It is committed to eachness: To *this* phenomenon *now* if and to the extent that it has been placed in the retort.

ous to remark that there are still people who believe that a psychoanalyst could be misled by lies of his patient. That is quite impossible. Lies are fantasies, *and we treat fantasies*" (*CW* 4 § 300 fn., translation modif., my emphasis). Fantasies, and not what they are the fantasies of, not mind independent objects! Objects, phenomena, contents only in so far as they are the soul's own contents, products, and concerns. This is our business. Psychology is relegated to interiority. It may be concerned with the self-sufficient father imago and the archetypal image of father, but not with the real father "out there", the father as mind independent reality. Entertaining the idea of the father as "thing-in-itself" would be psychology's self-undoing. Even if psychology turns to realities, its interest goes nevertheless solely to the *fantasy* embodied in them, solely to their interiority. "There is nothing without spirit, for spirit seems to be the inside of things" (C.G. Jung, *Visions Seminar*, vol. 1, Zürich [Spring Publ.] 1976, p. 164). And this "*inside* of things" is the exclusive concern of psychology.[29]

Marlan's problem in this whole area seems to be that he has not discriminated, indeed does not want to differentiate, let alone *emancipate* psychology from philosophy, on the one hand, and from everyday experience and the human, all-too-human, on the other. Also in this sense there is no alchemical *vas*. Why would he go into a discussion of views of Kant, Hegel, Heidegger, Derrida, to mention only these, in support of his views or, as the case may be, as counter-example?[30] What is Hecuba, i.e., what are these philosophers and their views to us, apart from their importance for the general training and differentiation of the mind and from their being part of higher cultural education (*unless* they, perhaps, here or there help us to a clearer understanding of the needs of *psychology*)? But in Marlan's text *one never senses a concern for the needs of psychology as a discipline in its own right*. His concern seems always to be either with much bigger, more general questions that are really of a philosophical nature or with his own

---

29 At the same time, this "spirit" that is the *inside* of things, is something totally different from Hillman's (and Marlan's) "*peaks* of spirit" that require a "heroic" mountaineering effort. And, secondly, psychology, committed to the Mercurial spirit imprisoned inside of the real as it is, is not operating with any idea of a truth *behind* the real. "Absolute-negative *interiorization*!"

30 By contrast, when I discussed Kant and Hegel, as I pointed out, it was only as figures in Jung's thinking and with the question in mind of what the consequences for psychology were of how Jung saw them and how he positioned himself towards them.

emotional and ideological needs (his own personal relationship to reality). He cannot see that psychology is merely a discipline, a methodological enterprise that, like each of the crafts and trades, has one limited special purpose: The goal of soul-making, and of soul-making *only* in *each* given actual, concrete case, concerning *each* "matter" *at hand* (be it dream, myth, fairy tale, a particular complex or symptom, a cultural phenomenon, etc.).

The predilection for ashes

Marlan insists that "there always remains a dark remnant in the retort after distillation". Leaving aside the fact that, for example, in the case of the *evaporatio* of H_2O as well as in the case of immaterial, i.e., *the soul's* or *mind's* or *the intellect's* prime matters[31] this can hardly be said to be true, and instead granting Marlan his dogma simply for argument's sake—can his claim be a psychological argument? Is the dark remnant of psychological interest and significance? Even if it were true that there always remains a dark remnant, who cares? Well, obviously Marlan for one does. He has a predilection, a soft spot for ashes and "heads of the dead" (*capita mortuum*) and things in themselves—which are all perfect embodiments of what Hillman would have called "literalism". No doubt, this love for dark remnants *can* be a person's concern.

But for us, for psychology, the point here is that it is not the soul's concern. The soul's aspirations go in the opposite direction, and psychology has the task and obligation to follow *its*, the soul's, needs and for that reason to disregard the dross (of course precisely not in the sense of repression, which would require effort and active involvement with it, but in the sense of simply not paying attention to it). No man, having put his hand to the plough, and looking back, is fit for the kingdom of God.

Our job is soul-making, not dross-making or dedication to dross. As far as C.G. Jung, for one, is concerned, it is clear that his whole effort was to move

---

31 Marlan regressively clings to alchemy's *chemical* and thus *physical, material* aspect and thus to what the alchemists called the *unio naturalis*, and what philosophically is the "ontology of substance", instead of following Jung in seeing alchemy as an endeavor that, to be sure, started out from its chemical base but was on the way to psychology (cf. the relatively late alchemist Dorneus: "The form, which is the intellect, is the beginning, middle and end of the procedure . . ."! *CW* 14 § 390). Jung devoted himself to *Symbols of Transformation*. Transformations don't leave a remainder behind.

towards making conscious, towards *sublimatio, distillatio*, and of course *co-niunctio*, and conversely away from what he called, e.g., the *Menschenstall* (the human stable) and from any focusing on the "hangover from the past, a *caput mortuum*" (*CW* 10 § 367). From early on his psychological thinking went into a definite direction, that of finality and future development, which is why he called his interpretative approach a "final-constructive" one. He viewed the soul's life in terms of "regeneration"; "rejuvenation", and "rebirth" as his guiding principles. By contrast, he warned of consciousness's becoming unconscious (*CW* 12 § 563)[32] and of losing one's "way among ever more tortuous back-streets of dubious repute" and of the "destruction of the bond between men and the gods" (*CW* 10 § 367).

Yes, certainly, when we burn wood in order to get a blazing flame and heat, there will be ashes, but: So what?! Nietzsche for example teaches us that psychologically ashes can be left behind without one's wasting a thought on them: "Yes, I know whence I have sprung! / Insatiable as a flame / I burn and consume myself! / Whatever I seize becomes light, / whatever *I leave, ashes*: / certainly, flame I am."[33] Jung, speaking about (the soul's) "primordial urge", said: "Nature . . . does not believe in shard-heaps and decay, but grass and flowers cover all ruins inasmuch as the rains of heaven reach them" (*Letters 2*, p. 590, to Read, 2 September 1960). The rains of heaven! Had not the soul's goal, and indeed its true home, for millennia been in Heaven or even in a *hyperoyranios topos*, or in Hades, but at any rate not with the ashes, the mortal remains, the *caput mortuum*? Marlan, it seems, reverses the one-way movement to which Hillman committed psychology, and Marlan's insisting on the difference of unity and difference and his devotion, at the cost of any love for the distillation product, to the dark remainder might have been criticized by Jung with the same (certainly all too extreme) words that he used when he criticized (in another context) the general attitude of modern man: "Such people, says Buddha, 'after their death reach the wrong way, the bad track, down to the depth, into an

---

32 The English translation in the *CW* renders this falsely and simplistically as "regression of consciousness into unconsciousness" although the process in question is not a regression at all. What Jung hints at is a logically much more complex process and much rather than a regression an—even if problematic or "faulty"—advance.

33 Friedrich Nietzsche, *Die fröhliche Wissenschaft*, Vorspiel "Scherz, List und Rache", # 62 ("Ecce homo"). My italics.

infernal world'".[34] Clearly, for Jung, just as for Hillman, there is such a thing as a psychologically *wrong* way.

Furthermore, does the dedication to the ashes and the dark physical, material remainder *in the last analysis* not even amount to the wish of an undoing of the fundamental upwards movement of hominization, described by Freud as "upright walking, nose raised from the ground, at the same time a number of formerly interesting sensations attached to the earth becoming repulsive"?[35] For is what Marlan wants not that we rub our noses in the ashes, the dross—and in it even find our spiritual delight? When you are in the business of soul-making you cannot have it both ways: Interest in the soul and commitment to the dross.

To conclude this section on the penchant for ashes and skulls, just one additional hint: According to 19th century poet and lecturer Edward Dowden,[36] writing about *Romeo and Juliet*,

> . . . the theme of tragedy, as conceived by the poet, is not material prosperity or failure: it is spiritual; fulfilment or failure of a destiny higher than that which is related to the art of getting on in life. To die, under certain condition, may be a higher rapture than to live. / Shakespeare did not intend that the feeling evoked by the last scene of this tragedy of *Romeo and Juliet* should be one of hopeless sorrow or despair in presence of failure, ruin, and miserable collapse. Juliet and Romeo, to whom Verona has been a harsh stepmother, have accomplished their lives. They loved perfectly.

And then follows the sentence that is the main reason for my quoting Dowden here: "Montague will raise in pure gold the statue of true and faithful Juliet". What is *celebrated* is not Juliet's mortal remains, not the ashes, not the *caput mortuum*, but her, as we might say, distilled essence, her inner divinity.

---

34 *Letters 2*, p. 532 f., to Charteris, 9 January 1960.
35 *The Complete Letters of Sigmund Freud to Wilhelm Fliess, 1887–1907*, ed. and trans. Jeffrey Moussaieff Masson, Cambridge, MA: Belknap Press of Harvard University, 1985, p. 279.
36 Edward Dowden, *Shakespeare: His Mind and Art*, 1887, quoted in Shakespeare, *Romeo and Juliet*, ed. by Oscar J. Campbell, New York: Bantam Classics, 1961, p. 170 f.

Materialistic misconception of psychology

Our topic in the previous section was leanings, preferences, interests, concerns, intellectual commitments that steer our thinking. Now we turn to the
concept of psychology. Marlan's operating with the ideas of a remainder,
of ashes and dross, reveals that his conception of psychology is stuck in a
materialistic fantasy. I already mentioned that we get ashes when we burn
wood. Companies mine the earth for ore in order to *extract* from the latter
pure metals or other valuable elements. The extraction process naturally
leaves a remainder or waste behind. The same applies to the refinement
of crude oil into gasoline and a large number of other consumer products,
from plastics to pharmaceuticals. Marlan's conception of psychological
work seems to follow such ideas of processing raw materials as his model
as well as of course more directly the idea of the work of literal alchemists in the laboratory. But as psychologists we are not in the business of
chemistry, not even of alchemy. Our job is (alchemy-inspired) psychology.
We do not mine ore and do not extract the valuable elements from it. We
do not take inferior metals and transform them into gold. In radical contrast to such a thing as "mining" and "extraction", our method is that of
absolute-negatively *interiorizing* a given phenomenon *into itself*—by *our*
penetrating deeper into it, our learning to see what all it involves inside
itself that was hidden to the first glance. We try to perceive the inner logic
of it. Nothing is taken out from it. So how could this process produce a dark
remainder, ashes, dross?

We are not involved with natural materials, with the physical. Hillman
introduced the idea of a re-visioning of psychology. I now add to this concept
that psychology *is in itself* (in what it does) a process of re-visioning, nothing but re-visioning. Psychotherapy has been ever since Freud's "Anna O."
a talking cure. We work only on the mind, on our ways of seeing and experiencing things, on consciousness's dominant perspectives, on our understanding of ourselves, life events, and reality as a whole. If a patient has
learned to see his father, or, e.g., "traumatic" experiences from which he
suffered, *differently*, if he has become able to see through certain prejudices
that had made life difficult for him and freed himself from the enthralling
power of his complexes, if he has acquired new insights about himself—
where are the ashes that result from this development? Psychology did not
do anything to his father "out there", did not change him, did not extract
anything from him and leave the rest behind as waste. No, it only changed

the patient's view of his father, changed his consciousness. But this real new view gave this patient *really* a fundamentally new father, a re-visioned father. It is still the real father, and the whole father—and nevertheless a different one because he is seen with new eyes. A formerly abstract, one-sided view has become refined, more complex, distilled, deepened.

Similarly, when I studied archaic blood-sacrifices and showed them to be a primordial form of soul-making (or rather the primordial making of soul in the first place), I did not thereby produce any dross. I merely opened our eyes for the soul view of the phenomenon of sacrifices, a shift in our seeing which really changes *them* for us *and yet* leaves them intact as literal realities. Because all that has changed is consciousness. Or, when I interpreted the slippery-glass-mountain fairytale and interiorized *into itself* its central motif of the older brothers' "always slipping down", how could I thereby have possibly produced a dark remainder in the sense of dross? Nothing was discarded or ignored or repressed. Absolute-negative inwardization means one's consistently staying with the given phenomenon chosen for one's study. It means one's devoting oneself to it and penetrating deeper into its essence, its internal logical life. The movement of "distillation" in the psychology of interiority is one from a prima facie assessment of a phenomenon to a subtle and more informed comprehension, ultimately one that might be capable of transforming the logical constitution of consciousness itself, of raising consciousness to a new logical status. Certainly, the superficial and primitive first opinion or external impression is thereby overcome and left behind, but precisely not left behind like a hard, dark remnant that does not want to go away, but rather like a superficial view or a seen-through error which the moment that it has become seen through ("aha!") has at once become null and void.

Nothing whatsoever is done *to* the "real" phenomenon studied. It is not processed and ipso facto fundamentally altered like raw materials in industry, corpses dissected in anatomy, or substances or specimens subjected to test procedures in alchemical or scientific laboratories. Psychology tries to transform only our views and ideas about phenomena. They, the ideas and conceptions about things and our consciousness are psychology's real prime matter, not the things themselves.

That Marlan obviously interprets "distillation" and interiorization in psychology along the lines of "extracting" and believes in unavoidable "remainders" must be due to the fact that his thinking is logically still staying "out there", in the (*fantasy* of the) natural world. It must be due to his mentally clinging to (the *fantasy* of) hands-on things, objects, or material substances. It is this unconscious prejudice, namely, the materiality implicitly and unwittingly set up by this materialistic fantasy, that *produces* the unavoidability of dross and ashes as dark remainders and the belief that "logical light" has a "dark other". It is the abstract reduction of "thought" to nothing but a particular, to a single psychic function among several, or, expressed the other way around, the incapability of comprehending "thought" as all-comprehensive and all-pervasive. Marlan has not come home to (*into*) psychology, to the preoccupation exclusively with man's mental *views* about the real and the *logical forms of consciousness* and the interiority of *soul*.

And his clinging to external things is in turn probably due to the suggestive power of and the seduction by the imaginal approach, the picture-thinking mode. This mode (in addition to his deep *predilection* discussed above) is what makes him take the *image* of literal laboratory-alchemy[37] with its possible residue in the retort as his inescapable model for his "psychological" thinking.

Simply not getting the "unity of the unity and difference" concept

A while ago I said: "When you are in the business of soul-making you cannot have it both ways: Interest in the soul and commitment to the dross." I could also have said: You cannot have both "unity of the unity and difference" AND "difference of the unity and difference". But this is precisely what Marlan proposes. In an earlier paper of his,[38] he wrote, speaking about the idea of "the unity of the unity and difference":

> . . . [B]ut even the idea of "the unity of the unity and difference" privileges unity, although at a higher "logical level." The "unity of the unity and difference" is still a tincture of the syzygy that emphasizes unity as the major trope. The syzygy can also be tinctured to choose difference. This would call out for the complementary idea of "the difference of the unity and difference" . . .

---

37 In contrast to its "oratory" and hermetic-philosophy aspect.

38 Stanton Marlan, "From the Black Sun to the Philosopher's Stone", in: *Spring Journal 74, Alchemy*, Spring 2006, pp. 1–30, here p. 12.

This plea of his corresponds to the fact that in the paper that we are concerned with here he insists that the former idea needs to be "supplemented" by the latter. *Two* tinctures. Complementation, supplementation! All this is most revealing.

He obviously thinks that the two phrases parallel each other. They are for him two alternatives of equal significance, but in such a way that each represents only one half of the whole truth, for which reason both need in his opinion to be heeded. In my opinion this is totally wrong. It amounts to a serious misconstrual of the phrase "unity of the unity and difference". If, as Marlan thinks, this phrase *privileges* unity and his own phrase difference, it means that the real issue for him is simply a *choice*, that between "unity" and "difference" (and then, of course, the complementation of the one chosen by the other). In contrast to his own acknowledgment that the former phrase does what it does "at a higher 'logical level'" he regresses to and stays at the lower level so that we are back at square one. Because with the choice idea, there are really only two terms, "unity" and "difference". We can prioritize either the one or the other of the two. But the third element, namely the first part of each phrase ("the unity *of . . .*" and "the difference *of . . .*"), is superfluous. It does not add anything, but merely expresses our subjective *preference* for the one or the other of the two. Its only function is therefore to *underline* one term in the simple two-term phrase, thus giving it its different "tinctures": in the one case "**unity** and difference", in the other "unity and **difference**".

The point is, however, that the phrase "unity of the unity and difference" does not privilege anything. In no way does it mean that "unity" is "the major trope". And the point, furthermore, is that this phrase indeed operates at a higher logical level, which Marlan verbally admits, but in his own thinking does not live up to and totally ignores. *He* gives a decidedly one-dimensional, one-level reading to the phrase "unity of the unity and difference". By claiming that it "privileges" unity, he must believe that the first occurrence of the word unity ("unity *of . . .*") in this phrase merely repeats and underlines *that same* "unity" from out of the pair "unity and difference" and ipso facto unfairly relegates the second element of this pair, "difference", to minor importance. In other words, the first occurrence of the word unity ("unity *of . . .*") stays for him at the same level as the part "unity and difference".

But in the properly understood phrase, the first "unity" is not at the same level. It is definitely not merely a "tincture" of a "syzygy". It adds something radically new and essential. It speaks on a higher level. One could call this, even if not quite adequately, a meta-level. To optically illustrate this quality we could rewrite the phrase in the following way:

the unity of
"unity AND difference",

or "(unity AND difference) *as* a unity". The "tincture of the syzygy" idea wants to obliterate this distinction of levels. The "unity of the unity and difference" formula, far from using unity as the major trope and far from prioritizing or underlining the one of the two elements of "unity and difference" at the cost of the other, refers to both at once and thus goes fundamentally beyond the level of the initial two opposites. Rather than choosing or privileging the one of the two elements, we are asked the impossible: To "*choose*" (to retain here this inadequate idea for the moment) precisely *both*, and *both at once* (not each one at a time, nor in two separate acts by way of complementation or supplementation), as well as *both uncurtailed with equal emphasis*; and this formula then demands of us to comprehend these opposite, mutually exclusive, peers as a unity![39] This is a shocking imposition. It is mind-shattering. It forces us to think something unheard of, namely a self-contradiction as a not faulty but valid one! And by forcing us to really *think* this "impossible" thought and let it come home to us, it expands or "revolutionizes" the entire constitution of consciousness. The "unity of the unity and difference", if and when consciousness has really managed to *think* it, amounts to a breakthrough through the sound barrier of "natural consciousness", through the commonplace mode of experiencing the world. It catapults the mind from the level of positivity to that of absolute negativity: From the standpoint of "ego" to the standpoint of "soul". The same, by the way, is true for Jung's notion of the "mysterium coniunctionis" as the "separation and synthesis of psychic opposites".

But here the problems begin for Marlan. He refuses, or is not able, to *think* "unity". As his repeated use of the word "tincture" reveals, he apperceives the whole topic of "unity and difference" only superficially, from outside. He does not want to go into the heart of the matter. Whether you

---

39 It is, by the way, interesting that Heidegger, one of Marlan's authorities (!), said that the inseparableness [or unity, in German: *Zusammengehörigkeit*] of identity and difference is that which needs to be thought.

say "unity of" or "difference of" "unity and difference" affects no more than its external coloring.

The thought of the "unity of . . ." phrase depends precisely on there not being any privileging or choice.[40] Marlan's "major trope" idea *thwarts* the very point of the unity phrase. It functions as a clear defense because it makes it possible for consciousness to escape the challenge of what this phrase demands of consciousness. His not wanting to *think* "unity" comes also out in his construing "the unity and difference" as a "syzygy". The idea of a syzygy refers to the yoking together of two, to a couple, possibly a married couple. From a psychological point of view there are two fundamental mistakes in this view.

The one refers to the definition of unity. What our phrase aims at is in no way a yoking together of two, not a "transcendent uni*fication*" (Marlan in his cited *Spring* article, p. 12, my emphasis), that is to say, a forcing of two different entities into a unity. In our case, unity and difference are opposites, which would make any unification especially difficult. If you want to join together two opposites without any separating partition they ordinarily cancel each other out (such as fire and water, +1 and -1, or yes and no) or end up as a compromise formation (such as black and white, which become gray). But the unity that we are interested in here is not that of the syzygy, of a couple (which belong to the domain of what Freud called family romance). Rather, it has the strict meaning of becoming one, of oneness, *identity*. In a union of the syzygy type the two remain separate (cf.

40 Psychology (as the discipline of interiority) is not Hegelian philosophy. But since Marlan seems to see them as more or less the same, it may be interesting to note that for Hegel the "identity of identity and non-identity" implies the "absolute difference of identity and difference" and that the identity *sustains* itself precisely *as identity* only in its opposite, the absolute difference. In other words, Hegel's *speculative* concept of "identity" has "everything it needs within itself", even its very opposite and, this must be stressed, it has this opposite, i.e., the absolute difference, within itself precisely as its internal animating and propellent element. Marlan, as it were, extrajects this "difference" from the full, living "identity" and sets it up as a cut-off separate entity, which he then wants to offer as fundamentally *external* "complementation" for that castrated, sterile notion of identity or union that was only produced by his splitting the full identity and depriving it of its heart. Because both "identity" and "difference" in Marlan's *decidedly dissociative* thinking (informed by the modern logic of the "unbridgeable difference") have dwindled to two separate dead *abstractions* that have their other outside of themselves does the feeling of a need for their mutual (likewise abstract, merely formal) supplementation arise.

husband and wife, anima and animus), retain their own identity, because they are merely yoked together in an external sense; a combination, an agglutination. Oneness is something else. It means a true unity and requires— imaginally speaking—consciousness's move from the thinking in terms of the "physics" of things (e.g., mixing black and white sand) to "chemistry" or "alchemy" (interpenetration and internal recomposition, reconstitution). And above all, in contrast to alchemical operations it is not produced, made, not a uni-fication. On the contrary, it demands of us to rise to the challenge of *comprehending* (insighting) the fact that unity and difference have in truth, in the depth, on the level of soul, been identical all along, that they are one and the same to begin with, that unity has difference *within itself*. The unity existed from the outset, it had merely not been seen; commonplace consciousness (the ego) had not been aware of it; and in ordinary life, in practical reality, in the empirical world, there is also no need for it.

The explosiveness of the insight into *this* unity lies in the fact that it is not like the insight that Pope John Paul II and Karol Józef Wojtyła were identical, but that what is here said to be identical relate to each other like fire and water, which we know in empirical reality to exclude and "negate" one another. If consciousness is capable of maintaining itself *in the contradiction* that unity and difference, instead of simply cancelling each other out like fire and water in reality, are identical despite their absolutely negating each other, it is initiated into absolute negativity.

The second just as serious mistake lies in the fact that the syzygy idea invites an "ontological" thinking (and psychologically it makes no difference whether literally "ontological" *or only metaphorically* "ontological"): What a syzygy unites or yokes together are persons, figures, forces, things, entities. But unity and difference are none of these. They are thoughts, *thought determinations*. They have no body, no shape, no subsisting reality, neither in the physical nor in the imaginal world. They are outside of time and space. They can only be thought and have to be thought. They are "categories", strictly logical concepts, nothing imaginal. And the unity of the opposites that is meant here is in the same way a strictly logical unity. By operating with the idea of a (differently "tinctured") syzygy, Marlan shows that, despite his protestations,[41] his thinking remains enclosed within, and

---

41 In his *Spring*-article (p. 5f.) he makes a big deal about the difference between image as "optical picture" and a more radical understanding of image as being "not what you see but the way you see". But this does not invalidate my thesis of the fundamental deficiency

limited by, the horizon of picture-thinking, which inevitably reifies and imagines in terms of entities, processes and behaviors. Even if the imagination may entertain completely fanciful images that have no counterpart in the real world, nevertheless the logic of the imagination and of the mode of imaginal thinking holds thought inevitably down in the form of an "*ontology*" of the natural world and does its imagining in terms of the ordinary reality. It necessarily objectifies.

Imaginal thinking is that thinking whose imperceptible logical form or syntax is such that it *within itself resists and disowns itself* and ipso facto forces its own thoughts *out* (away from itself as thinking consciousness or subject), namely into the *form* of contents or objects of consciousness, that is to say, it keeps them in the form of *projection*. (It is only thought proper that does no longer project, because true thinking is that mode that has no "about" but is the form of its reflecting *itself*. Subject and object, form or act and content are the same.)

Picture-thinking is the mode in which Marlan approaches also the phrase "unity of the unity and difference". He treats "unity" and "difference" as if they were items, entities, positivities in syzygial union. In the *Spring*-article mentioned (p. 8f.) he explicitly professes his resistance[42] to thought on the ground of his belief in the imagining mode (". . . my belief that Jung and Hillman brought about a major advance in consciousness by revisioning image and imagination, both of which have been in the shadow of Western thought and metaphysics since Plato". To my mind the tendency of this belief is decidedly reactionary). He claims there that "the dominant historical process" "had depotentiated images and reduced soul to rational intellectual spirit", thereby presenting an interpretation of history which I believe is factually untenable. But this is not our issue here. I merely quote it because it shows his commitment or bias. At any rate we see that this bias prevents

---

of the imaginal mode for doing justice to the deepest concerns of the soul. Regardless of whether optical image or way of seeing, of whether the image is consciousness's object or informs the subject, regardless also of whether the image is taken literally or seen through, the problem of the imaginal mode remains: That it is inherent in its inner logic that it stays inevitably tied to the *logical form* of the "natural" world-conception in terms of things, shapes, figures, events and has no access to concepts as concepts. Psychologically speaking, the real contrast to "what you see" is not "the way you see" but would be "what opens the eyes".

42 Very strange, coming from a psychoanalyst.

him from approaching *thinkingly* the thought of the "unity of the unity and difference" and from receiving it on its own level, namely as a thought, as a strictly conceptual, (psycho-)*logical* issue. Because he refuses to rise to the level of thought he simply does not get the message of that formula; he misses the point of the "unity" expressed in it.

Furthermore, because of his refusal to think, he also has to completely misunderstand even the very concept of "thought". He apperceives it reductively in his imagining way as the one part of Hillman's binary opposition of the "valley" of the soul and the "peaks" of spirit,[43] which shows us once more picture-thinking at work and the projective and naturalistic nature of the imagination—and of course also the insufficiency of the imagination to comprehend thought. The latter is beyond its horizon. This viewing thought in terms of the peaks of spirit (or, even worse, of "the poisonous state of splendid solar isolation") is reminiscent of the naive retrogressive "cargo-cult" logic of primitives confronted with phenomena high above their head: With phenomena of modern technological reality.

As a counterexample to Marlan's image-fixation let me remind you of the youngster Jung, who, when he came across the paragraph on the Trinity in confirmation class, described his reaction as follows: "Here was something that challenged my interest: a oneness which was simultaneously a threeness" (MDR p. 52). We see here the future psychologist emerging; here it was the soul that stirred from within the boy Jung and had captivated his consciousness with *its* deepest concerns. It was a strictly

---

43 Another issue is that he somewhere says that I prioritize thought. This shows what he thinks about thought: Just as for him it is something segregated on the peaks, having no place in the vales, so it is also psychically for him only one function or activity in contrast to others. But for a non-psychic, in a not everyday-sense, i.e., for a *psychological* understanding, there is nothing truly human without thought. To be sure, thought is also in our literal thinking (even if mostly only in an inferior form). But it is just as much in our dreams, our desires, our feelings, in our sexual life, in our illnesses, in language, in crimes, in politics, in pyramids and paintings, in perception and volition, even in our complexes. "The fact that consciousness does not perform acts of thinking does not, however, prove that they do not exist. They merely occur unconsciously and make themselves felt indirectly in dreams, visions, revelations, and 'instinctive' changes of consciousness, from whose nature one can see that . . . they are the result of unconscious acts of judgment or unconscious conclusions" (*CW* 11 § 638, transl. modified). So how can one prioritize thought? As humans, we are always already embedded in, surrounded, and overtaken by thought.

(psycho-)*logical* problem that fascinated and troubled Jung: What we have here are just thoughts, logical concepts: oneness, threeness, and their unity. No persons, no entities, nothing "real" or figurative, nothing that belongs to the sphere of positivity nor anything imaginal, no metaphor. For the same reason late Jung could interpret alchemy as an implicit psychology, because what alchemy is dealing with, in the tradition of hermetic philosophy, are thoughts proper, *although*, admittedly, thoughts and logical issues still not seen through as such, but concealed in the (inadequate) *form* of projection onto material substances or processes and garbed in wild imagery. The inner logic of alchemy is once and for all beyond the imaginal. It is conceptual and logically negative, and this conceptual nature is also reflected in the style of its images, which are no longer logically innocent images in the vein of the traditional mythic imagination. Rather, the inherited form of "image" has been repurposed, and the outcome of this is usually surprisingly weird or even self-contradictory, at any rate in itself reflected, more allegorical than imaginal.[44] This weirdness is a result of the discrepancy between (still seemingly mythological) *form* and (already decidedly post-mythological, strictly logical, abstract-conceptual) *content.*

Now turning our attention to Marlan's own phrase that he proposes as complementation, the formula "difference of the unity and difference", we have to characterize it as a mindless phrase, an un-thought: An empty tautology or pleonasm. It is rightly no more than a *tincture* of the syzygy. His formula does not really *say* anything, does not introduce anything new or unknown and does not present a challenge (the way the "unity" phrase does). Its message is a simple repetition: For that there is a difference, indeed an incompatibility, between unity and difference is from the outset already inherent in the simple juxtaposition of these two concepts. Even to the everyday consciousness of the man on the street it is self-evident that unity and difference are mutually exclusive opposites. No need to make a big deal about their difference by dressing this ordinary and self-evident truth up in the linguistically fancier, more complicated garment of Marlan's three-term formula.

But this tautological formula is of course needed for the purpose of mimicking the "unity of the unity and difference" formula (which indeed adds something

---

44   The stone that is not a stone; *aurum nostrum non est aurum vulgi; vinum ardens, aqua permanens, aurum potabile, cauda pavonis, unus mundus, spiritualis sanguis,* etc.

new and totally unexpected to the two-element phrase) and thus of creating the impression as if the tautological formula were on a par with it. But in reality it can only produce a peerage between them by conversely having castrated, banalized the unity formula, and downgraded it to the level of Marlan's own formula, conceiving both versions as mere "*tincturings*"! But more than that: The "difference" formula is supposed to create the impression that it is going *beyond* the concept of the "unity of unity and difference" and truly presenting an *answer* to the former, a *corrective* to it, a supplement or complement—while in reality, as we have seen, it has not even sighted it. It falls back behind the challenge that the notion of a union of the opposites represents and merely returns to the commonplace view of things, even if, perhaps, with more élan and an additionally created impression of a higher philosophical aura.

But apart from the fact that Marlan's formula does not *do* what it claims to be doing because it simply does not rise to the plane of the idea of the "unity of the unity and difference"—a revolution of consciousness (and, as we have seen, our formula does revolutionize consciousness) does not have "sides", cannot be said to be one-sided and thus is not in need of supplementation, simply because as revolution it transforms the entire *constitution* of consciousness and, in the present case, does equal justice to both unity and difference—by the same token, Jung's version of the "unity of unity and difference" formula, namely, "mysterium coniunctionis" as the "separation and synthesis of psychic opposites", is not in need of any supplementation. It also gives both separation and synthesis their due.

With his insistence on the tautological phrase "the difference of the unity and difference" Marlan, instead of complementing the other phrase, digs his heels in and in the last analysis merely firmly establishes his unyielding commitment to the *standpoint*[45] of positivity and externality, to the fantasy of the tangible and concretistic: The thing-in-itself, the dross, the ashes, the unassimilable remainder. And thereby rescues commonsensical consciousness's logical innocence.

A dictum of the alchemists says: Don't begin any operation before not everything has become water. Another one advises us to dissolve the matter in its own water. We could say similarly: Psychology does not really

---

45 He argues on the object-level (the resisting remainder as an experienced fact, etc.), but he is unwittingly doing something for the subject: He establishes and defends its *standpoint*.

begin before not everything has entered the status of absolute negativity and thereby has come home to the soul from its exile in the state of projection and thing-likeness. Jung declared: "Every other science has a point outside of itself; not so psychology, whose object is the very subject that produces all science" (*GW* 8 § 429, my transl.).

When imaginal psychology tries to view image as a "metaphor without a referent" (Hillman[46]), it seems nicely to be doing justice to the referent-lessness of psychology expressed in the first part of Jung's statement. As such, image is self-contained, and as metaphor it is certainly not unassimilable. The unassimilableness thesis, by contrast, lustfully reinstates the external referent, the rigid object that resists consciousness and thus irrevocably remains vis-à-vis it, just as the idea of a necessary supplementation of the one "tincture" of "the syzygy" ("unity" tincture) by the other ("difference" tincture) amounts, to say it in terms of Marlan's "syzygy" image, to complementing a successful marriage bond with the couple's estrangement or divorce. This may produce a fitting portrayal of our social reality. But is devotion to everyday reality the task of psychology?

Be that as it may, we learned from Hillman that in imaginal psychology image qua metaphor is without a referent. However, this is not enough. It refers only to a literal referent. But metaphor has not fully overcome externality; it still harbors within itself, and further transports, the *logical form* of "referent" or "object", inasmuch as it has itself become the new object of consciousness instead of any literal object. Whether literal gold or imaginal, metaphorical gold—both the thing-character and the "content of consciousness"-character of the "gold" have not really been overcome. And this is why "metaphor" does not do justice to the *second part* of Jung's statement.

Alchemy, by contrast, explicitly negates, cuts into, the very "images" it uses or lets them openly contradict themselves and thus prevents even a possible metaphorical understanding of them: The stone that is *not* a stone, the aurum *non* vulgi, the "tail-eater, which is said to beget, kill, and devour itself" (*CW* 16 § 454) cannot be mistaken as metaphors.[47] They all, and

---

46 James Hillman, "Silver and the White Earth (Part Two)", in *Spring* 1981, 21–66, p. 49.

47 Metaphors do not come with an *explicit* "not" or other form of self-negation and self-reflection. They do not deliberately and from the outset cut into their own flesh as an explicit warning against misunderstanding them. They enjoy (and require) their innocence.

even more unambiguously our "the unity of the unity and difference", leave the orientation towards, and form of, object behind and aim directly—and thus *reflectively*—at the (perceiving, experiencing, interpreting, imagining, all-sciences-producing, . . .) "subject" alone, at the mind, at the transformation of the constitution or logical form of consciousness, trying to raise *it* to the *standpoint* of soul, the *standpoint* of absolute negativity. The philosopher's stone, for example, is not an object out there and not an entity, neither literally nor metaphorically. "Transmute *yourselves* from dead stones into living philosophical stones!"[48] Of course, "yourselves" could still be personalistically misconstrued in terms of *people's* psychic self-development. But Dorneus also preempted such a misunderstanding by saying: "In truth the form, which is the intellect of man, is the beginning, middle and end of the procedure. . . ."[49] Let us remember: We are doing *psychology*.

The black sun's home in psychology (as the discipline of interiority)

Now I can at long last offer a very different, namely *psychological*, non-literalizing interpretation of the image of the black sun. *Above* I showed that this image is most likely to *appear* (to happen), as an explicit experience, to a white-soul consciousness and that it then functions as a fundamental challenge and ipso facto as an invitation to this consciousness to go through the entrance gate opened by, and in the form of, the black sun. It is, above all, the invitation to "see through" its imaginal character. *Now*, however, my question is what this image can mean for psychology, that is, for a consciousness that is not informed by the anima alba, but is *logically* from the outset already on the other side of the entrance gate and has its standpoint there. Here the black sun does of course not represent a challenge, nor does it produce "experiences of brokenness, incision, wound". And it does not have the explicit form of *object* of consciousness (something *to be* seen and experienced) in the first place, nor does it—literalized instead of seen through—seduce consciousness to mystifications, so that it comes

---

48 Dorneus, quoted in Jung (*CW* 9i § 264, my italics). Soul in general is not an object, a substance, something subsisting.

49 The *form*, the *intellect*! We would say: The logical constitution of consciousness. (The quote is from *CW* 12 § 366.)

up with the firm (allegedly "psychological") belief in "mind independent object" and thing in itself. Instead of object and content of consciousness, the black sun in psychology (as the discipline of interiority) is much rather like an "archetypal perspective" (in Hillman's sense), a way of seeing, one that structurally informs consciousness as if from behind. This means more concretely: The "black sun" is the spiritus rector of psychology's *methodological* approach, this approach *expressed* in concretistic (symbolic or imaginal) form.

How is this to be understood? For psychology (as the discipline of interiority), every phenomenon of psychological interest in its immediacy *is* at first (i.e., right after having been placed in the retort) Marlan's "black sun", as it were, and needs to be seen and appreciated as such: As dark, black, ununderstood, an enigma. It could even be said that our placing it in the retort is the act that ipso facto *constitutes* it as "black sun".[50] But persevering devotion to its blackness (often) leads to the experience that the phenomenon in the retort as this "black sun" indeed emits, as Marlan says, "an odd light, what the alchemists called the 'light of darkness itself'" (p. 34). This process from darkness to slowly deepening insight describes precisely the method (and experience) of our working with dreams, myths, symptoms (and other material). What Marlan ignores and denies is that this "odd" light of "darkness itself" *is* truly *light* and as such the very opposite of an "ultimate 'no' to consciousness"; and what he neglects is to *keep seeing* in this light. He does not seem to be interested in this *inseeing* and instead to prefer to look out and away ("pro-ject") and to end up standing in awe in front of the resulting *yonder* of an obscure, on principle unassimilable a-rational enigma or abstract "wonder". In reality, however, this light of darkness itself is a light that can dawn on us and illumine the initial darkness of the material at hand for us and allow

---

50 This is the fundamental difference of the psychological phenomenon to the scientific objects of study, which are never constituted as "black sun", but as "what is the case or fact". No "dark light", let alone a bright light, shines from out of them. The sciences see the phenomena in the general light that falls from outside on them, in daylight, the light of common sense. Placing phenomena in the retort deprives them of their "fact" or "being the case" character, and forces them to appear in no other than the very special light that is exclusively the respective phenomena's own light. It is a light that ipso facto reflects them into themselves, and turns them into the soul's self-expression, into what Jung in the above quote called "fantasy" and Hillman "image".

us, step by step a little more, to see it in its very interiority, its inner logic
and truth.

I have to add that it is indispensable for any true psychological work
that the light we see in is, precisely and only, the light *of the original
"darkness itself"*, because only then is it the phenomenon's own light,
and is our insight really its *self-illumination* and in this sense that which
allows for our true soulful understanding of it (and the "odd"-ness at-
tributed to this light by Marlan consists in nothing else but the fact that it
is the phenomenon's [qua dark sun] *own inner* light and not the familiar
general daylight shining upon it from all around it). I need to stress this
because so often in the practice of psychotherapy analysts try to throw
the external, essentially foreign "light" of their preconceived psychological theories or of their personal free associations upon dreams and case
material, mechanically identifying patients, as cases, for example with
ready-made abstract DSM diagnoses or with theoretical constructs such
as the oedipal complex, libidinal stages, infantile trauma, etc.,[51] as well
as identifying this image with the phallus, that with the Great Mother,
"the unconscious", the shadow, the *puer*, the anima, or what have you, as
their ready-made props. The discipline of interiority conversely requires
the black-sun darkness of each real phenomenon at hand as the starting point of its psychological work of absolute-negative interiorization,
which includes our leaving behind, as far as is humanly possible, all our
theoretical baggage and preconceived ideas as well as our conventional
simplistic everyday understanding of the images. And it is a *discipline*
also in the sense that it requires the self-discipline of our patient perse-
verance in the phenomenon's original darkness and our strict refusal to
let any alien light come in from outside. Now we also understand better why I said that the, let us say, "post-imaginal", logical approach of
psychology as the discipline of interiority has the character of a "dark"
seeing.

Far from being the "dark *other*" of "the logical" and of psychology
(as the discipline of interiority), the "black sun" has always already tac-
itly been at work in it as its own methodological principle that guided it
in its understanding of the soul's logical life. Here, in psychology and as

---

51 With an expression Jung used to criticize the abuse of his typology we could say:
   They stick labels on people.

its methodological principle, the black sun is really at home, fully integrated into the structure of its consciousness, fully *assimilated*—and thus also fully realized, that is to say, here it is true and real, because it has been released into its truth and thereby come home to itself from its exile in objectified imaginal form. Marlan's not having seen this is due to the blindness that resulted from his consciousness's having become overly impressed and infected, in its own constitution, by the blackness that it saw in its literalized object or content and by having become its (the blackness's, the *not*-inseeing's) subservient ardent prophet. It is not the black sun that resists conscious assimilation. It is Marlan. He rejects the *existing* assimilation to be found in psychology. Yes, indeed, as Marlan himself put it in the last three words of his paper: "black light matters" (p. 40). However not as he meant it: Semantically, literally, objectified and externalized as imaginal contents ("a dark sky marked by tracing a dark light, stars in a night sky, an Egyptian goddess Nuit . . ." [p. 40]), but syntactically: *psychologically*, interiorized into itself.

In psychology, where the black sun is the spirit and form of its methodological *procedere*, all the mystifications clinging to Marlan's version of the black sun topic have disappeared. It is no longer the object of external reflection. It has been "vaporized", distilled, absolute-negatively inwardized into logical form, into the style of seeing. As a method or mode, it is, on the one hand, something concretely real and practical, down to earth, not a yonder, also not an unassimilable wonder, and yet, on the other hand, it is not either concretized or positivized as a be it empirical or imaginal object.

This is a truly psychological (and not a would-be philosophical) interpretation of the image of the black sun, because this interpretation lets the soul speak in this image about itself and its own needs, rather than about an objective reality.

The necessity of distinguishing oneself from one's truths

As we have seen, "making conscious" or "conscious assimilation", does not mean "overcoming" or "bleaching" (in the sense of turning everything into "logical light") and lifting phenomena up into the heroic heights of "peaks of spirit" beyond their concrete reality, which is how Marlan seems to understand Hegel as well as psychology (as the discipline of interiority).

If consciousness is under the domination of the white soul, "making *conscious*" much rather means: Seeing *it*, the black sun (or whatever other soul phenomenon may happen to be in focus), more deeply, seeing through it, getting into it, and letting *it* lead the way wherever it may lead, which in such an extreme case as that of the black sun may even be into a whole other dimension or other status of consciousness. This, however, can only happen if that consciousness maintains itself as a seeing one all the way through.

But consciousness's preserving itself as a seeing one and penetrating into the depths of its experience is not all that is implied by "making conscious". Making conscious also means *distinguishing* oneself (one's consciousness, one's psychology) *from* the truths of all particular images that one may experience, instead of *letting them go to one's head* and simply "buying" their message. Jung stressed the importance of our learning to free ourselves from the suggestive power of unconscious images.

What a difference! Jung opts for the liberation from the *suggestive power* that the image exerts on consciousness, its hold on us, i.e., he opts for liberation from the image's possible effect; Marlan opts for the liberation from ["dissolution of", "going away of"] the *inner quality* of the image itself: before his about-turn that changed him into the defender of unassimilability he had expected the experienced *object* (the black sun) to become assimilated and not consciousness [the experiencing subject] to free itself *from* the black sun's power while respecting its nature. He wanted the change to happen "out there". His favoring externality is consistent.

Liberation from the suggestive power of an archetypal image that tends to enthrall consciousness does of course not mean to reject it or fight it. As a *psychological* liberation it is not an act of the *will*, an ego act, in the first place. It does not have the literal form of an attempt of holding it away or, conversely, of immunizing oneself against it. Through a directly negative relation to a psychic image or reality we stay as much under its spell as through a positive, loving one. Psychologically, the only way to free oneself from the enthralling or inflating influence is, dialectically, through one's getting closer to it and one's embracing, "owning" it, in the double sense of *our* being initiated into it (which is tantamount to *its* being seen through) and *its* being distilled, changed from the form of imaginal content or substance to that of perspective of consciousness, style of seeing, logical form. Both aspects are necessary. Because if consciousness has not liberated itself from their suggestive and enthralling power, archetypal contents also become consciousness's logical form, what Hillman called a "dominating archetypal perspective" that determines one's seeing and evaluations from behind. But *this* logical form of consciousness is one that consciousness is totally unaware of. It is taken by consciousness to be absolutely self-evident, unquestionable, *the* true one—the only one that's possible. The change from archetypal content to form of consciousness or style of seeing, if it happens totally unconsciously, all by itself as a background process, is precisely the way how the suggestive power that Jung warned of exerts its influence and how consciousness gets inflated. Consciousness's initiation (its real entrance into the archetypal truth in question) and therefore its seeing through this content is indispensable for the liberation. Only through it the "archetypal perspective" ceases to be an unconsciously dominating one and becomes a *human* perspective, consciousness's own property. Consciousness is then self-critically aware of its perspective and in this sense free. And the perspective in turn has then the status of a *methodological* approach that consciousness can choose to employ or not, as it sees fit.

Since Marlan's attack on Hegel and on psychology's absolute-negative interiorization—an attack in the name of the unassimilable remnant and *ad maiorem capitis mortuum gloriam*—has revealed itself to us as actually being the unwitting defense of what he calls his "psychological narcissism", it has an ulterior purpose: It has the task of performing a function in or for his personal psychological economy and for his "highest value", i.e., this belief of his in the remnant and in mind-independent object. Therefore this attack does not come from Marlan as the *professional* that he is too; it does not really have the status of a *theoretical* (be it philosophical or psychological) counterposition, as which, however, it tries to present itself with his citations of numerous philosophical writers as authorities supporting his views. It is, as I pointed out at the very beginning of this paper, *ideological*—in fact, a "postmodern" metaphysics of otherness and exteriority.

Or should I not much rather say: A kind of "'postmodern' religion"? For one cannot help but get the impression that he speaks with a deep (even if faint) sense of religious ardor when he comes to such notions as "gateway back to the beyond, at the root of imagination, wonder, and transformation" (p. 29), of a "dark enigma" (p. 34), and "an erotic presence calling

us toward her [i.e., to the Egyptian Goddess Nuit, the dark night sky[52]]
to an absolute that is not an absolute, seducing us to a wonder beyond
the language of truth" (p. 40).[53] It is "postmodern" because it is just the
empty form and subjective *feeling* of religion, its zero-stage, a completely
abstract contentless "religion" without God or gods, without heaven or
hell, redemption and eternal life, without meaning and truth—just a void,
pit, or darkness of wonder and enigma.[54] The erotic seduction by the dark
Night goddess could also be interpreted as consciousness's letting itself be
enticed into the situation of the Platonic cave-dwellers who, like passive

52 It is very revealing that the Egyptian Goddess, whose real Name is *Nwt*, generally tran-
scribed as *Nut*, appears in Marlan's text as the Goddess *Nuit*, a transcription which, according to the relevant Wikipedia entry accessed in May 2017, is "certainly erroneous",
but of course allows itself to be easily associated with French *nuit*, night, although this
Goddess is by no means exclusively "the dark night sky".
53 "Beyond the language of truth": A fitting accompaniment to the Donald Trump era.
54 More than ten years ago Greg Mogenson, at the very end of his review of Stanton Marlan's *The Black Sun*, entitled "Marlan's Bardo Thödol", in *The San Francisco Jung Institute Library Journal*, 2005, Vol. 24(4): 1–10, had already clairvoyantly detected and
highlighted the central problem of Marlan's approach to the black sun topic by quoting
very pertinent statements George Santayana had made by way of a critique of mysticism:
Mysticism "consists in the surrender of a category of thought on account of the discovery of its relativity." Mogenson continues:

> Eschewing the specific and finite, the mystic deserts reason and judgment on account
> of their share in these. The upshot of this is that [now with Santayana's words again]
> ". . . instead of developing our minds to greater scope and precision, it would return to
> the condition of protoplasm—to the blessed consciousness of an Unutterable Reality."

In a further comment, Mogenson adds: "As psychologists we must not leave the black
sun a mystical object, or bring a false prestige to our patients' despair and depression
through the strange grandeur of its name." Yes, indeed, *theoretically* the diagnosis
"condition of protoplasm—the blessed consciousness of an Unutterable Reality" and
therapeutically the warning against "mystical object" and "bringing false prestige to
our patient's despair through the strange grandeur of its name" hit the nail on the head
concerning the problem and danger of Marlan's position! At the same time we understand all the better why concrete, spelled-out elaborations, such as in psychology (as the
discipline of interiority) or in Hegel, of the logic at work in phenomena can appear to a
"blessed consciousness of an Unutterable Reality" as expressive of a "splendid solar isolation" and this splendid solar isolation in turn as a "poisonous state", since it represents
a serious threat to the blessedness of consciousness (that blessedness that Jung called
consciousness's having become unconscious and that philosophy might call an ontology
of agnosia, of not-knowing).

movie or TV watchers, look enthralled and in ecstasy at the absolutely ir-rational, language-transcending marvel of the truthless shadows projected onto the cave wall.[55] Jung said about Freud that he was *ein Ergriffener* ("a man touched and taken hold of in his innermost depth", my transl., cf. *MDR* p. 153). The same may be true of Marlan: *ein Ergriffener*.

---

55 I discussed the Platonic Cave parable in my "The Occidental Soul's Self-Immurement in Plato's Cave", in: *Technology and the Soul, Coll. Engl. Papers Vol. II*, New Orleans, LA: Spring Journal Books, 2007, now London and New York: Routledge, 2020, pp. 213–279. There I suggested that the *Cave situation* is not so much to be seen as the starting point from which Plato's philosophical thinking pushed off and which he left behind, but *conversely* as an unwitting utopia, a first vision of or general blueprint for a future possibility, i.e., as a totally unconscious *project* which only now in modernity is being realized. What Marlan is striving for seems to provide additional evidence for my thesis about the Cave story.

Chapter 4

The psychologist as repentance preacher and revivalist[1]

Robert Romanyshyn on the melting of the polar ice

Jung opened his early main work, *Transformations and Symbols of the Libido*, later revised as *Symbols of Transformation*, with a chapter on "Two Types of Thinking". He must have felt that in order to really start upon the work of psychology one had to draw a clear dividing line between the type of thinking it required and the generally prevailing different type of thinking. This was early in the 20th century. But this clear demarcation of a particular style of thinking necessary for psychology did not once and for all settle the question of psychology's self-constitution. Obviously, psychology is a truly precarious field. Throughout his life, Jung needed to contrast the approach and thinking of psychology proper with those of theology, metaphysics, philology, the natural sciences, strictly technical and medical approaches to psychotherapy, and socio-political ways of thinking. Psychology is, however, not only in need of marking its borders to other fields. It also needs to draw clear dividing lines between different types of thinking that come up within its own precincts, and this time and again. I could not help but be reminded of this latter necessity when lately becoming aware of a growing tendency in the Jungian field to advocate what has been called ecopsychology. It gives me rise to propose another and different differentiation of "two types of thinking".

Although I don't know whether Romanyshyn would himself use the label "ecopsychology" for his work, his well-argued paper on "The Melting Polar Ice: Revisiting *Technology as Symptom and Dream*"[2] could be

1 Written in 2009.
2 All references to Romanyshyn in this chapter are taken from the following publication: Robert D. Romanyshyn, "The Melting Polar Ice: Revisiting *Technology as Symptom and Dream*", in: *Spring, A Journal of Archetype and Culture*, vol. 80, Fall 2008, 79–112.

DOI: 10.4324/9781003611417-4

considered as a high-level example of it. It nicely exemplifies, and thus allows me to demonstrate, one type of thinking based on certain premises and
tenets, displaying certain attitudes, and leading to certain strategic moves
that I find incompatible with what I would consider psychology proper, a
"psychology with soul" in the tradition of C.G. Jung.

Anxiety

The first section of Romanyshyn's paper is entitled, "Anxiety and Ice", and
right at the start we are informed, "So I begin to write in this anxious state, . . .
remembering that anxiety was also the beginning of my book, *Technology
as Symptom and Dream* . . . The anxiety then was the imminent prospect
of a nuclear winter; the anxiety now is the prospect . . ." (p. 79) of the new
catastrophe of melting ice caps. Anxiety as the explicit *archê* and principle
of his writing and thus as the *spiritus rector* for all that follows. The author
does not see this as a problem, but gives a psychological justification for
beginning in this emotional state. Anxiety is ennobled as the "proper starting
point for the discovery of integrity" (p. 80). Staying in touch with it is even
claimed to be an "ethical process in which 'one's infinite obligation to the
other is expressed'" (p. 80). "To stay with the anxiety of the moment is to be
responsible, able-to-respond, because I am listening" (p. 80). This is the view
of the one type of thinking.

The other type of thinking would say that emotions in general inevitably
make us unfree to the extent that we are under their spell. They tend to blind
us. Let us hear Jung on emotion:

> And you always have emotions where you are not adapted. If you are
> adapted you need no emotion; an emotion is only an instinctive explosion
> which denotes that you have not been up to your task. When you don't
> know how to deal with a situation or with people, you get emotional.
> Since you were not adapted, you had a wrong idea of the situation . . . to
> be emotional is already on the way to a pathological condition.[3]

In quoting Jung I do not wish to suggest that because Jung said this it must
be right and everyone has to accept it. In his long life Jung said so many

3 C.G. Jung, *Nietzsche's Zarathustra. Notes of the Seminar Given in 1934–1939*, ed. by
   James L. Jarrett, vol. 2, Princeton University Press 1988, pp. 1497f.

things that all sorts of views, at times even opposite ones, could be supported with quotations from his writings. It is the other way around. I quote his statement because it hits the nail on the head.

This passage serves here merely the purpose of showing the other type of psychological thinking. According to it, there is nothing ethical about staying with one's anxiety. On the contrary, it is the ethical obligation of any writer striving for insight to first free himself of any emotion so as to become able to study his subject *sine ira et studio*, to become "up to his task".

Also, as a therapist I know that when I have a new patient whose deeply suppressed but powerful fury uncannily fills the whole atmosphere of the consulting room or who seems to be threatened by a psychosis *and I become anxious*, I have ceased being his therapist, his analyst. In my fear of him or of his threatening material I can no longer do justice to him, because I am no longer free. I am not adapted to the situation, not up to my task. It is vital for the therapy that I struggle to overcome my anxiety and gain my freedom vis-à-vis what made me afraid. If I don't succeed, I cannot continue this therapy. In a very similar sense, how can I write on technology if I am under the spell of anxiety caused by the imminent prospect of a nuclear winter or the melting ice? It would be unprofessional.

Strangely, very strangely, the possibility of *overcoming* one's anxiety seems to have no place in the first type of thinking. The only way that Romanyshyn can imagine to deal with this emotion, other than staying with it, is "numb[ing] myself against this feeling", "going to sleep, benumbing myself", entertaining a "comfortable illusion". In other words, the only other option for him would be repression, avoidance, escapism, which psychologically is of course out of the question from the start. But the possibility to truly *overcome* one's fear, to rise above it, and this means to honestly face the threatening reality without illusions but precisely with a wakeful mind, does exist. For example, to free myself as analyst of the anxiety evoked in me by threatening aspects of my patient means anything but going to sleep, closing my eyes to what may be dangerous, or cherishing illusions. No, it means my conscious willingness to allow what caused the anxiety to *be* and to show itself the way it is in the consulting room unhindered, without my need to inwardly defend myself against it, without any resistance against it on my part (and my anxiety would be of course a form of resistance). I let it be and expose myself to it. In full awareness I allow Pandora's box to be opened.

But of course, as Jung said, "We don't like to control our emotions because we enjoy them".[4] People relish anxieties. They thrive on them—just remember how most of America wallowed in anxiety after the terrorist attacks on the Twin Towers in New York. Hysteria. And why do we enjoy our emotions? Probably because emotions make us feel much more intensively alive than normally. They strengthen the *unio naturalis* for us. This is why Jung was right to continue by saying it is felt to be "partial suicide when we control them". Because it cuts into and dissolves our natural oneness with ourselves, and so "[w]e regret[5] ourselves; we are sorry for ourselves . . ."[6]

Formerly, by contrast, to control one's emotions, to overcome oneself was generally expected of people as a matter of course, as part of being civilized, educated. And in the spirit of this latter view, the second type of psychological thinking still now believes that the first step and *sine qua non* of the psychological *opus* is the dissolution of the *unio naturalis*, and that the Work itself is an *opus contra naturam*.

In 1975 James Hillman, on the first page of his *Re-Visioning Psychology*, quoted Ortega y Gasset saying: "Why write, if this too easy activity of pushing a pen across paper is not given a certain bull-fighting risk and we do not approach dangerous, agile, and two-horned topics?"[7] One can hardly imagine a greater difference than that between the bull-fighting spirit vis-à-vis a dangerous topic and one's purposely rooting oneself as author in one's own anxiety. With the avowal of one's anxiety one has *psychologically* from the outset succumbed and given in to what is feared. No risk-taking any more, no willingness to hold intellectually one's place vis-à-vis it. The mind has already given up. And so it is no surprise that Romanyshyn's paper ends with his confession that he is writing "from this place of near despair" (p. 113). "The pull to go numb, to fall asleep . . . is strong" (p. 113). One is tempted to console him by saying *requiescat in pace*. The quest for insight is drowned in emotionality, in a sinister *mood*.

---

4 C.G. Jung, *Nietzsche's Zarathustra. Notes of the Seminar Given in 1934–1939*, ed. by James L. Jarrett, vol. 1, Princeton University Press 1988, p. 158.

5 "Regret": Jung was probably thinking of German *bedauern* which can both mean "regret" and "feel sorry for".

6 C.G. Jung, *Nietzsche's Zarathustra. Notes of the Seminar Given in 1934–1939*, ed. by James L. Jarrett, vol. 1, Princeton University Press 1988, p. 158.

7 James Hillman, *Re-Visioning Psychology*, New York: William Morrow & Company, 1992, p. 1.

I mentioned that the first section of Romanyshyn's paper is entitled "Anxiety and Ice". But this is a misnomer. There is no ice in this section. There is only the mood of anxiety. Moods are warm, emotions are hot. Psychologically the ice, the soul's icy coldness, is already melted to begin with; it is dissolved prior to the feared melting of polar ice out there. Ice is cold, hard, crystal clear, sharp-edged. And I would think that an icy mind would be needed to do justice to the topic of polar ice, since only like can know like. But in this paper what is "like" on both sides is not the ice, but the melting, the crumbling away. A mind that has some ice in it, a mind that is willing to take a certain bull-fighting risk, does not need to get hysterical or depressed over the insight that melting polar ice may have terrible, disastrous effects. For millennia people in most parts of the world have lived with the firm belief that there would be an end of the world, apocalypse, doomsday, Ragnarök, the grand finale of the Kali yuga. What is so special about a coming doom? *Media in vita in morte sumus.* We all know that we will have to die. Is this a reason to make, *in advance*, a huge fuss and bother about it? Let's keep both feet on the ground.

This whole anxiety business is in my opinion a case of what Jung once termed, with a drastic, vulgar expression, *Hosenscheißerei des Ich.*

> Question: is it an object worthy of anxiety, or a poltroonery of the ego, shitting its pants [*eine Erbärmlichkeit i.e. Hosenscheißerei des Ich*]? (Compare Freud, "The ego is the seat of anxiety", with Job 28:28, "The fear of the Lord, that is wisdom".) What is the "anxiety of the ego", this "modestly modest" overweeningness and presumption of a little tin god, compared with the almighty shadow of the Lord, which is the fear that fills heaven and earth? The first leads to apotropaic defensive philosophy, the second to γνῶσις θεοῦ.[8]

This quote nicely contrasts the two types of thinking I am speaking about, although only in the one specific area of fear, namely the anxiety of the ego versus "the fear that fills heaven and earth". It is a small example of the general difference between a psychology construed as ego-psychology and one as a psychology of soul.

8 *Letters 2*, p. 333, to Arnold Künzli, 16 March 1943.

A German proverb states that anxiety is not a good advisor. But the very thesis of Romanyshyn is the very opposite, namely that staying with the anxiety is an ethical obligation and precisely connects us with the other. It makes him, he says, "responsible, able-to-respond, because I am listening". I think this is a great illusion. Of course I admit that anxiety, because it is a fear *of something*, in a literal and superficial way connects us with this something, this other. But that is psychologically absolutely irrelevant. *Psychologically* anxiety inevitably makes us circle around ourselves, it constellates the ego that wants to survive and fears for its life. Anxiety makes us ego-centered, if not downright selfish, egoistic; it does precisely not open one's psychological ears to the other. To the exact same extent that anxiety rules, the other has no chance. It has only a chance to that extent that one has overcome one's own anxiety and is willing, in the sense of Ortega y Gasset, to face the bull. Is it not symbolic for this ego-centeredness that the first as well as the last paragraph of his paper begin with the word I, and, mind you, not with the I of the *author* who may at the beginning wish to outline what he intends to do in his paper or to present his first argument or the like, but with the private I of the ordinary empirical human being and his subjective inner state?

Sin

In Romanyshyn's paper this ego-centeredness certainly does not show as selfishness or egotism, not even as focusing on himself. No, on the level of contents he goes away from himself and indeed bases his reflections on a very interesting and substantial exploration of important objective soul events, above all that of the invention of linear perspective during the Renaissance. They are later further backed up by more or less detailed discussions of aspects of works of literature from the Romantic period. So the way the ego shows must be different in his case. It appears in the style of viewing, in the perspective with which he approaches linear perspective. His apperception and interpretation are informed by "the anxiety of the ego" and are thus guided by an ego perspective. He does not perceive the phenomena he studies from the point of view of soul, that is, as the soul's own further development, its further-determination, its advancing to new statuses of itself, but from an ego bias. Instead of merely describing and analyzing what happened, allowing the material itself to provide for him the categories and criteria by which it is to be interpreted, he interferes with a subjective moralistic judgment of his own that he brings to bear on the material from outside.

He rightly observes certain essential historical changes, but the condemnatory evaluation that these changes receive from him is his own addition. Of course, he himself denies that he condemns anything or, conversely, that he judges the condition prior to those changes as being better:

> I am not arguing here that the pre-linear perspective world was a better world. On the contrary, my argument here is that while this way of dreaming the world as it moves toward the vanishing point has produced many benefits and has given us a great deal of power and control, it has exacted a price. In the face of the melting ice it is our task to know that price.[9]
>
> (p. 93)

However, this way of putting it does not correspond to what he actually presents in his paper. The price to be paid is something different from what he is talking about. When I desire an object and buy it, then afterwards I have this object but I have less money than before, because I had to pay the price it costs. Similarly, when I leave the home of my parents in order to stand on my own feet, I acquire a certain degree of adult maturity, but have to pay for it by the loss of all the advantages of containment in a family. The price is the particular loss that is concomitant with a gain or acquisition.

But the melting polar ice caps in the twenty-first century are not the price for the invention of linear perspective in the fifteenth century. In his scheme it is more like punishment for a crime. A criminal usually does his deed with the hope of being able to reap for himself only its benefits and, blinded by the dream of the benefits, either scotomizes his knowledge that there might be punishment or at least is pretty sure that he will escape punishment because of his clever precautions. If he nevertheless gets caught, his punishment comes to him as a later new separate and external event. For this reason (the external nature of a punishment) the model of crime and punishment is not completely suitable in our context either. Rather, the fantasy that Romanyshyn seems to be working in is more adequately described as that of a sin that has its punishment as its inherent unintended consequence within itself. An example might be one's starting to take drugs

---

9 I would say, to *pay* that price.

for the sake of an exciting experience and later finding oneself a hopeless addict on an inevitable path to ruin. According to Romanyshyn's logic, we might say that the people who invented linear perspective gave in to an extremely promising, but sinful temptation, he calls it "a dream", without any idea as yet of what they let themselves (and all future generations) in for, and only now, six hundred years later, do we become aware of and find ourselves stuck in the disastrous consequences of the development that they set in motion.

It is in the light of those disastrous consequences that Romanyshyn ap-perceives the achievements of the Renaissance artists who invented linear perspective. The presently felt threat of impending disaster (climate change and melting ice) provides the gauge with which in retrospect the early be-ginnings are to be judged. This is how the "the anxiety of the ego" becomes the lens through which one can assess the historical phenomenology of the soul—and, of course, assess it *as* a terrible sin.

Romanyshyn himself generally does not speak of sin (except that he says that Coleridge's Ancient Mariner "sins against nature" [p. 106]). But he names the sin, and with numerous names: Abandonment of the body of the earth, flight from nature, taking leave of the flesh and of the senses, breaking the erotic bonds (and freezing our feeling connection) with nature, becoming oblivious to what matters, a kind of imperialism, a forced colo-nization of the natural world by the light of a mind that knows no darkness, a solely masculine mind generating what it creates apart from the feminine, the despotism of an eye that sheds no tears, a consciousness without flesh, a nature dreamed as inanimate and a soul as un-natural, the broken connec-tion between body and world, the fragmentation of the world into its divis-ible parts, being above and unmoved by what is experienced, and so on. The end-result is: "We have all of us become trigger-happy cowboys ready to fix our gaze, not blink, and take aim at what is other to ourselves" (p. 108): Point-blank killers.

All this he reads into the invention and cultivation of linear perspective in the art of the Renaissance, which becomes for him embodied in imaginal figures that he calls the Spectator Mind and the "despotic eye" (p. 81). His view is moralism pure, but I think it is also a terrible misconstrual of the historical telos and achievement of the invention of linear perspective, a misconstrual that needs to be contradicted (although this is not my main point and interest in my critique of his paper). Phenomenologically and historically this evaluation is untenable. While it is of course true that linear perspective goes along with a distancing and a fixed, unmoved viewpoint, one must not single out this one abstract aspect, see it in isolation, completely apart from the whole context and spirit of Renaissance art, philosophy, science, apart also from the treatises of the artists themselves, and blow it up as the central or even the one and only feature. Such an interpretation does not become any better even if it is backed up by (likewise untenable) quotations from an art historian, Samuel Edgerton.

Romanyshyn and Edgerton are unable to see the dialectic of the creation of distance, the dialectic of the vanishing lines. It is as if neither of them had looked at actual paintings that were inspired by the spirit inherent in and underlying the invention of linear perspective and had not read Nicholas of Cusa, Ficino, Pico della Mirandola, Dürer, Leonardo da Vinci, etc. Flight from nature? Taking leave of the flesh and the senses? A dream of nature as inanimate? The opposite can be seen in the work (and thinking) of the artists. Whereas in earlier pre-linear perspective paintings of the Middle Ages, rather stiff figures had been depicted as abstract types, now all of a sudden there is an interest in the real looks of people as individuals. For the first time, painters tried to capture the exact hue of the color of skin as well as the real facial expression of people with all their emotions, as well as their wrinkles and dimples. The many nudes that were drawn and painted from then on (absolutely unthinkable during the earlier Middle Ages) show the celebration of sensuality—just think, for example, of Giorgione, Lucas Cranach, Rubens.

The painstaking attention to detail, to the individual hairs of fur, to the surface structure of materials like silk, brocade, linen, marble, and wood shows the dedication to the natural world that inspired those painters, and the numerous studies of hands, feet, faces, of trees, rocks, and even something as trivial as grass painted or drawn from nature are unmistakable evidence of a loving devotion to nature. The goal of the artist was to learn from, be taught by nature. Whereas in the Middle Ages the depicted scenes were usually set off against a gold background that denoted the otherworldliness of divine light—their not happening in our natural, earthly world—Renaissance painting shows that the soul has come down to earth and situates even sacred scenes here in the real world, such as the Annunciation in a real 15th century interior equipped with all the practical items of daily life, and other scenes in real-looking landscapes or architectural sites.

By talking of a "despotic eye" Romanyshyn smuggles his subjective value judgment, his moral condemnation, already into the very designation of the phenomenon to be described, which is of course manipulative, espe-cially because phenomenologically there is really nothing despotic about the eye in the Dürer woodcut in which Romanyshyn claims to see this despotism. All one can phenomenologically say is that the depicted art-ist practices a disciplined, concentrated, and controlled looking. Discipline practiced by somebody is not despotism. Yes, this eye is held fixedly in place. Yes, distance is thereby created. But in itself there is nothing wrong with that. Distance is the condition a priori of the human possibility of hav-ing a *world* and being in a "world" instead of merely being, like animals, factually involved with, and an integral part of, the *environment*.

Romanyshyn finds fault with the fact that Alberti, when painting, first draws a rectangle, a rectangle that Alberti says he regards as an open win-dow through which the subject to be painted is seen. Although on a very dif-ferent level and in a very different context, this act seems to be structurally analogous, for example, to the ancient city-building ritual of first drawing a sacred furrow in the earth around a square within which the city was to be built (as, e.g., practiced by Romulus in his founding Rome), or to the alche-mist's enclosing (even imprisoning!) in a hermetically sealed glass vessel the matter to be worked on and carefully observed. Romanyshyn seems to forget that an artist is an artist, that his work *per definitionem* is something "artificial", and that, as a matter of course, he is not living in "sensuous proximity to things", does not have an immediate but a reflected relation to the world. And is it astonishing that a painter privileges the eye as the mode of relation? After all, he's making pictures. *C'est son métier.* The musicians and poets of the time did not privilege the eye.

The vanishing point, Romanyshyn claims, "was prerequisite for taking leave of the earth". But no, the leave-taking of the earth, the longing for the beyond, and the mortification of the flesh, had been the medieval soul's ardent desire for centuries prior to the Renaissance invention of linear per-spective, and it was conversely now, along with this invention, that the soul for the first time truly *entered* the world, rooted itself in the earth, really, carefully opened its eyes to it in its sensuous beauty. What begins here is a *conscious* relationship to nature, instead of people's merely unconsciously living in and with it, taking it for granted (because their eyes and soul were turned upwards, to heaven, to eternity).

It is the dialectic of the vanishing lines that they go both ways. They do point to infinity, but they also show the real natural world in unbroken, continuous contact with the infinite, the finite as permeated by the infinite, and the infinite as the ultimate source of everything created. This is why the natural world had become an *explicatio dei*, as Nicholas of Cusa put it.

But Romanyshyn walks into the trap of Edgerton whom he quotes as saying, "space capsules built for zero gravity, astronomical equipment for demarcating so-called black holes, atom smashers which prove the existence of anti-matter—these are the end products of the discovered vanishing point". In other words, for Edgerton the vanishing point is, *in nuce* and *avant la lettre*, in itself already a black hole. What a lack of historical sensitivity! A clear case of a retrojection of the logic of modernity into the psychology of earlier and totally differently structured ages. A retrojection across the fundamental divide, the great historical rupture that separates all the ages in the Western tradition prior to the 19th century from the modern world. Through the 18th century, the world as a whole had been an intact order permeated by God's spirit. No broken connection. No emptiness, no nothingness at the vanishing point and thus no vanishing in the nothingness of a black hole. Human life and all human striving ultimately had a clear *substantial* goal. The vanishing point was the symbol of the undepictable infinity and fullness of the creator God, whose spirit permeated all of the natural world and was—potentially—revealed for the *mens humana* through its (the *mens's*) *lumen naturale*. Spinoza would later even speak of *deus sive natura*.[10]

It is silly to retroject our modern godlessness, nihilism, and centerlessness and our disjunctive logic of unbridgeable difference and différance way back into the invention of linear perspective by viewing the latter as the starting point of the former and the former as the end product of the latter. A false genealogy. The "black holes" as *our modern* "vanishing points" (in quotation marks!) and the vanishing points of Renaissance paintings are totally different, unrelated things. The broken connection with nature has a fundamentally different origin. The prerequisite for the possibility of the broken connection with nature is precisely that the divine order of the world, of which linear perspective and the whole art executed in its spirit was expressive, and thus also linear perspective's vanishing point (fulfilled infinity), had absolutely crumbled away and thus left a great hole,

---

10 Much would have to be said about these things, but inasmuch as what I want to show is a different matter I will have to leave it at these few hints.

a fundamental lack, an unbridgeable difference. It in fact happened—in the depth of the soul—around 1800–1830, with the transition from the handicraft mode of production to the industrial mode of production and with the transition from the logic of the *copula* (which had prevailed throughout classical metaphysics) to the copula-less modern logic of the *function* (as it would later be called by Frege).

It is of course noteworthy that for Edgerton and Romanyshyn there is, on the one hand, in the depth a *historical* connection, the unbroken continuity of a dream prevailing from the 15th century to the present, while, on the other hand, what gives this history its continuity is for them precisely the fact that it is the history *of* the dream of a *broken connection*. The historical rupture of the connection between man and nature that occurred in the 19th century in *their* theory reappears, safely encapsulated, as the *content*, *project*, and *nature* of the continuous dream from the invention of linear perspective to the present. A displacement.

In the light of what I will show below, I think it likely that the deeper unconscious reason for this displacement is the ego's wish to escape the painful insight that there has in fact been a real irrevocable rupture of the connection with nature, an irreparable rupture that happened *in the soul*, truly *happened* "to us" and simply has to be endured by us (rather than its being the result of a "dream" or world design on the part of the Spectator Mind), and to substitute for it a man-made disconnection as a faulty development that we can be condemn (and maybe correct). A syntactical change is reduced to a semantic one. Factually, Romanyshyn and Edgerton of course have to accept and endure the historical rupture, too. But psychologically, they try to rescue for themselves the old consciousness, the idea of a unity between man and nature, by moralistically rejecting the broken connection as a mere mistake or crime. "Ontologically" or logically, nothing fundamental has changed: Nature, the flesh, the senses, the earth are still as real as ever; only our human views, attitudes, behavior have changed in the direction of the "Spectator Mind" and the "despotic eye". The problem is merely our human abandonment of the body of the earth, our taking leave of the flesh and the senses, in other words, our sin, not a real rupture of the *unio naturalis* itself. Instead of our having to live with a fundamental rift in the very logic of the objective soul itself, both in its own historical process and between the psychic opposites, we get a grand narrative of a history of psychological degeneration and aberration.

Interestingly enough, the second half of Romanyshyn's paper focuses on a poem by Percy Shelly, Lord Byron's *Manfred*, Mary Shelley's *Franken- stein*, and Coleridge's *The Rime of the Ancient Mariner*—all works of the early 19th century and as such reflective of the great severing of the *unio naturalis* that happened at that time and was sensed as a deep shock by the more creative minds of the time. It is the absolute shock, to the sensitive poetic mind, at what had happened in the depth of the soul (or the depth of the logic of the world) at the time of these writers that led to a first interpre- tation of this change in terms of an outrage, a crime, just as the 19th century is in general the time of the invention of the crime and detective novels, which earlier would not have been possible because they would not have made any sense since the "crime"—the dissociation of the soul's copula, the dissociation between the psychic opposites—had not yet happened. The unity had still been intact. Only with this poetic material from the Romantic period, does Romanyshyn's thesis about our present-day situation get some sort of a phenomenological backing, since *this* material, in contrast to the linear perspective, is itself concerned with the modern dissociated condi- tion. But instead of realizing from his own material that it is the beginning of the 19th century when the decisive fissure happened, he wants to see it as a continuation of what had begun in the 14th century. And of course, he also interprets the event moralistically, from the point of view of the modern ego rather than of the objective soul, taking literally the early 19th century shock-induced misinterpretation of what had happened as a *crime* and making it his own.

Let us imagine for a moment that all he asserted about the Renaissance beginnings of the Spectator Mind and the "despotic eye"—the broken con- nection between body and world, the exclusion of the feminine and dark- ness, the dichotomy of inner and outer, the flight from the earth, the taking leave of the senses and the flesh, etc.—were true. What would justify us, insofar as we are psychologists, in condemning it? Who are we to claim that we know what is right or wrong for the soul? Does the soul have to follow our ideals, our normative ideas of health, wholeness, unity of masculine and feminine, and a feeling connection to the body and the senses . . .? Is it we who dictate to the soul the program that it ought to follow in its history, or are we not much rather at the receiving end and simply have to take note of how it in fact historically developed and develops, in order to take it from there? I think we have to let each new event and manifestation of soul teach

us afresh what "soul" and "soulful" means. Eachness rather than preconceived standard definitions.

There is no good reason other than our childlike naivety (which, however, is precisely not a *good* reason), why the soul at certain points in its
history could not need to become purposely one-sided and, for example,
insist on abandoning the earth, divorce itself from nature, overcome the
flesh and the senses, and exile the feminine. Why could it not need at
times to marginalize certain aspects? It is absurd to expect that the soul
follows our modern principles of political correctness. All this insistence
on a *wrong course of history* only shows, I quote Jung again, "the inten-
sity of our prejudice against the actual development, which we obstinately
want to be as we expect it. *We* decide, as if we knew" (*Letters 2*, p. 591, to
Read, 2 Sept. 1960, adapted). Had not already Pseudo-Democritus taught
us that "Nature rejoices in nature. Nature subdues nature. Nature rules
over nature", in other words, that it is inherent in the dynamic of the soul
to negate and overcome itself, so that this turn against itself is part of its
soul-making?

Furthermore, when talking about soul, do we mean the soul as something
really real in this our real world, as a possibly ruthless and fearful dynamic
that goes its way without concern for our human wishes and throws us at
times into unexpected and undesired predicaments, the soul as the dynamic
Mercurial spirit *in the actual historical development*—or do we only mean
an imagined and ideal soul *apart from, above, and over against*, the real
development, as a second world, an ego ideal—soul as nice and sweet, morally good, with the opposites light and darkness, masculine and feminine,
mind and matter always perfectly balanced in the wonderful pop-sense of
"wholeness", so that any deviation from this wholeness could only be a human fault and psychologically wrong (soulless)?

We can sense a desire and great effort in Romanyshyn's paper to construe the history of the last 600 years as a wrong development. We see
this same need also in the *theologian* (not the psychologist) Jung,[11] namely
when he charges Christianity as one-sided, with the shadow, evil, darkness,
and the feminine radically split off (which, by the way, is a sign that Jung
had simply refused to follow the revolutionary logical move of Christianity

---

11 James Hillman was probably the first to make the significant distinction between
Jung's theology and his psychology.

beyond the psychology of paganism and not grasped what it is really about, not entered the spirit of Christianity; instead he approached it with crude pre-Christian categories; but this is not our topic here). Romanyshyn gladly cites these views of Jung's. However, the *psychologist* Jung knew that such value judgments are misplaced. Calling a historically real religion wrong or deficient is an ego-trip. In psychology the categories of good or bad, right or wrong amount to an "artificial sundering of true and false wisdom". Jung speaks of one's succumbing "to the saving delusion that *this* wisdom was good and *that* was bad".[12] He frequently attacks the old idea that, *omne bonum a Deo, omne malum ab homine*, which follows the same logic. Why is it a *saving* delusion, a defense-mechanism? Because by blaming a *real phenomenon* or *development* of the soul for being bad, wrong, one-sided, the ego succeeds in rescuing *its own ideal*, its wishful thinking, its own program, value system, and categories from being refuted and sublated by the soul's actual development and ipso facto escapes the *psychological* challenge of the present, the psychological task that its own historical locus confronts it with.

As I pointed out, Romanyshyn stated that the development he discussed had a price. But it seems to me that he does his best to avoid truly *paying* the price, where "paying" could be understood psychologically as well as literally. Psychologically it would mean without reserve and resistance allowing the irrevocable rupture of the *unio naturalis* or the loss of the unifying bond between the opposites to come fully home to consciousness *as* the *soul truth* of modernity, allowing it to work on, decompose, and distill the inherited logical form of consciousness with its traditional expectations. This would be tantamount to giving up the narcissistic illusion that our situation is merely the result of a faulty development, of our outrageous aberration from soul, of our crime (*nostra culpa, nostra maxima culpa*) as well as to giving up the *unus mundus* delusion. Literally it would mean facing, for example, the melting of the ice caps without flinching[13] and understanding that our response to this threat has to be *only* a sober pragmatic

---

12 *CW* 9i § 31, transl. modified.

13 Interestingly enough, Romanyshyn accuses the "despotic eye" of the Spectator Mind of not blinking (which, by the way, is not convincing given what we see in the Dürer woodcut; there is no reason why the depicted artist could not blink). The condemnation of "not blinking" goes well together with his not facing our situation without flinching.

(technological, scientific, rational) one, very much down to earth, without any higher aura of having a soul meaning.

But Romanyshyn proceeds the opposite way. He starts out with the melting ice (or the prospect of a nuclear winter) and a priori apperceives it as a *corpus delicti*, evidence of a crime. In other words, his is not a psychological, phenomenological, but a criminological consciousness that deals with it, and a *corpus delicti* naturally immediately incites the interest of consciousness in *Who dunnit?* After a careful search for the "traces" and "footprints", both "carbon and lunar", left by the perpetrator and now "leading us to the melting ice", the suspected culprit is quickly found and arrested: It is the Spectator Mind with its despotic eye that, still juvenile, during the early 15th century with the invention of linear perspective—allegedly—committed the first crime of a long criminal record.

A good policeman, however, would (a) not only catch the dogsbodies, but would try to get the brain behind the whole operation, and (b) would not arbitrarily arrest just any one of the usual suspects, but identify the actual perpetrator. As to (a), if the "crime" is the distance to the earth and the appearance in history of the Spectator Mind, in order to find the "brain behind it all" a good detective would have to go way back to Adam and Eve and their original sin—to the moment of hominization, i.e., of the initial emergence of a reflecting consciousness, an emergence which is tantamount to what in mythological parlance is called the expulsion from paradise. From the very moment that *Homo sapiens* became human and, as *zôion logon echon*, started to speak, he had already left the "sensuous proximity to things", had also learned to "kill at a distance", and lived, high above "the earth", in language, myth, ideas, notions. Already then and not only from around 1400 B.C. onwards "the world (was turned) into a double of itself so that what it [the mind] thinks about the world is what the world is". This is how it had always been. The soul is "un-natural" from the outset. If it were not "un-natural", if it were itself a piece of nature, there would not be soul at all. As Jung never tired to point out, we are hopelessly enclosed in an exclusively psychic world (e.g., *MDR* p. 352, *CW* 8 § 680); we live in images, and only see the world through them. What happened later at different times in the course of history, such as during the Renaissance, was only the further unfolding of this "original sin", *if* you want to view it as sin.[14]

14 On p. 107 Romanyshyn writes: "My point, therefore, has not been that only with the development of linear perspective has this ability [to distance oneself from nature] arisen.

To the extent that this "original sin" is the fact of hominization, "sin" in this case is not a moral category, but a logical one, man's logical (not biological) always-already having pushed off from the animal state or, in mythological terms, the expulsion from the paradise of animal existence; it is not a particular deed, but the very nature of man (as *logon echôn*), part of the logic of being human. Inherent in the very idea of original sin is that it is inescapable, has to be borne by every single human being as a fact that is absolutely out of reach for us, because it is our logical a priori.

And concerning (b), the real psychological problem of a rift in the very logic of our being-in-the-world, of the loss of a copula that connects heaven and earth, man and nature, etc. came up as late as the early 19th century after the conclusion of Western metaphysics and along with the Industrial Revolution, and not earlier. It is likewise inherent in the very concept of this historical rupture that it is both inescapable and out of reach for us because it is a rupture brought about by the objective soul and thus amounts, as indicated, to a radical change in the logical constitution of our modern being-in-the-world. There is no possibility of going back behind the radical loss of *mater natura* and behind the broken connection between the psychic opposites brought by this historical rupture and no chance of possibly undoing or correcting them. The cards of the game of life have been mixed anew by the soul for us, and they are the only cards we have. As it has always been, so it is also for us today: We have to prove ourselves in this new

---

On the contrary, my point has been that with that development we have transformed a possibility into a metaphysics, a condition into a method . . ." This comment appears inserted in a discussion of the arrow motif in *The Ancient Mariner*, after about 27 pages (out of 34) of trying to convince us that this ability did arise with the development of linear perspective. His point *has* certainly *not been* what he now all of a sudden claims, claims by way of a mere afterthought necessitated by the sudden realization that arrows and killing at a distance predate the invention of linear perspective by millennia. If it *had been* his point (and "on the contrary" so), there would have had to be some trace of it before, nay, he would have had to start out with it and describe the "dream" of linear perspective against the backdrop of this always prevailing truth of the human condition, which would have shown it in a very different light. But he does his best to make what began with linear perspective appear as absolutely singular. And besides, distance from nature was not a "possibility" but is *the* human reality, and metaphysics is the reflection and articulation of the inner truth of the actual mode of being-in-the-world (and the logical constitution of the world) at a certain historical epoch and not something that "we" make out of a possibility.

situation. *Hic Rhodus, hic salta.* That's all there is to it. Everything else is illicit speculation and wishful thinking.

Against the backdrop of this foil, the function and achievement of the criminological mind's moralistic condemnation of the rift (which was a *happening* in the history of the soul) as an alleged *doing* (the Spectator Mind's "dissolving" the tension between mind and nature and its "aligning itself on the side of mind split off from nature") and of the search for the criminal responsible for this doing becomes clear. It is the wish for the revival of what was lost or destroyed by the invention of linear perspective.

Repentance

It is the task and purpose of the police to secure and restore the old order. The psychological equivalent to the police, the moralistic and criminological mind, has correspondingly the task to rescue an obsolete consciousness. In the case of our material, moralistic condemnation has the psychological function to construe what happened as merely caused by a false attitude, false views. Inasmuch as attitudes and views are only ego perceptions or interpretations, human perspectives and ideas, they are only an overlay over reality. They happen in and belong to the ego, to the human intellect, but do not necessarily reflect the truth. Since what happened is according to Romanyshyn merely caused by *false* views, the underlying truth is not really affected, but only obscured, forgotten, discarded, ignored, and mistaken. So in the soul, logically, the breaking of the bond between mind and matter did not really happen. In the depths, the old order, the connection, the *unus mundus*, still exist intact, and all that is needed is to "radically alter our view of the world". The function of this moralism is to uphold the *dream* of paradise *not* totally lost, the dream of the unity of mind and matter, man and nature, light and darkness. For this dream to become powerful, the construal of history as a faulty and morally bad development is needed. Because only if there is sin—here the sin of the Spectator Mind's "dream" of an ideal spirituality, of power, control, and dominant mastery over the forces of the natural world, of leaving the earth, etc.—will there be need for repentance. And only in the preaching of repentance does the new dream become psychically effective, the dream that there has not been a rift in the objective logic of the world and that the world is still undissociated.

Romanyshyn's dream is a counter-dream to what he thinks was the "dream" of the Spectator Mind, of which he says, "We are the inheritors of that dream". But his is, I believe, not only a counter-dream to that earlier "dream", but also a *counter-factual* dream, an idle ego fiction without any psychological, phenomenological basis. Just wishful thinking. A new belief system or ideology.

John the Baptist preached, "Repent ye: for the kingdom of heaven is at hand". (The Greek has for "Repent ye" *metanoeite*: "About-face! Radically change your minds".) Romanyshyn preaches: We must radically alter our views for the melting of the polar ice caps is at hand. And just as the medieval repentance preachers happily availed themselves of the terrifying plague epidemics in their time to present them as a clear sign of God's punishment for our sins and as evidence of the imminent end of the world, so Romanyshyn makes use of the melting ice as proof of the crime of the Spectator Mind and as an apocalyptic threat that gives urgency to his call for repentance.

Let us hear a bit of his sermon:

> There can be no solution to this crisis without some radical change in the fixed attitude of the Spectator Mind, . . . no solution without . . . an ego-cide of sorts . . . For this transformation to take place we will have to develop new rituals, which make room for what has been discarded and ignored . . .
>
> (p. 111f)

It is clearly the activist ego, the technological mind, that is speaking here. There is a will to change things, to solve the problem, to correct and better (if not rescue) the world. This impulse is of course very common (it also clearly comes out, for example, in the title, cited by Romanyshyn, of the book by Hillman and Ventura, *We've Had a Hundred Years of Psychotherapy—and the World's Getting Worse*), but it is not a psychological one; it is even incompatible with psychology and (truly psychological) psychotherapy. What is it to a psychologist—*to the extent that* he is really the representative of the standpoint of soul—whether the world is getting worse or better? The psychologist knows himself not to be the healer, the doer. He only accompanies and "attends to" the real process. He knows that *if* there is to be a healing that deserves this name it has to come from the soul, to be the work of the soul itself.

Although Jung himself is not always free of the world-rescuer impulse, he nevertheless expressed the *psychological* attitude very clearly when he said, we "want to see the world as it is and leave things in peace. We do not want to change anything. The world is good as it is" (*CW* 18 § 278). The world is good as it is *even* in view of the melting ice and other possible disasters. This statement about the goodness of the world is neither a sign of total blindness to illness, misery, dangers, to all that is wrong in the world, nor a religious dogma or a metaphysical assertion, but merely an articulation of the psychological, psychotherapeutic methodological as well as ethical principle to leave things in peace, abstain from meddling in the process by intruding with our own moral norms, recipes, wishes, or activism. Just as the cobbler should stick to his last so the psychologist should let the soul do its own thing, whether it be pathologizing or healing a pathology. That Jung's maxim also applied to work in the consulting room comes out in his repeatedly stating that when asked by patients in distress what they should do, he was wont to answer that he did not know either and that the only thing to do was to look at and attend to the dreams. The psychologist is not a problem-solver, not a politician, a technician, social engineer, not a healer or savior, educator or reformer, not a do-gooder. He is *only* a "careful observer" of and attendant to the products and processes of the soul, without salvational program of his own.

Only the ego wants solutions. Only the ego can think that *we* should or could develop rituals. A psychologist knows that true rituals have to come from the soul, from the objective psyche, in order to *be* rituals in the first place. Just like gods, rituals are not of our making, not our inventions. And how could we possibly develop rituals if it is their purpose to first make room for what is the a priori condition of the very possibility of rituals, namely the missing connection? A *petitio principii*. Without the copula between the opposites, without the actual living connection between the sensible and the notional, any so-called ritual could only be an empty ego ceremony. But for Romanyshyn *we* have to *make* this connection. "The melting ice is a symptom that calls once again for us to bridge that divide between inside and outside" (p. 85). But soul bridges cannot be made. They are logical bridges. And if they do not exist for us, as is the case in modernity, then all our attempts at bridging the divide are idle acrobatics at the one bank of it. A *Pontifex maximus* can only build those bridges that logically already exist and allow him to be logically on both banks at once.

"We will have to", "there can be no solution without": Rhetorically mild ways to express a commandment, a "Thou must". It is the ego that is speaking here; and it, this ego, with its demand of a radical change also constellates only the ego in the reader and speaks to it; and it furthermore tries to press its own ego program upon the latter, just as it started out from an ego emotion (anxiety) and approached its theme with ego moralism. This stance is all ego, an ego completely cocooned within itself. Soul does not figure here. On all counts it is the very opposite of the stance of psychology: Psychology as the careful listening to the soul's speaking to *itself* about *itself* and only for *its own* sake (*not* to us and about us or about the world and for our sake, our better). "In myths and fairytales, as in dreams, the soul speaks about itself, and the archetypes reveal themselves in their natural interplay, as 'formation, transformation / the eternal Mind's eternal recreation'" (*CW* 9i § 400, transl. modified).

Small wonder that a standpoint that is so exclusively steeped in ego comes up with the demand for an ego-cide. This idea would be absurd in that stance that inspired Jung's statement just quoted, because in it the ego did not figure at all from the outset. The ego had dropped out altogether. This stance was psychological to begin with. It had taken its position on the standpoint of soul. But the fact is that the called-for ego-cide would not change anything, could not reach its goal. It would by no means bring an end to the ego and take us to the land of soul. Paradoxically, an ego-cide would only confirm and build up once more that same ego that is to be killed, because this whole fantasy is itself a desperate ego move of a technical problem-solving mentality. You can only get to the soul if you are already in it, have begun with it, have left the ego behind.

The ego's fifth column undermining psychology from within

But the soul is of no concern for our author. He has no interest in that *self*-contained "interplay" that Jung, with a poetic allusion, characterized as "the eternal Mind's eternal recreation". *This* soul is *fundamentally* "absent", distant, cold. And it even requires distance. By contrast, Romanyshyn wants our *immediate* involvement with the facts of this world, the ecological crisis.

"The melting ice is, in Al Gore's term, an 'inconvenient truth' because the soul and its symptomatic speech remains an inconvenient truth" (p. 85). I have no difficulty with letting a politician get away with calling the melting ice "a truth". But in psychology this would be a frivolous use of the word. The melting ice is not a truth, but an external empirical fact, a positivity.

The very purpose of Romanyshyn's paper, however, is precisely to oblit-erate the psychological difference between soul truths and external facts of nature, as we can see from the quoted statement about the inconvenient truth, which tries to suggest that the melting ice is *the soul's* "symptomatic speech", as well as again from the very last sentences of his paper: "The collective, archetypal unconscious at the core of the melting ice is an incon-venient truth. But it is truth we cannot afford to ignore. Depth psychology has a special obligation to this truth" (p. 113).

A fact of nature is, just like that, an expression of the collective, arche-typal unconscious, and, mind you, not due to that rare, mysterious, because by definition *acausal*, connecting principle which Jung called synchronic-ity, but directly and, according to the author, obviously caused by human attitudes and behavior! A positive fact of nature is here not just happening as an event, but it is also *speaking*, just as in animistic, magical, or mytho-logical times the soul spoke through thunderbolts, trees, rivers, the flight of birds, earthquakes. Instead of viewing the melting ice as an *unintended consequence* of human behavior, it is immediately claimed for the soul, as the voice of the collective, archetypal unconscious. I would call this super-stition or mystification. Without any need, what is completely satisfactorily explained as a practical consequence of certain long-term actions[15] is in-flated with soul importance. Here even the founder of the theory of the col-lective, archetypal unconscious would feel the need to apply Occam's razor (*principia non sunt multiplicanda praeter necessitatem*).

But we would misunderstand Romanyshyn if we viewed this as a slip. No, it is his program. He wants to bring down and reduce the relation be-tween man and soul to a positivistic level, the level of the relation between inner attitude and outer fact. A telling symptom of this is his use of the idea of an *Axis Mundi*.

"The polar ice caps are the *Axis Mundi* of the world and the Polar Re-gions of the soul" (p. 93). It is odd that ice caps, broad thick masses of ice, are said to be an "axis", which is something linear that goes through and connects, normally, two wheels or, in a figurative sense, also two regions or perhaps two poles. But it may well be that this strange mixture of im-ages is already indicative of a tendency in Romanyshyn's paper to identify

---

15 That the melting of the ice is caused by human actions seems at least to be what most scientists think.

an imaginal or logical idea with, and stuff it into, the thick materiality of an external fact. The *Axis Mundi* is actually the very ancient, hallowed and nearly universal mythological idea of a cosmic tree that went through the three regions of the cosmos, the underworld, the earth, and heaven, and that above all both connected and held apart (distanced!) heaven and earth. This tree did of course not exist anywhere as a positive biological reality in nature. It was exclusively the property of the mind, an *imaginal* reality that was the early mythological equivalent of the later *logical* copula that connected and held apart subject and predicate, the particular and the universal. In Romanyshyn's version the *Axis Mundi* gets stuffed into the literal geographic or geological reality of the earth, the positively existing ice caps. The archetypes are now out there in actual things.

This positivization is the one problem. The other problem is that now the *Axis Mundi* does not hold apart and connect two *logically different* realms any more, earth versus heaven, the particular versus the universal. The whole tension is gone. The psychological difference is canceled. The polar regions of the earth are "the *Axis Mundi* of the World-Soul" (p. 97). The entire dimension of heaven, mind, *logos*, transcendence, and God has disappeared from this scheme. The *Axis Mundi* has become flat, earthly, utterly meaningless. It has no other anymore. With the loss of its function to bridge the psychic opposites it has also lost its soul. If it still holds apart and connects two "opposites", it is the literal realities of the polar ice caps, which are twice the same thing, merely at different locations on this empirical-factual earth.

Apropos the topic of dream interpretation Jung once said,

> . . . we see that behind the impressions of the daily life—behind the scenes—another picture looms up, covered by a thin veil of actual facts. In order to understand dreams, we must learn to think like that. We should not judge dreams from realities because in the long run that leads nowhere.[16]

The same applies to all psychological interpretation. Our author, however, views the important pieces of poetry from the Romantic period that

---

16 C.G. Jung, *The Visions Seminars*, From the Complete Notes of Mary Foote, Book One, Zürich (Spring Publications) 1976, Part One (Lectures October 30–November 5, 1930), pp. 7f.

he devotes himself to and the invention of linear perspective precisely in the light of present-day ordinary realities and conversely applies the poetic motifs directly to our modern empirical facts, as if "ice" in the one sense and "ice" in the other were the same thing. It is his express purpose "to bridge that divide between inside and outside" (p. 85), to proclaim that "The ecological problem . . . is a psychological problem . . ." (p. 80), and his ecological anxiety is his psychopomp, his only bridge, expressly so: "[I]n this moment of anxiety I know in a way that deepens its uneasiness that the melting ice is more than a reasonable problem . . ." (p. 80) and "We cannot imprison the melting ice within the confines of our technological ideas and treat it only as a problem that is out there" (p. 85). As we already heard, the polar ice caps ARE for him, quite literally, the polar regions of the soul. The soul is literal fact out there. It has now been buried in *mater natura*, or no, not in the divine Mother Nature of old, but in modern physical reality. What for Jung had still been a thin veil of actual facts has completely solidified and is *tel quel*, as the *prima facie* impressions of daily life, supposed to be soul. And so the new divide to be bridged is no longer between heaven and earth, God and natural world, the universal and the particular, but, completely secularly and positivistically, between inside and outside.

As to what happened in the Renaissance over against the earlier Middle Ages, Jung wrote that the heavenly goal was exchanged for an earthly one and the vertical orientation of the Gothic style turned into the horizontal one of the discovery of the world and of nature. And he implies that this shift led via the French Enlightenment and French Revolution directly to our present clearly "antichristian" condition (*CW* 9ii § 78). Although I do not think that this view does justice to the *psychology* of this change, on the surface this is an adequate description, and I mention it here because it can serve us as an image for what happened to the *Axis Mundi* in the hands of Romanyshyn. It is a shift from verticality (heaven–earth) to horizontality (the poles of the earth as well as inside–outside, subject–object, consciousness–natural world).

The psychological difference is not one between inside and outside, which is solely an ego problem, a problem of personalistic psychology and also of "ecological psychology" (which is an oxymoron or even a downright contradiction in terms). How could inside/outside be a problem for a psychology based on the insight that "the soul speaks about itself, and the archetypes reveal themselves in their natural interplay, as 'formation, transformation / the eternal Mind's eternal recreation'"? For such a psychology, the entire inside/outside issue has dropped away and along with it both inside and outside. Because "inside" is the opposite of and as such dependent on "outside", what is "inside" is itself inescapably *external* and unfit for a psychology that is defined as the discipline of interiority. An "ecological psychology" makes externality—in Jung's just-cited terms the earthly, horizontal orientation, the banalities of everyday life—even its very principle. It exclusively celebrates the ego's interests in its own and the earth's survival and transfigures them as if they were a *soul* interest, thereby eroding the very concept of soul. Psychology's interiority is absolute, i.e., absolved, *freed*, from the whole inside-outside opposition. It comes about through the methodological process of the absolute-negative interiorization into itself, into its concept, its soul, of any phenomenon that happens to be of psychological interest.

The soul's images have therefore everything they need within themselves. They do not refer to anything outside, but only to themselves. The psychological difference properly understood is, for example, the difference between "the thin veil of actual facts" and "the other picture that looms up behind it", or that between *aurum nostrum* and *aurum vulgi*, and so also between "*our* melting ice" and "the melting ice as an *ecological* problem".

But the new dogma is precisely: *Aurum nostrum* IS *aurum vulgi* and the ecological problem IS a psychological problem (and vice versa), the melting ice IS in itself "a symptom and dream". This is the dogma of a secular, but pseudo-religious doctrine of salvation, one whose sterile components are boosted up and fired solely by ego emotions and ego desires to give them the appearance of truth. Emotions: Fear, despair, hope, moral condemnation, guilt feelings. Desire: That our flat positivistic reality be "*more* than a reasonable problem", *more* than unintended consequences. The demand for MORE as a substitute for the eliminated psychological difference, for absolute-negative interiority, for the soul's verticality and for what is "behind the scenes". More means: What is by definition secular and systematically apperceived as an external problem ("outside") ought nevertheless to have a religious aura, and the nihilistic ought to have a depth of meaning.

The psychological response to this desire would be that the *soul* (as what is behind the impressions of daily life, behind the scenes) would make us realize that the melting ice outside is "*only* that!"—*only* one of the empirical facts or of the banalities of life that make up Jung's "thin veil".

Salvation

The ultimate aim of Romanyshyn's paper is to cultivate the dream of the possibility of (psychological) salvation, the possibility of restoring and reviving all that was lost and destroyed by the Spectator Mind. We learn in more detail what "all" can be restored, because the melting ice, we are told, is not only a terrible threat but also

> a chance to heal the split between mind and nature, a chance to reanimate an aesthetic sensibility that unfreezes the feeling connection that has been lost . . ., a chance to remember the feminine principle in the work of creation, a chance to recover a sense of the sacred within an integrated spirituality that honors the darkness in the light, and a chance to restore the symbolic attitude that . . . is able to witness in the albatross [an allusion to Coleridge's *The Rime of the Ancient Mariner*] the extraordinary in the ordinary, the miracle in the mundane, the numinous in nature.
>
> (p. 112)

New Age kitsch. All the faddish slogans of the ecological variety of pop psychology are gathered here.

So we are said to have now all these many wonderful *chances*. But what does the author have to offer to back up his huge salvational promises, other than his admonishment at the address of the ego to repent, to "radically alter our view of the world"? What does he have to show that would raise all these marvelous chances beyond mere wishful thinking and turn them into *real* chances, concrete options for which the conditions of possibility are provided? Does he say *how* we could in fact go about radically altering our view of the world and *how* we could actually achieve this? For obviously, we cannot change our views like we change our jackets. Views are deeply ingrained in us, in our institutions, and in the entire organization of social life. Jung might have said, *we* do not have those views, they have *us*.

Aside from the blame for what he considers a wrong development and aside from the call for repentance we hear nothing that would give convincing reality to the alleged chances mentioned, unless one considers the construct of a "deep unconscious of the *unus mundus* world of soul where psyche and matter are one" as something. But this idea does not make those chances more credible. Both "the unconscious" (let alone a "deep" unconscious) and the *unus mundus* are fictions, "metaphysical" assertions without empirical or phenomenological basis, irresponsible clichés that come up here only as a *deus ex machina*. Since I am speaking as a psychologist and not a metaphysician, I would of course not want to claim on my part that it might not possibly turn out at some point in future history that psyche and matter, in some way, are one. I simply have no knowledge about that issue either way, and it also is none of my business since the task of psychology is to devote itself to *what actually shows itself (has shown itself) of its own accord*. But in our present situation it is completely out of the question for me to frivolously assert the unity of psyche and matter when, in this our present situation, this idea is contrary to our actual experience and remains absolutely speculative, mere ideology, a thought-thing.[17] By relying on this spurious product of the intellect's wishful thinking, Romanyshyn himself precisely "align[s] [him]self on the side of mind split off from nature", split off from the real! Ego wishes for a *retour à le paradis* of absolute unity are given out as "the deep ground of existence, the deep unconscious of the *unus mundus* world of soul where psyche and matter are one" (p. 96). The actually existing rift is simply pasted over by an assertion, an ideological belief.

This his new belief-system IS his having given in to the very "pull to go numb, to fall asleep, . . . to grasp at . . . easy solutions" that he said he wanted to resist. Because the easiest "solution" is to indulge in wishful thinking and to turn it into a doctrine. It is *consciousness's* going unconscious.

There is one passage in his text in which he seems to give us a hint about how he possibly imagines what the healed split would look like. He speaks of what he calls the "negative gnosis of a metaphoric sensibility" which "is responsive to this de-stabilizing influence of the unconscious. It is a linguistic alchemy, which always dissolves the certitude of 'is' in the possibilities of the 'is not' and thus holds the tension between the dogmatic arrogance of the fixed mind and the cynical despair of the postmodern mind" (p. 96). This sounds to me pretty similar to the stance of Nietzsche's *last man*, who, by the way—Romanyshyn will rejoice—*blinks* (in contrast to his "despotic eye" that does not blink). The ideal here is: A little bit of this and a little bit of the opposite, of "is" and "is not", of "dogmatic arrogance of the fixed mind" and "the cynical despair of the postmodern mind" (p. 96). It is the trick of

17 The very fact that even if we radically changed our views of the world it would not make any difference to the melting ice points to the *really experienced* disunity of psyche and matter.

switching back and forth between two disconnected rigid stances, playing the one against the other, and thereby creating the *impression* of flexibility and life. It is this "undulating" that is called by him "metaphoric sensibility" (p. 96).

The undulating is the expression of the fact that the I reserves itself. It does not make either position fully its own so as to be fatefully exposed to the negation coming from its own internal opposite. Rather, the I stays aloof, uncommitted, it holds its place vis-à-vis the two positions as a separate third party which thus is free to alternate at will between them untouched. Since the I only switches back and forth, it preserves the "is" and the "is not" in their initial form, locking them firmly in undialectical opposition, and preventing their possible clash and thus the resolution of the contradiction. The dogmatism of the fixed mind here is just as much as the postmodern cynical mind over there preserved intact, indeed, both are (alternatingly) being subscribed to by the ego, but they are also kept abstract, I-less: Not real *minds* at all but abstract theoretical positions. Since the I does not take a stand, stake itself, and own up to its dogmatism (or, conversely, to its cynicism) as its own stance, it must not and cannot die as dogmatic I (or as cynical I, respectively) and thereby become a truly psychological I. The psychological I is not dogmatic (it does, for example, not indulge in ideologies like that of an *unus mundus*) and it is not cynical (it does not just switch between positions without committing itself). It is committed, determined. *Hic Rhodus, hic salta.* But it knows the position that it takes with determination to be "*only* that!": This one mortal I's personal view today.

I mentioned that Romanyshyn's paper ends on a rather pessimistic note, "near despair". He wonders, "Is there still time to approach the melting ice at the poles of the world as a symptom and dream?" (p. 112). Probably not. But I think this whether or not is only of subjective, *psychic* importance. Regardless of what will factually happen, all that *psychologically* counts is that he established and confirmed for himself the belief in the *unio naturalis* as a present possibility and passed over the really existing split by condemning it as false. Whether all the chances he sees will come true in real life or not makes psychologically no difference. An idea or illusion, such as the dream of the oneness with nature, is psychologically "true" inasmuch as it exists. It does not need factual corroboration. Even if this belief would be refuted by reality and there would have to be utter despair on the *psychic* level (i.e., for the ego personality)—on the *psychological* level, for the salvation of the soul (*if* the latter happens to be so inclined), it is perfectly sufficient that the ecopsychological ideology of those chances is being *entertained* and *promoted*.

Chapter 5

A serious misunderstanding

Synchronicity and the generation of meaning[1]

In the sphere of academic and scholarly work, it is expected as a matter of course that anyone who discusses an author bases his study on the latter's original texts. A theologian's theses about Biblical passages would not be taken seriously if he only knew the Bible in the King James version, and not the Hebrew Old Testament and the Greek New Testament. A philosopher writing about Plato must of course have read Plato's dialogues in Greek. A scholar who dared to interpret Shakespeare's dramas exclusively on the basis of their French translation would be the laughingstock of his profession. But it seems that this rule often does not apply when it comes to C.G. Jung. Numerous articles and books about Jung are published by authors who rely for their knowledge of Jung only on the English translation of the *Collected Works*. Even dissertations written at universities and academic "Jung studies" usually betray their authors' unfamiliarity with Jung's original texts: What are actually "R.F.C. Hull studies" are given out as "C.G. Jung Studies". Now one could probably say that the damage is not so great as long as it is only a question of the broad outlines of Jung's thinking. But it becomes problematic indeed when the discussion of some Jungian topic hinges on the wording of particular passages or phrases. And this is especially the case when it comes to a topic like synchronicity, which is defined in terms of "meaningful coincidences", in other words, a topic that immediately involves the question of the meaning that "meaning" has in this case.

Synchronicity understood as meaning-making

Looking, by way of example, merely at two articles about synchronicity that recently appeared in the same issue of the *Journal of Analytical*

---

1 Written 2011.

DOI: 10.4324/9781003611417-5

Psychology (2011, vol. 56, no. 4) we find that Warren Colman thinks about synchronicity in the light of "the meaning-making psyche".[2] In synchronistic experiences "there is a confirmation of the internal event which gives it 'meaning' in a way it did not have before . . ." (p. 473). Synchronicity "generate[s] meaning for those involved", it (often) "generate[s] 'strong transcendence' and a shift into non-rational states of mind" (p. 474). One of his sub-headings reads: "Strong synchronicity: an experience of transcendent meaning" (p. 475). He speaks of "the creation and attribution of meaning" (p. 478) and "the meaning-making aspects of synchronicity" (p. 484). ". . . [S]ynchronicity works by the same process by which metaphor operates—the use of congruence between two or more factors to produce a meta-meaning that might be described as 'emergent' or even 'transcendent'" (p. 486). The "meaning in synchronicity is a function of human meaning-making" (p. 472). Colman quotes a definition given to synchronicity by another author, G.B. Hogenson, which fits this whole conception: "a juxtaposition of a psychic state and a state in the material world that resulted in the emergence of meaning and a transition in the individual's state or understanding of the world" (p. 476). Angeliki Yiassemides in her paper in the same journal issue likewise speaks of the "meaning-making of synchronistic events" (p. 466) and concludes that "Synchronicity could thus be regarded as a *manifestation* of Jung's meaning-making quest" (p. 467).[3] And just as Colman operates with the idea of a shift into non-rational states of mind, she evokes the idea of the employment of "faculties beyond intellectual thinking and causal explanation" (p. 466).

This whole line of thinking seems to have come about because the authors were led astray by the phrase "meaningful coincidences" in the English *CW*, which must have suggested to them that the "meaning" Jung talked about here was the meaning that synchronistic events *produce* in and for people who experience them: Synchronicity as the bringer of meaning. Defined as a not accidental but meaningful coincidence of two events, it means for them that the coincidence itself, the fact of the uncanny *coinciding* of two

2 All references to Colman in this chapter are taken from the following publication: Warren Colman, "Synchronicity and the meaning-making psyche", *Journal of Analytical Psychology*, 2011, 56, 471–491.
3 All references to Yiassemides in this chapter are taken from the following publication: Angeliki Yiassemides, "Chronos in synchronicity: manifestations of the psychoid reality", *Journal of Analytical Psychology*, 2011, 56, 451–470.

events, is meaningful, and meaningful at times even to the point of generating a transcendent meaning. The emphasis is on the (subjective) *experience* of people induced by the coincidence, on what synchronicity does *to them*, on the "impact created by the experience" (Colman) or the effect it has.

When we now turn to Jung's text we find that he did not say "sinnvolle Koinzidenz" at all, which would be the German equivalent to "meaningful coincidence". He said, "sinngemäße Koinzidenz" (*GW* 8 § 827 and *passim*). The difference between *sinnvoll* and *sinngemäß* is crucial. When one reports what someone else said, adding that the report will be *sinngemäß*, one indicates that what follows is not a verbatim quotation, but merely "roughly the same", a repetition 'faithful to' (*gemäß*) the basic *Sinn* (intended meaning) of what had been said, but now presented in the present speaker's own words or summary, sort of the speaker's version of the gist of it. Whether what you cite in a *sinngemäß* way also happens to be *sinnvoll* (meaningful) or not is another question entirely. It could also be one's report of the other person's downright trivial, stupid, or nonsensical statements.

With "sinngemäße Koinzidenz" Jung is merely stating that in the case of synchronicity (the way he saw it) the inner and the outer event "mean roughly the same thing". The scarab in the dream and the flying insect tapping on the window, which was not a real scarab but nevertheless "the nearest analogy to a golden scarab one finds in our latitudes" (*CW* 8 § 843), exemplifies what Jung means by *sinngemäß*: That each of the two components that make up the synchronicity have *roughly* the same meaning (here the *notion* of scarab-likeness); they are comparable or equivalent *to each other* in this regard. Meaning in this context has absolutely nothing to do with Meaning with a capital M, with human *experiences* of meaning, with what is meaningful *for us* and makes existence meaningful, let alone with transcendent meaning. In his entire synchronicity essay the big question of meaning in the sense that the word has in the phrase "quest for meaning" has no place. Rather, the sense of meaning is here quite sober, down to earth, close to "concept" or "notion". It is roughly the same as when we speak of the meaning of a word. Synchronicity as "sinngemäße Koinzidenz" could be likened to what in linguistics is the phenomenon of the synonymity of two words. Two synonyms have roughly but not quite the same meaning. But the occurrence of two synonyms is not an event of Meaning with a capital M; it does not "give new meaning", not bring meaning. If it did, we would merely have to open a thesaurus of synonyms to be overwhelmed by a flood of "emergent" or "transcendent" meaning.

This point becomes highlighted by the fact that there are certain cases without involvement of the psyche in which Jung nevertheless recognizes the principle of synchronicity but, because of the absence of a psychic factor, avoids the word "meaning" (Sinn) altogether, in other words, also the phrase "sinngemäße Koinzidenz", and instead prefers to speak merely of "*Gleichartigkeit* oder Konformität" (*GW* 8 § 932, note 126. *CW* 8 § 932, note 72: "equivalence or conformity". "Gleichartigkeit" means "being of the same kind"). This extreme possibility throws a light on the particular meaning of meaning even in the ordinary *psycho*physical cases of synchronicity, which is also why Jung, later in his text, repeatedly uses the term "Gleichartigkeit" and equates "sinngemäße Koinzidenz" directly with it: "Die sinngemäße Koinzidenz oder die Gleichartigkeit eines psychischen und eines physischen Zustands . . ." (*GW* 8 § 955, corresponds to *CW* 8 § 956). Very sober. No "higher" meaning, no transcendence. No quest. Just a description of what shows itself of its own accord, a description of the objective relation of the two events to each other. Jung's word "cross-connection" (*CW* 8 § 827) makes this very clear. All this "higher Meaning" sense of "meaning" has to be kept out of one's discourse if one wants to understand Jung's concept of synchronicity. But it seems that the word "meaningful" in the English translation of "sinngemäße Koinzidenz" put the wrong ideas into people's mind and sent them on a completely wrong track.

The difference between the synchronicity of two events and the subjective experience of synchronicity

There is a second aspect in which the initially cited views about synchronicity have gone off track, in addition to the "meaning of meaning" aspect. Hogenson includes the *result* that a synchronistic experience has for the individual in his very definition of synchronicity. Colman focuses likewise on "the *impact created* by the experience" (pp. 476–477), on the meaning that is *generated* by it and on "the meaning-*making* aspects of synchronicity" (p. 484, my emphases) and lets himself even be carried away to the view that "the meaning in synchronicity is a function of human meaning-making" (p. 472). I say "carried away" not because I want to denigrate any interest in human meaning-making, but because his discussion of synchronicity has left the discourse within which Jung discussed it and, while retaining the word synchronicity, substitutes a different, incompatible concept for Jung's concept of synchronicity. Jung's "cross-connection" between the events is replaced by the relation between the synchronicity (the coincidence of two events which display this *sinngemäß* cross-connection) *and* the experiencing human subject, a relation which does not figure in Jung's concept of synchronicity at all, so that the resulting discourse can ultimately even turn into a transcendence discourse.

Jung did not include in his concept of synchronicity the results and effects that synchronistic experiences have or may have. In this area Jung was not at all concerned with the human person and what such events or experiences may mean in and for them, what alteration of mental states may or may not be brought about by them, what may "emerge" from them. It was the other way around. He was exclusively concerned with where the *sinngemäß* cross-connection came from or how it came about. The difference between these two stances is in formal regards similar to the one between an interest in where a train came from (~ Jung's interest) on the one hand and where it will depart to (~ the interest of the cited Jungians), on the other.

It is interesting to note that Colman has clearly seen that Jung viewed synchronicity as pointing to "an objective principle of meaning in Nature", but, probably misled by the word "meaningful" in the English phrase "meaningful coincidences", he was put on the track of meaning in the sense of experiences of meaning and ultimately of transcendent meaning, so that he could not grasp and do justice to what Jung was struggling with under the title of "synchronicity". This inflated sense of meaning (cf. "strong transcendence") instead of Jung's (in this context) low-key, quasi-linguistic sense of meaning made Colman interpret Jung's work on synchronicity in such a way that it became for him an illegitimate metaphysical attempt ultimately to provide a new kind of proof of God, God as objectively subsisting in nature. ". . . [T]he guiding spirit behind Jung's project is God Himself" (p. 482), Colman writes, a thesis which may be true in many regards of Jung's psychology, but certainly not with respect to his theory of synchronicity—because transcendence, "higher" meaning, and God do not figure here at all.

The fact that Jung stressed "that the ultimate nature of mind, meaning and matter remain forever unknowable beyond the phenomenal world", is for Colman no more than "a Kantian fig-leaf for the real achievement which is to have put spirit back into matter—*as if they were divided in the first place*" (p. 483, my emphasis). Concerning this last clause, he charges

Jung with remaining "in a dualist Cartesian way of thinking about mind and matter while at the same time attempting to describe a phenomenological reality that is non-dualist" (p. 482). First of all, the oft-repeated, only hearsay-based, and misguided attack on the philosophy of Descartes as being *dualistic* is a prejudice which by being parroted time and again does not become any more true. But this need not be a topic for us in the present context. Secondly, and this is indeed relevant here—does the assertion implied in the clause "as if they [spirit and matter] were divided in the first place" hold true, and not only in a general philosophical sense, but concretely with respect to the question which Jung tried to solve in his study on synchronicity?

The division between spirit and matter

Jung started out from specific experienced phenomena. And so I will likewise use one case of a synchronistic event (not taken from Jung) as a concrete example by means of which I can more plastically elucidate what Jung was concerned with in this area.

During World War I several women of an extended family joined by individuals from next door were sitting together knitting, sewing, and mending. Suddenly one of the women who had been deaf for several years said she had heard a loud bang. And from that moment on she could hear again. The next day she received a telegram informing her that her son had been shot dead in battle around the time she had heard that bang.

Quite independently of one's general philosophical commitments, are there here not *phenomenologically* indeed two entirely separate events belonging to two incommensurable spheres divided by a gap, the one physical, a gunshot in external reality, the other psychic, internal, a loud bang in the consciousness of the woman? Can we leap over this gap just like that and simply pretend that it does not pose any problem because, allegedly, "mind and matter are *already* united in an experiential reality" (Colman, p. 484)? On the contrary, the irreconcilable division between the inner (the loud bang heard by the woman in her mind [it was heard only by her!]) and the outer (the real gunshot on the battlefield), between consciousness ("spirit") and physical fact ("matter"), is what we really experience. It is our truth, and Colman himself indirectly admits this duality when he once speaks of an "interaction *between* mind and Nature" (p. 472).

Synchronistic experiences are a slap in the face of our deepest spontaneous convictions. And to try to brush this experienced division aside with a
casual "as if they [spirit and matter] were divided in the first place" would
in turn be a slap in the face of *our own* real experience. Jung was perfectly
justified in seeing in synchronistic events an (on the face of it) unbridgeable difference between the world of external fact and the world of the
mind. This is not a question of philosophical dualism at all, but one of phe-
nomenality. Descartes and Kant need not be evoked. And that the "archaic
mind" did not sharply distinguish between inner and outer reality is neither
here nor there, because, first, we live in modernity and have a much more
differentiated mind, and, second, the issue that Jung tackled with his synchronicity theory was not one of the experiencing minds, man's subjective
interpretation, but an extremely puzzling, intellectually challenging *objective* problem: The problem given with the *events* themselves.

The only two accepted ways of getting out of this objective problem
are: (a) To explain the synchronicity in terms of causality, which, however,
would be absurd (in our example: How could sound waves from a gunshot
travel over a distance of a thousand kilometers, actually penetrate the ears
of this deaf [!] woman, and if so, why should she hear only one single gunshot when there must have been the din of millions of simultaneous shots),
or (b) to declare it to be "mere chance, *mere* coincidence", i.e., to deny that
there is any connection whatsoever, which also does in no way do justice
to what happened here. Obviously, there *is* a connection between the two
events. We *cannot* pretend that there was none. It would require a *sacrificium intellectus*. So we are stuck with a real dilemma. And far from involving the question of Meaning, the idea of transcendence or even "strong
transcendence", or the individuals' shifts into non-rational states of mind,
and far from requiring faculties beyond intellectual thinking, far also from
any "emergence" and any function of human meaning-making and symbol
creation, this is a strictly intellectual problem, a challenge for the scientific
mind. And the solution offered by Jung is also a rational one. The whole
mystifying and sentimental waffle by so many Jungians today about the
unus mundus, about an opening to the sacred and to transcendence and
the corresponding anti-intellectual attacks against the rational mind totally
miss the point of Jung's theory of synchronicity and its spirit.

All Jung does is to wrestle with the question of how two events can be intrinsically related if it can neither be a connection of cause to effect nor "no

connection at all" ("mere chance"). All he is interested in (in this regard) is this question of *connection*: The "cross-connection" between the two events that make up the synchronicity phenomenon, the "Acausal Connecting Principle" from the sub-title of his essay. It is a problem that requires an *explanation* (e.g., *CW* 8 § 827) in the scientific sense of the word. By contrast, whether and how people experience a synchronicity and what they feel and make of it is irrelevant, just as it is irrelevant for a *causal* explanation whether people are subjectively aware of the connection between two events or not. There is a rumor that certain primitive peoples did not know about the causal relation between pregnancy and sexual intercourse. But their possibly not knowing about it does in no way imply that at their time this causal relation did not exist.

The fact that what is at stake is the cross-connection between the two events highlights once more my claim that the result that synchronicity may have for (or in) the minds of people and what may "emerge" for them from it is no topic in the sphere of synchronicity. In the particular example I used, synchronicity did not *bring* any meaning, nor did it induce any "human meaning-making"; it was, as synchronicity by definition always is, just an objective occurrence of a *sinngemäß* coincidence; and the "result" it, too, had for the human subject was in this case itself a physical one (the restoration of the woman's hearing). But of course, it is always *possible* for people in their subjective feeling and thinking to *make* something deeply meaningful out of it or *construe* it as pointing to the transcendent and sacred.

The fact that in the scarab case Jung went on to say that this experience "punctured the desired hole in [his patient's] rationalism and broke the ice of her intellectual resistance" (*CW* 8 § 982) does not mean that he considered this aftereffect to be an integral part of the concept of synchronicity. It is merely an additional piece of information about the serendipitous subsequent course of events and remains external to the synchronicity event itself. (And, by the way, one may wonder whether this result was therapeutically really desirable, because the breakthrough was brought about completely irrationally by external force, by the suggestive power of a "miracle"—by "magic", as it were—and not, so to speak, alchemically, by a true intrinsic transformation of her consciousness, a veritable insight or illumination. Does an *Überrumpelung* of consciousness, its being taken by surprise, count psychologically? Are we interested in technical results or not much rather in *fermentatio* and *sublimatio*?)

Incommensurability of the topic of synchronicity with a true psychology

I personally have no stake in synchronistic *experiences* (which to my mind have to be listed under the heading of curiosities without any great psychological dignity; no fuss needs to be made about them), nor do I have a stake in the *theory* of synchronicity along with its ideas of a psychoid level of reality and of an *unus mundus*. And so I do not want in any way to stand up as a proponent of these ideas. But I do think that when one discusses Jung's synchronicity theory one has to do justice to him and not obfuscate what he was concerned with on account of one's own obsession with Meaning. Given the truly puzzling intellectual dilemma with which genuinely synchronistic events confront us, as the one I cited, Jung's hypothesis of a *sinngemäß* coincidence and an underlying subsisting factor of meaning in nature is certainly one intelligent, reasonable attempt at an explanation—and, as far as I can see, the only explanation available to date that makes at least some sense. As such it can be respected. Without Jung's explanation we are left with the nebulous and baffling feeling of something miraculous. Jung's explanation removes the dumbfounding miracle quality and makes the unusual event a bit more *intelligible*. The *theory* of synchronicity is not without merit, but only intellectually so. However, whether we buy Jung's theory or not is another question.

I said that I have no stake in it, and the reason is that my own commitment is to psychology, psychology as the discipline of interiority. Psychology and the theory of synchronicity are not commensurable. We have to be very clear about this: The person who came up with the theory of synchronicity was not *the psychologist Jung*, that Jung who opted for a "psychology with soul" and said that "Psychology, however, is neither biology nor physiology nor any other science than just the knowledge of the soul" (*CW* 9i § 63, transl. modif.). Nor was it *the theosophist Jung*, that Jung who developed the "Myth of Meaning" according to which the Meaning (purpose, the What-for) of human existence consists in the fact that man is needed for God to become conscious in him. No, it was *the rational scientist Jung*, Jung *the quasi-physicist* who left the precincts of psychology proper and, from the standpoint of externality, expanded the world-picture of modern physics by logically *deducing* (mind you: Purely *hypothetically*) that an additional factor or dimension might have to be added to it to enable us to explain the empirically observed facts of synchronistic events, namely, the level of the so-called psychoid, an acausal arrangedness, orderedness, an a priori and objectively subsisting factor of meaning—where, however, as we already know, "meaning" does precisely not imply meaningfulness, the way the meaning-fetishists among the Jungians misunderstand it, but simply an additional natural *explanatory* factor, in itself no more (but also no less) metaphysical, numinous, or irrational than, say, Newton's likewise merely *deduced* principle of gravitation. "Faculties beyond intellectual thinking" are not needed nor evoked.

Nothing can be derived from his theory for the benefit of our psychological experience of life. Whether there is an *unus mundus* OR whether body and psyche, matter and spirit are irreconcilably divorced systems—in either case nothing changes for us with respect to how to live life and whether it is meaningful or meaningless, just as little as do questions of whether time is absolute or relative, whether the big bang was the absolute beginning of the universe or whether there was something before it, or whether there is or once was water on planet Mars or not. These are intellectually interesting questions, question essential for the advancement of scientific understanding and a challenge for the human thirst for knowledge. But psychologically they are irrelevant. Our daily practical problems and our moral conflicts, our joy and pain, our feeling (or not feeling) at home in the world and our death, and the big question of the purpose of life as well as of God and transcendence are not affected. Even if the proposed (merely *postulated*) existence of a self-subsistent objective factor of meaning could be proven, it would not make existence meaningful, *if* it is not meaningful on the basis of some other ground in the first place. It would not open gates to the sacred or the transcendent.

On the contrary, one could possibly even argue that the positing of such a natural meaning factor is destructive for *Sinn* and spirit, inasmuch as, by being defined as a natural factor, the very meaning of meaning becomes positivized and meaning thus *in itself* meaningless, "spirit" spiritless. Then, of course, there would really *be* meaning, but it would not really *mean* anything anymore, having become reduced to the facticity of an orderly, more or less mathematical arrangedness on the same level with and parallel to the other natural principle, causality. This is the pitfall of Jung's fraternizing with physics.

When Colman writes that "Such experiences generate an uncanny sense of what I can best describe as a feeling that the universe is alive" (p. 475), and when he focuses in general on human meaning-making (as comparable to metaphor production), we have to say that what he is concerned with belongs all to the subjective mind, to personalistic or ego-psychology. Our feelings and what *we* make of experiences is of course interesting to ourselves. But psychology proper is concerned with what the soul, not the ego-personality, thinks and feels and what events indeed ARE and MEAN from the point of view of soul. Psychology has a responsibility towards truth. Likewise, Jung's theory of synchronicity aimed for knowledge, cognition, even if not as a psychological theory, but as a scientific one. It was, or is, concerned with what IS, not what we feel or what meaning we generate from it. Whether specific experiences give rise to a feeling that the universe is alive and whether they generate for us transcendent meaning is largely dependent on how impressible and credulous a person is and on his or her ideological-emotional needs, theoretical prejudices, and superstitions. Anything can "emerge" in the subjective psyche. For some people even the most ordinary things, such as hotel rooms with the number 13, generate a powerful "meaning"; paranoid persons have been known to ascribe "transcendent" meaning to such trivial every-day behaviors as a certain person scratching his nose, and in modernity many people simply like to *indulge* in emotional "experiences" of meaning. Colman describes himself as at a certain time having been "much impressed by the idea that all actions were unconsciously motivated and that anything that happened to a person had a hidden significance for them, as if it was 'meant to be' in some way" (p. 475). Small wonder that under the conditions of such a craving for hidden significances, such a *petitio principii*, the subjective psyche (not the soul) has an easy time of utilizing synchronicity both for "generating (transcendent) meaning" on the experiential level and for making consciousness also cultivate a *theory* of transcendent meaning.

* * *

Having started this paper with the issue of "Jung in the translation of the *CW*", I want to conclude it with an additional example occasioned by Colman's article, although it does not contribute directly to the synchronicity topic. In footnote 1 of his text, Colman says, "In a strikingly disingenuous footnote [it is a footnote to *CW* 8 § 946], Jung contrasts his interpretation [of certain dreams given in Jung's preceding text] with others who may 'indulge in wishful thinking about dreams'. That is, others may be mistaken but Jung is not" (p. 471).

The *CW* translation of this footnote is misleading. It begins with the phrase, "Those who find the dreams unintelligible . . .", whereas what Jung wrote (*GW* 8 § 936, fn. 132) is the equivalent of "Those to whom this statement might appear unintelligible" (i.e., those who cannot follow it), namely the statement to which Jung had attached this footnote. It is his claim (after his having given his reading of those dreams) that "This is what the dreams are obviously saying". In other words, Jung is not talking about whether the *dreams* are intelligible to others or not, but whether those others can concur or not with his *assertion* that these particular dreams "obviously" mean what he said they mean. Not his particular interpretation but his (general and, for any student of Jung, familiar) approach to dreams is the issue.

And then Jung explains why he could make this claim, by revealing the principle of this his own approach to dreams. He prefers "to keep as close to the dream statement as possible, and to try to formulate it in accordance with its manifest meaning". This is what was meant by his phrase about what the dreams "obviously mean" and harks back to his old dispute with Freud about the latent vs. the manifest meaning of dreams. As Jung repeatedly tried to impress on us, "the dream is its own interpretation". "What the dream, which is not manufactured by us, says is *just so*. Say it again as well as you can" (*Letters 2*, p. 591, to Herbert Read, 2 Sep 1960). Precisely this "saying it again" is what Jung believes to have done in his discussion of those dreams, and this is what he explicitly expressed in his sentence that gave rise to his footnote, the sentence "This is what the dreams are obviously saying". He did not wish to give an interpretation in the sense of his subjective views about some meaning *hidden* behind the manifest dream text (here, too, no "human meaning-making"!), but merely rephrased what they themselves said. He took the phenomenon the way it showed itself.

Jung contrasts his own approach with that of others, but he does not at all say about them that they "indulge in wishful thinking about dreams", the way the *CW* have it. No, what he says is that "on the basis of preconceived opinions" (i.e., their belief that they *know* what dreams must in truth be speaking about; we may think here, e.g., of repressed desires and traumas, personal conflicts, transference aspects, etc.) they see "a very different hidden meaning" in those dreams (i.e., the famous *latent* meaning), and he denounces this searching for a hidden meaning as "fantasizing" (*not* as "wishful thinking"), i.e., as people's coming up with ideas of their own *about* the dreams, *their* speculating, *their* "interpreting" in the usual sense (when for Jung it is merely a matter of amplifying, *highlighting*, the dream text *as it stands*, letting it speak for itself).

So there is nothing "strikingly disingenuous" in this footnote. Jung simply puts his cards on the table and shows that he is fully aware of, and as a matter of course allows for, the fact that other people will not see it his way. All he does is in all brevity explain the theoretical foundation of *his* stance on dreams, thereby at the same time justifying the claim that occasioned his footnote and, of course, standing up for it, while rejecting the opposite one. But in no way does Jung claim infallibility concerning the dream interpretations he had presented. All he suggests is that they follow his own approach to dreams.

A glance at Jung's own text might have prevented this misunderstanding which led to such a severe accusation. And possibly, a proper understanding of Jung's footnote might even have opened Colman's eyes to the content of those few dreams that Jung had introduced as supporting evidence for his hypothesis of a self-subsisting meaning in nature. But then again, Colman's commitment to the theory (in Jung's terminology: To his "preconceived opinions") of egoic meaning-*making* and subjective experiences might have proven invincible.

Chapter 6

Saban's alternative

An alternative?[1]

In his paper given at the ISPDI Berlin 2012 conference, "The Tautegorical Imperative: Mythos and Logos in Jung and Giegerich, Hegel and Schelling", Mark Saban wants to "offer an alternative approach informed by Schelling's philosophy of mythology" in contrast to "Giegerich's arguments against a myth-based psychology".[2] I have responded to his views more or less briefly both orally during the conference and afterwards in a written exchange with him in the ISPDI online discussion forum. But I think that these discussions were mostly concerned with individual arguments only so that the central and crucial issue has still not been clarified sufficiently enough. There is still more in Saban's position that can help us to get a better, fuller understanding of our own position. We can learn something from it. And so now, I want to turn to his paper and his subsequent substantial online posts once more, this time focusing on what is ultimately at stake in this dispute. My purpose is not so much a response to Saban, but rather an *analysis* of his scheme, the sharp contrast of which to our own lets us see our own standpoint all the more precisely.

Exteriority

In his rich, detailed post of August 2, 2012 to the discussion forum, Saban writes at one point apropos of dream interpretation,

> The mantra "nothing to be let in that does not belong there", seems plausible because of its wonderful simplicity, and indeed it can be hugely

---

1 Written in August 2012.
2 This paper remained unpublished but was, when this essay was written, available on the ISPDI website. It is now inaccessible.

DOI: 10.4324/9781003611417-6

fruitful when applied to a dream or a myth or a fairy tale, but of course even there it can only be applied in a relative sense. After all, who is to decide what 'belongs'? In the case of the dream do we not let in the associations of the dreamer, our psychic and somatic countertransference reactions, synchronistic events, our half-remembered knowledge of myth etc etc. Do these belong? Could we exclude them even if we wanted?[3]

Saban's initial high praise ("hugely fruitful") for Jung's abbreviatedly cited alchemical dictum—so essential for a "psychology as the discipline of interiority"—is immediately thereafter relativized by him and ultimately reduced to absurdity. It is reduced to absurdity because it is thought that we should not, and indeed simply would not be able to, exclude material that clearly comes from outside, *regardless* of whether it may belong or not. Why not? Simply because there is no way how to determine whether it belongs or not.

However, this absurdity is not inherent in Jung's dictum. It is rather the result of a refusal on Saban's part to let himself thinkingly in for what it says. A sign for this refusal is already the word he chose for this adage, "mantra". In our Western, non-religious usage of the word, "mantra" suggests a mindless, mechanical repetition, if not rattling-off, of the *sounds* of a phrase without awareness of or attention to *what* it says. The mind is closed to the inner meaning of the sounds, not intently present in and tarrying with it, just as conversely the inner meaning of the sounds does not reach the conscious understanding and feeling of the person. Both sides are immunized against each other. By using this word, Saban inadvertently tells us how he relates to this sentence, namely, as if it were merely a dead formula that one can mechanically apply just like that. He does not relate to it the way we relate, for example, to a book by opening, reading, and understanding it.

In the first post to the ISPDI discussion forum in which he introduced himself (July 22, 2011), he stated that he did not want this society to be "a place where we all [. . .] sit around competing about who can use the word sublation most often". This fantasy of a completely mechanical, unthinking activity fits well to his later "mantra" idea that we are here concerned with. This is his *fantasy* and reveals *his* mindset: How close such mechanical *procedere* is to him.

3   The posts on the discussion forum were also available on the ISPDI website but are no longer accessible.

Similarly in his "The Tautegorical Imperative" he warns against "accepting them [Giegerich's writings] uncritically as a new dogma to replace the old", where "old dogmas" refers to the teachings of Jung and Hillman. Again a strange imputation. Who would want to "accept" (whatever) "uncritically"? To whom does he speak, to churchmen, to believers? Why does he feel the need to imagine these psychologies as dogmas? And instead of offering ways how to dissolve the alleged rigidly dogmatic form into the fluidity of living thought, Saban has nothing better to propose but an "alternative", simply something else (his own dogma?).

Jung did not establish dogmas. He had, on the contrary, reproached Freud for having made, as Jung saw it, a dogma out of his sexual theory. And with all his innovations, Hillman did not want to simply replace Jung's psychology, providing an *alternative* for it. He wanted to *re-vision* it. The "re-" shows that he wanted to rework the same: A kind of alchemical further refining and deepening of the same prime matter. Similarly, I did not want to externally substitute my scheme of things as an *other* for that of Hillman's archetypal psychology. I offered to archetypal psychology much rather a way of how to critically re-think *itself*. The same, not an other.

Returning after these additional examples of a "tough-minded" mechanical style of thinking to our alchemical dictum, we find that in the quoted text this apperception receives confirmation by his attributing a "wonderful simplicity" to it.

But is it really that simple? Or, if we were to accept the predicate of simplicity, would we not have to be mindful of Schelling's, Jung's, and Heidegger's insistence that, as Jung once put it, "the simplest is the most difficult of all"? The alchemical adage would be really simple if it demanded of us not to let in *anything at all* from outside. *That* would be a clear-cut commandment that we could apply just like that, mechanically, without further thought. But our dictum says: "Nothing from outside *that does not belong* should be allowed to enter". It does not flatly prohibit any external associations whatsoever. On the contrary, it confronts us with the idea that *certain* external material could, despite its externality, be internal to the image itself! In some special cases, what is outside is nevertheless intrinsic to what is inside. And because it has, despite its factually emerging from outside and as something external, psychologically nevertheless always already been inside (i.e., the inner property of the dream image), according to our adage it is allowed also to *explicitly* enter.

This is an amazing idea. Here our thinking is needed. What can possibly be meant by this at first glance unlikely dictum? It is an open question that requires our concentrated effort to understand it, because the idea of something external that is nevertheless actually internal, and something internal that in fact appears only from outside, does not make any sense to our everyday commonsensical understanding. It cannot be imagined or represented (*vorgestellt*), it can only be thought. Even more difficult is the other absolutely necessary question, rightly raised by Saban, "who is to decide what 'belongs'?" It is a *question* raised by him, but he also right away dismisses it with his concluding purely rhetorical questions, "Do these belong? Could we exclude them even if we wanted?" Instead of devoting himself thinkingly to the question, he contents himself with the naturalistic objection, worthy of the New Testament sceptic Nicodemus, that in practical reality it does not work.

Saban has to dismiss those questions because obviously nowhere is there any expert judge in sight who could decide what "belongs". Nobody, even if he were Jung himself, can claim to legitimately function as this judge. And so we can see why the naturalistic mind feels that we simply have to apply to the dream images whatever external material happens to come up ("the associations of the dreamer, our psychic and somatic countertransference reactions, synchronistic events, our half-remembered knowledge of myth etc."). The mere *positive fact*, the *natural event*, *that* associations have popped up is here thought to be sufficient reason to let them into the dream image in our interpretation of it. We could formulate the net result of Saban's reflections on the alchemical dictum in the following statements: "Forget the question of whether the external material belongs or not. That's all there is to it. For we could not even exclude it even if we wanted."

We see in all this a perfect example of the standpoint of externality and everyday naturalistic thinking. It shows here in several regards.

1. Saban approaches the alchemical dictum externally, taking it thing-like as a mantra, or as an instruction by an external authority to be either simply obeyed (acted out) or not, and thus like an unopened package. He does not enter it thinkingly. He stays outside as an external observer and views and reflects *about* the possibility or impossibility of its practical application.
2. He thinks that the question of whether something external belongs would, in order to be tenable, require a decision by a likewise external judge (or perhaps, instead of a literal judge, by external distinguishing marks objectively to be found in the external material itself).
3. The external material (the associations, countertransference reactions and so on) is taken up in its factualness and positivity, as natural occurrences—"as they come off the street", so to speak.

4. When this external material is let into the image in our interpretation of it, the *relation* of the external associations, etc., *to* the image is also an external one, a mere juxtaposition or combination, or an external reflection of the one in the other, because if the question of whether it belongs or not is not answered, the relation cannot be an intrinsic one. It is "physical", not "(al)chemical". Accordingly, in another part of his post Saban expressly opts for "the holding together of the logical and the naturalistic, seeing one through the other, and maintaining their conflict, however messily unassimilable they are to each other". An avowal of and commitment to *disiunctio*. The analyst brings dream images and associations together much like a billiard player lets different balls bump into each other. *Bang!* For Saban, "the richness of psychological life consists precisely in the complex and ultimately unresolvable relationship between thought and world. The endless excitement of that relationship depends upon surprise, a surprise generated by the fathomless alterity against which we always find ourselves bumping". This clashing even becomes his very definition of soul. ". . . [S]oul is to be found in the mythic [why mythic?] conflict at the heart of the modern individual", in the *bang!* between "the apparently exclusive and contradictory ideas of myth on the one hand and individual experience on the other". No soul-making. No opus. No putrefaction, sublimation, distillation. Just the positive-factual event of the surprise or clash.

And finally,

5. the notions "inner" and "outer" themselves remain radically external to each other. They are conceived as literal, completely abstract (and thus mutually exclusive) binary opposites, an external dichotomy. They are then like things in space, just as in our everyday thinking a piece of jewelry is either inside a box or outside of it. *Tertium non datur.* The imposition of Jung's alchemical adage to us, by contrast, is to actually *think* the thought of something that can be verily external and yet intrinsically belong inside the image—and thus to think the thought that, pictorially expressed, inside and outside are yin-yang-like one in the other. But such an intrinsic relation can here not be thought. Consciousness has not overcome the naturalistic standpoint of externality and apartness—and, as we heard under point 4, *on principle* does not want to overcome it. It is committed to alterity as its supreme principle.

All five points are interrelated facets of one and the same psychological standpoint.

To Saban's question "Could we exclude them [the associations of the dreamer, our psychic and somatic countertransference reactions, synchronistic events, our half-remembered knowledge of myth etc.] even if we wanted?" Jung would have answered, "Yes, absolutely." When Jolande Jacobi published a paper in a psychological journal in which she discussed Jung's views in contrast to those of Freud, Jung objected: "*I don't use free association at all* [Jung's italics]. . . . In dream analysis I proceed in a circumambulatory fashion, having regard to the wise Talmudic saying that the dream is its own interpretation" (*Letters 2*, p. 293f., to Jacobi, 13 March 1956). The dream its own interpretation! The dream as a self and relating to itself by interpreting itself!

If this is the case, would it not precisely imply that *all* external material has to be kept out? But surprisingly, the Talmudic dictum, although it is as difficult to think as our original one, can pave the way to the answer to the questions how something that is clearly external can intrinsically belong to the dream itself, and who is to decide what belongs.

A dream, considered as a text in the sense of positive fact, does of course not interpret itself at all. It does not do anything. It is written on a piece of paper and just sits there mute. If it is to interpret itself, *we* must circumambulate it, which also means that through forming this hermetical circle around it we close it over against what is outside. But true circumambulation means even more than this negative stance to the external. It means, positively, our dedication to the dream, dwelling with it, abandoning ourselves to it. Our interiorizing ourselves into it. Or conversely, harking back to the idea of circumambulation as the formation of a circle around it, we could also say that it means enclosing the dream within our mind and heart and in this sense *going pregnant with it*.

Only then is the dream a real dream in the first place. The written dream as such, the dream as an objective fact, as a mere text on paper, is not a dream in the full psychological sense at all. As fact, the dream is fundamentally mute and also does not have a meaning. The real dream, the dream as psychological reality, originates only in our dedication to it. It is fundamentally subjective-objective.[4] It *is* the *relation* between ourselves and the dream text. The dream needs us to be a dream in the first place and to come

4 In this context I disregard that things are more complicated: That the dream is actually subjective-subjective-objective. I discussed this more complex relation, for example, in "Imaginal Psychology Gone Overboard", in my book *The Soul Always Thinks*, CEP 4, New Orleans: Spring Journal Books, 2010, pp. 480 ff.

alive. Only once we have given ourselves over to it and interiorized ourselves into it can *it* begin to speak and, at the same time, to interpret itself.
It speaks and interprets itself only in and through us.

But it is only truly *it* that interprets *itself* if we have really entered it, are
really in the image in its inner complexity, in the spirit and logos of the image, so that we, our mind, our soul, our feeling, can become, as it were, its
musical instrument through which it can make itself heard. *Oportet opera-
torem interesse operi* (the one who works the work, the adept performing
the opus, must be *in* the opus, *CW* 12 § 375), the alchemists said—which
is of course the very opposite of Saban's psychological commitment to
aloofness.

Entering the dream in the sense given must not be confused with our
becoming one of the actors in its inner drama, the way we are supposed to
enter a fantasy in the Jungian method of active imagination. If this were
how we entered, the dream would not interpret itself. It would be changed,
the drama it displays would go on. The clue for what "entering" means we
can get from a passage in a late letter of Jung's. "It is quite possible that
we look at the world from the wrong side and that we might find the right
answer by changing our point of view and looking at it from the other side,
i.e., not from outside, but from inside" (*Letters 2*, p. 580, 10 August 1960,
to Earl of Sandwich). Of course, the right way to look at the world is not
our concern. It is a philosophical, not psychological concern. But the move
itself that Jung proposes, if applied to our relation to dreams, can tell us
what entering the dream would have to mean. It is the shift of our standpoint from outside to inside. We have to get to a point where we can see the
dream *from within itself*, with its own eyes, so to speak. Our interiorizing
ourselves into the dream is, as I pointed out, tantamount to our going pregnant with it, and thus it is the dream's taking hold of us and emerging in our
consciousness from within ourselves. It is our being touched in our imagination and feeling, our consciousness's being deeply affected and permeated, *by the spirit and logic of the image*. The dream is no longer the object
of *our* reflection *about* it. No longer a vis-à-vis. And thus also no external
juxtaposition of dream and associations, no "holding together of the logical
and the naturalistic".

As the simultaneity of "interiorization into" and "going pregnant with",
this type of relation between the dream (or the *opus*) and the interpreting
real human being (or the *operator*) is a repetition of the yin-yang-like relation that we found between inner and outer.

But when (and if) this inwardness in the dream image's logos (I could also say: In the *soul* of the dream image) has happened, then the dream ceases to be the literal dream text as a positivity (merely the letters and words) and turns into something that *within itself* opens up into a world. The field is wide open. The dream image then possibly *resonates* and *reverberates* with seemingly remote personal or historical memories, with amplificatory images from mythology. And *then* the answer to the question "who" is to decide what belongs and what not is clear. It is the dream itself, the *living* image that decides, *it* as its productive, generative internal logical life. *Only* those associations or amplifications are permissible that are *its*, the dream's memories, not mine. "It has a say now, not you" (Jung in *Letters 2*, p. 532 [to Charteris, 9 January 1960]).

Our inwardization into the dream means our (methodological, temporary!) going under into the dream, our emptying ourselves, so that we can go pregnant with it and so that, ipso facto, the inner spirit or logic of the dream image itself may be given free rein in us to productively unfold itself, its inner complexity and potential. This is why it is so vital not to allow anything from outside in, not even the idea of *the dreamer* (!), and on the contrary altogether dissolve the naturalism of the *unio naturalis*, because external associations would inevitably serve as a distraction and inhibit, maybe even quench, the image's further thinking itself in us. As Jung insisted time and again, free associations only lead back to *people's* personal complexes and away from the dream. Literally external material merely "held together" with the dream is deadly. Psychological dream work in the Jungian spirit is the *art* of letting the dream interpret itself, which, in order to exist, presupposes our having given way to it so that *it* can do its thing in and through us. An art! A subtle art. "PDI"[5] is a *discipline* of interiority, the art of methodologically going under into the "matter" at hand.

But since it is an art, it is also always possible that we do not succeed, or not enough. And even if we have truly interiorized ourselves into the dream (or should I say: If the dream has absorbed us into itself?), this interiorization is probably never total. We are finite human beings and exist as the psychological difference, the difference between ourselves as biological organism and naturalistic consciousness, on the one hand, and ourselves as

---

5 PDI refers to Psychology as the Discipline of Interiority.

soul, on the other, between our psychic and our psychological realities. So there is never any guarantee that what we do when working with a dream is in fact letting the dream interpret itself.

This is why we have to be on guard and try, using our feeling function and relying on our psychological conscience as the only guidelines available to us, to consciously *discriminate* between all associations and amplifications that in fact may come up concerning the question of whether they really belong or not. "Believe not every spirit, but try the spirits whether they are of God . . ." (1 John 4:1). *Whose* memory is it, *who* has the association or amplification, me or the image? Does my amplification really come as *its*, the dream image's, self-interpretation, self-articulation, or is it my external reflection about it? We need to risk ourselves.

Conversely, with respect to Saban's charge that our dialectical thinking results in total sameness and thus in "the absence of remainder", the fact that we can never be certain that it is truly the dream that is interpreting itself through us, means that we do not really need to worry about a total disappearance of any "remainder". On the contrary!

* * *

The standpoint of exteriority naturally entails a disinterest in inwardness, even a blindness to it. Inwardness and inwardization are too subtle, sophisticated for it—not positive and commonsensical enough. At one point Saban makes a kind of confessional statement:

> For me this massive labour of transforming one's logical status from one point of view to another, from the semantic to the syntactic etc., seems not only unnecessarily *over-determined* for everyday psychological work (and is there psychological work which is not in some sense everyday?), but also in a sense *inappropriate* to the task.
>
> (my emphases)

A momentous confession. Ultimately—it tells us—he feels committed to the everyday perspective, to the naturalism of ordinary, conventional psychological consciousness. By contrast, what the discipline of interiority aspires to is for him overly extravagant, hyperbolical, off-beam, and ipso facto misses the real practical needs of psychotherapy. This is the return, on an intra-psychological level, of the skeptical objection with which depth-psychological therapy in the early days used to be confronted by the commonsense of the man in the street: It is completely unnecessary to talk about dreams and childhood memories and spend so much time on feelings and fantasies as is spent in analysis; all that the patient really needs is to pull himself together, to go out into the fresh air, to get some good advice and maybe some educational measures. The particularly Jungian thesis, by contrast, goes even beyond the ordinary depth-psychological approach and insists that a patient is best served precisely through attention to the *hinterland* of the soul, that is, the soul in its absolute negativity—but as such, it now meets, in Saban, with equivalent objections by the common sense of the conventional depth-psychologist.

Saban asks, "But what is the justification for committing to PDI? Why interiority rather than exteriority?" And revealing his utilitarian orientation he contrasts this with the situation in science: "If you say to the scientist, 'why commit yourself to science" he or she will say, 'well, just look at what science has done'. . . ." For me this would, however, be a surprising answer coming from a scientist, because for me the reason for going into science, i.e., the motivation (and precisely not the "rational *justification*" from the point of view of its usefulness), would be something like curiosity, the passionate desire to *know*. But it is true, science can also point to its amazing achievements and the practical usefulness of its results. Psychology in the spirit of inwardness has nothing like that to show for itself. It cannot, and does not desire to, prove its efficacy and usefulness, the way the behaviorists tempt to do. And it does not have an external utilitarian justification at all, which does, however, not mean that it is totally without rational justification. Rather, its justification lies within itself. How else could things be for a psychology as the discipline of interiority? By its colorful tunes the lark blissfully climbs up into the air. No physical ladder. No external foundation. No solid ground.

When asking, "why are we required to commit to PDI?", Saban shows that he does *not all along* know by himself why psychology in the spirit of inwardness is important. He wants an external reason. This in turn shows that he is simply not the right person for it. As a matter of course, nobody is obliged to be committed to interiority. This psychology is only for those who love it, who are deeply touched and reached by the inwardness and absolute negativity of the soul, who do have a sense of *soul* (in contrast to psyche and to the practical affairs and conflicts of daily life). The psychology as the discipline of interiority does not proselytize. It does not want to claim others for itself nor approach them with a "you should, you ought to join". It is perhaps like with poetry. Nobody is required to write or appreciate poetry. The spirit of Schelling's statement about his later "positive philosophy" (in contrast to his earlier "negative philosophy") applies mutatis mutandis to PDI, too. Schelling said:

> Positive Philosophy is the truly free philosophy; he who does not want it, may leave it alone. I leave it up to each individual. I only say that if someone wants, for example, the real process [*Hergang*], if he wants a free world creation etc., then he can have all this only by means of such a philosophy.
>
> (*SW* vol. XIII, p. 132, my transl.)

In the same way, PDI leaves it up to each individual. But for PDI it is not only a question of whether one wants it or not. It is above all a question of whether one is *able* to *see* what it is about in the first place or not, to see the *aurum nostrum* in contrast to the *aurum vulgi*.

And as to Saban's questioning "this massive labour of transforming one's logical status", we have to say that the word "massive" is, of course, absolutely misplaced (we are not in the realm of heavy industry), but apart from this, the alchemical refining work indeed happens to be a long *opus*; becoming proficient in the *Art of Archery*, or in the art of playing a musical instrument musically or in the discipline of interiority happen to require effort. Even an ordinary trade must slowly be learned. But whereas in most trades, there is a time when the former apprentice has become master, in PDI we generally start out from natural consciousness and, vis-à-vis of every new dream, symptom, or patient story, have time and again to work ourselves up to the appropriate standpoint of interiority from scratch *while* we work with the material, in the doing of it. And it is precisely a sign of a "master" of PDI that he can, with methodological awareness, each time go honestly back to square one whenever he is confronted with a new phenomenon to be worked.

* * *

So far I have exemplified the standpoint of exteriority in the area of practical psychological, our working with dreams. But this standpoint makes itself also felt in the area of the very categories of psychological thinking. Saban blames me for "a persistent tendency in [my] writings to dichotomise or binarise: Interiority vs Exteriority, Opus Magnum vs Opus parvum, the syntactic vs the semantic, the horizontal vs the vertical etc etc." Again, as with the above "mantra", while at first being able to acknowledge the usefulness of these distinctions, but only partially "from an heuristic point of view",[6] ultimately they result for him "in conceptual sterility or absurdity". His charge is that they "become sedimented into absolute ontological categories", and that for me ". . . a phenomenon is either to be included in one of the two dimensions or it is in the other, but never both". This is nonsense. While it is true that these categories *as such* exclude each other, *phenomena* can participate in both at once, without in any way compromising the respective absolute difference between the categories. Let me elucidate this point only with one, the semantic/syntactical, difference. Obviously, already on a positive-factual level, one and the same sentence has a semantic or content aspect and at the same time a syntactic structure, and the absolute difference of the categories congeals in the really existing distinction between dictionaries and grammar books. To speak of dichotomizing makes no sense.

And *in psychology* this distinction is not merely of heuristic value, but vital for making ourselves conscious, conscious of soul. When Nietzsche, for example, said, "I fear we cannot get rid of God because we still believe in the grammar",[7] he made us aware of the fact that it is not enough to say, "God is dead". This semantically clear-cut, unambiguous message is, according to Nietzsche, contradicted by the belief in the substantiality of the sentence subject *unwittingly invested in*, and thus confirmed by, the syntax of this very sentence! In other words, psychologically viewed, the person who with full conviction says "God is dead" or "God does not exist" says nevertheless at the same time, but completely unwittingly, "God exists". Did Nietzsche here dichotomize, binarize? Is this distinction conceptually sterile or absurd? Or did this distinction serve him only as a heuristic tool? No, it is psychologically indispensable. By means of it Nietzsche *opened our eyes* to a deeper, more fundamental but heretofore unnoticed, unthought, level, the level of *psychological* reality, or, to say it with Jung's words from another context, to the picture that looms up "behind the impressions of the

6 Or "however useful it may be sometimes to talk as though the two are separate phenomena".
7 Friedrich Nietzsche, *The Twilight of the Idols: Or, How to Philosophise with the Hammer*, trans. Anthony M. Ludovici, in *The Complete Works of Friedrich Nietzsche*, vol. 16, ed. Oscar Levy, Edinburgh and London: T.N. Foulis, 1911, p. 22.

daily life—behind the scenes".[8] He left the naturalism of the commonplace mind and advanced to the "psychological difference", the difference between the psychic and the psychological, the semantic and the syntactical, and thus to the interiority of soul. Much the same could be shown for the other distinctions mentioned by Saban.

This example from Nietzsche could *in nuce* also provide the outlines of an answer to Saban's consternation about my general idea that, as he puts it, "there is no necessary relation between what individuals think, say and do, and the so-called logic of their culture". The person who thinks that God is dead is contained in, but unaware of, the logic of his or her culture, in this case of the syntax of this culture's language. Because his explicit thought is contradicted by the culturally provided logical form of his thought, it is obvious that the two aspects (individual thought and logic of the culture) are here radically separate (and in general separable). This, however, does not at all mean that the logic of the culture is "a disembodied logical abstraction hovering above humanity", as Saban imagines it, *needs* to imagine it on account of his one-dimensional, only-horizontal dualistic set-up. No, in this case that person even actually performs that very logic of the culture in practical life by thinking this semantically deviant thought, but totally apart from the explicit thought. Language is certainly "anchored in concrete reality", indeed, it is itself a concrete reality.

What Saban does by defaming these distinctions as illegitimate dichotomizing and as ultimately absurd, is, in the last analysis, to deny the psychological difference and to opt for the external picture of "the impressions of the daily life" (which for him is, of course, to be *externally complemented* by the fundamentally unrelated, even contradictory ideas of myth) while altogether eliminating the whole concept of "what is behind the scenes", in other words: the soul as it is understood in psychology in the Jungian tradition.

What for Jung, Hillman, and me is the phenomena's (vertical) relation to their own internal depth and thus an internal otherness of the same, for Saban has obviously been replaced by the external (horizontal) relationship of literal alterity, the bumping into each other of inner and outer, thought and world, personal experience and myth. Pointing to a passage in which I state that while the psychology of an individual in a given culture might be

8 C.G. Jung, *The Visions Seminar*, Book One, Zürich: Spring Publications, 1967, p. 8.

consciously rational, the collective psychology of the culture in which this individual dwells, can simultaneously be in a state of "participation mystique", Saban counters: "Surely the relationship between individual and collective cannot really be as dissociated as this? Are the two not entwined to such an extent that they are ultimately indistinguishable . . .?" Ultimately indistinguishable! Here we see that his attack on the various distinctions listed above boils ultimately down to a leveling out or obliterating of the differences altogether. Here the advocate of "unfathomable alterity" reveals *his* type of sameness.

Misconceptions and insinuations

Saban's construal of the logical form of a culture, if it is considered being clearly separate from what individuals think, as "a disembodied logical abstraction hovering above humanity", and the relation between the individual and the logic of the culture, if so conceived, as "dissociated" is already one example of his several misunderstandings and misconstruals.

A major one is his view of what dialectics in Hegel is. Having referred to Lévinas and Derrida and "an ethics based upon the call of the other" he says that "it is in this context that I see the relationship of the dialectic to otherness". First of all, viewing Hegel in the context of those thinkers, who never let themselves in for the *thought* that was thought by Hegel, is unproductive from the outset. When Derrida believes to be critiquing Hegel, he does not critique *Hegel*, but much rather merely further displays *his own* position, only this time against the foil of his preconceptions about Hegel. Like Heidegger, and in fact all modern thinkers since Feuerbach, Derrida acts *as if* the metaphysicians up to Hegel had been standing on the *same* ground as the one that he and the modern thinkers know to be theirs, so that critical objections of the modern thinkers to the earlier ones might theoretically be feasible. He is unable to see that Hegel (and the entire tradition of Western metaphysics including, by the way, Schelling) are fundamentally *other*, that an abyss, a discontinuity, separates him from them and that only if he were ready to cross over this abyss and let himself in for this Other could he be in a position to do justice to the metaphysical thinkers. The thinking committed to the unbridgeable difference and to ineradicable otherness is apparently not capable of seeing *its own other*, but interprets it merely as a *mistaken, faulty* version of the same.

This is also why the phrase "relationship of the dialectic to otherness" does not make any sense. It is a meaningless combination of words. It is the apperception of the concept of dialectics from the viewpoint of externality. This thinking starts out from the presupposition of ineradicable otherness and ipso facto ruins its chances of ever understanding what dialectics in Hegel's sense is about. Saban's thought is here informed by the binary opposition of same and other. But what is dialectics? Dialectics begins with whatever it happens to begin with and unfolds this "matter's" internal contradictions and their consequent process, or rather: Lets them self-unfold. Just as in alchemy the prime matter is enclosed in the hermetically sealed alchemical vessel and the adept's full concentration goes exclusively to what is inside the retort so that any external other *has always already been* left behind and simply is no topic anymore; so it is, mutatis mutandis, also in the case of dialectics. The talk of a "relationship to otherness" is simply out of place, a crude misunderstanding of what be it alchemy or dialectics are about. Much as, in the sphere of externality, anatomy, physiology, and biochemistry reveal the hidden internal complexity of the living organism and the function of its parts, substances, and processes (organs, cells, genes, hormones, etc.), so does dialectics reveal, in the sphere of the spirit, the internal complexities of concepts, beliefs, and cultural realities, the only difference being that in the realm of externality violent force is necessary (anatomy dissects the body), whereas dialectics works nonviolently by letting the complexities self-display. It works merely by one's devoting oneself intensively to a chosen topic and, rather than *operating* upon it, taking it absolutely seriously, i.e., *taking it at its word*. Then it will show what it entails, namely that it involves complications that were not expected. These complications or, more specifically, contradictions can then again be taken at their word, and so on. It is a process of learning by experience.

But Saban construes dialectics in a totally different way. "To negate, to negate the negation, to sublate is to force the other into a digestive process whereby it returns as same. Hence the absence of remainder. Nothing is left outside, nothing is so other that it cannot be fully sublated into sameness." Many things are wrong with this statement. *Nobody* negates anything in Hegel's dialectics. *Nobody* sublates anything. Negation or sublation in dialectics is not a technique performed by us upon some other. It is not our doing at all. Dialectics is, as indicated, merely our observing how an idea (or what one's topic happens to be), *if taken at its word*, does not work as promised, and it is this experience, that is, the original idea's own self-contradiction, that negates this idea and leads by itself of necessity—in the sense of learning by experience ("aha!")—to a revised, corrected idea that takes what has been experienced into account. No force at all. And where is there anywhere here an alleged "other" *that* is allegedly forced? The real work of the dialectical development is done by the idea to be examined itself, all by itself and upon itself. There is from the outset only a "same", the idea at hand, since everything external that does not belong, I could also say: Every "other", is excluded from the beginning, which, however, conversely implies that it is false to say that there is no remainder, that nothing is left outside. Of course there is: Everything else that is not in focus remains outside.

From the cited passage we also learn that for Saban the dialectic means a forcing (!) the other *into a digestive process*. This view is connected, in his fantasy, with the idea of an "attempt to depotentiate the other through appropriation". "The animus (logos) seeks to appropriate anima (image)." ". . . consciousness seeks to transcend everything that does not correspond and is not adequate to the concept." Saban warns against the idea of "the sublation of the old into the new, so that it is swallowed up entirely in order to create a new all embracing total myth". All this shows that Saban's interpretation of dialectics is informed by an imperialistic expansionist fantasy, by the dream of conquering the world, the All. There is a seeking, a program; a will to transcend, overcome, subsume, and subdue, to incorporate; a compulsive attempt to devour and assimilate everything heterogeneous and to force it into a sameness.

This way of seeing things again betrays the standpoint of exteriority, inasmuch as, with its orientation *outwards* to what is all around it ("the other"), it is a political power fantasy, modeled after the image of great conquerors, like Alexander the Great, Caesar, Genghis Khan, Napoleon. It is *Saban's* imperialistic fantasy; even, or precisely, by fighting it, Saban nevertheless also confirms it. This imperialism is probably the unacknowledged shadow of his (and Lévinas') "ethics based on the call of the other" (Derrida already pointed to the sublime *violence* of Lévinas' Other). Be that as it may, this imperialistically interpreted dialectics has certainly nothing to do with Hegel's dialectic nor with dialectics as practiced in psychology. They both perform the exactly opposite movement to the movement of expansion, conquest, swallowing, and appropriation, namely, the mind's absolute-negative interiorization into a "matter", into one single topic, concept, or phenomenon at hand, the mind's abandoning itself to and going under in it so as to allow the matter's internal complexity to emerge and unfold step by step. Not expansion but depth. Not "the other" and the manifold of what all there is all around, but merely "this".

Apropos of the "ethics based on the call of the other" and Saban's idea of "an urgent need to rediscover a primal ethics behind logos" we can see again that his standpoint is that of externality. Ethics in the traditional (in contrast to the special *psychological*) sense addresses and constellates "the civilian man" in us (as Jung called it) and not the psychologist qua psychologist in us. It has its place out there in the social arena, in the literal world, outer reality. It is concerned with interpersonal relations, "the relations between the ego and the external other (i.e., people or the environment)", not with "The Relations Between the Ego and the Unconscious", or, as I would prefer to say, the relations between the I and the soul. "People" are by definition outside of psychology's sphere of vision, provided that one has a rigorous notion of psychology and abides by it. The only ethics *relevant for and in psychology* is the ethics of soul itself, the ethics of soul-making, of the image, of logos, of dream interpretation, etc., an ethics of which Jung's dictum discussed above—not to allow in anything that does not belong—is one exemplary maxim.[9]

* * *

I come to another type of misconstrual. Referring to both Hegel and Giegerich (it is silly to put these two authors into the same sentence and connect them with "and" as if they were on the same level and of the same rank. But this is done by Saban), he says, "Consciousness seeks to transcend everything that does not correspond and is not adequate to the concept. . . . Myth, as a mere form of *phantasie* must be seen as a moment on the way to truth." Then, ". . . Hegel and Giegerich [. . .] reduce the content of mythology to a clumsy, pre-logical attempt at expressing logical forms". And finally, "For Hegel and Giegerich the images and stories of myth resemble the shadows on the wall of Plato's cave: all we need to do is turn around and see the reality and truth of the notion".

---

9 Other maxims are, for example, the related one about our having "to stick to the image" (our obligation to pay attention to the sensual precision and exactitude of the image), as well as: "It has a say now, not you", "Say it again, as best you can", "Tarry with the negative, with what has been *in via ejectum*", "Don't mistake daily-life impressions for manifestations of soul dignity; don't judge dreams from realities", "Inwardize the matter absolute-negatively into itself", "Beware of the physical in the material", etc.

What an absurd misrepresentation! For me, myth is itself the *appearance* of the truth and not a mere moment on the long way to a final truth. Neither for Hegel nor for me is there, in the overall development of history, a progression from clumsy to perfect, from mere shadow and "chaotic darkness" to truth.[10] Myth is perfect in itself and has everything it needs within itself. For Hegel the absolute is always, and always already, present, just as for Jean Gebser there is an "ever-present origin". Instead of a linear upwards move, a rise in the sense of improvement, from illusion to truth, there is in history (and *as* history) only a form change, a metamorphosis, *of truth*. Truth goes through a historical process, passes through different stages, appears as different truths, according to the statuses of consciousness and the actual modes of being-in-the-world, above all the forms of production. The truth of Stone Age hunters is different from the truth of Greek polis-dwellers at the time of Plato and again from the truth of Medieval man as well as from that of industrial modernity. But in each case it is the authentic manifestation of the full-fledged truth and of truth as such. Truth is in itself historical, dynamic, a living process: Part of the soul's logical life. It is *absolute* truth, which is the opposite of the abstract, static idea of truth as otherworldly, supratemporal, and self-identical that Saban seems to work with. Truth is always. We cannot ever fall out of it, we are always encompassed by it. However, it is not always easy to see it. It requires dedication, effort, and a certain soul depth of apperception. And it becomes the more difficult to see it the more complex and diversified the culture is becoming.

The idea of a linear historical progress from clumsy beginnings to final truth and to the glory of the notion is a crude, simplistic idea in Saban's mindset. He did not find it in Hegel or in my work, but projects this (his own) fantasy of linearity upon it. His assertion that, for Hegel, "consciousness seeks to transcend everything that does not correspond and is not adequate to the concept" betrays a shockingly un-Hegelian, namely abstract, concept of the concept, which is nevertheless ascribed by him to Hegel. Myth and religion are for Hegel from the outset relative to and exist only for "the existing concept" (in Hegel's sense). Religion, just as art and philosophy too, is the manifestation of the absolute spirit, the spirit that knows itself. What Saban suggests, the move from the "clumsy, pre-logical" to

---

10 The only idea of historical progress in Hegel is that there is an advance in the "consciousness of freedom", an idea that does not seem altogether implausible in view of the actual historical changes in the West.

pure "logical form", is, by contrast, conceived as a process of abstraction, of stripping, so that in the end only an *abstract*, emaciated, formal-logical, concept is left, in other words, precisely that which Hegel vehemently criticized as the abstractions of *Verstand*. I find these allegations intolerable because they are based on ignorance.

There is nothing wrong with a critical reading, but everything wrong with a crude misreading. Where is here the lauded "ethics based upon the call of the other"? Would such an ethics—as, by the way, any ethics in a more traditional sense—not require that one only talks about something if one really understands it, and that otherwise one remains silent? Where is the respect of Hegel (and of Schelling as well!) as *philosophers*, as *thinkers*? What Saban says about them makes me ask if it is based on a real study of their works, or only on hearsay? At any rate, it appears that their work is seen by him as consisting of propositions and opinions (opinions that one can pluck out and concur with or reject, as if they were building bricks, rather than being integral living thought, thought that needs to be entered *thinkingly*). Saban's *real* other (to whose call he should, according to his own principles, respond) is in the last analysis not so much Hegel and Giegerich as it is *thought*, the inwardization into living thought.

* * *

This same fantasy of an upwards development comes out in his description of my thesis of "the birth of man" as a "development which allows for the beginning of reflective thought, the commencement of the soul's logical life". This is a crazy statement. As the informed reader will remember, I located what I called "the birth of man" at the threshold of the 19th century, the time of the Napoleonic era, at the beginnings of the Industrial Revolution and after the end, or better: Conclusion, of the age of classical Western metaphysics with Schelling and Hegel, and I described it, for example, as the radical shift from the uroboric logic of the copula or of identity, the logic of the judgment, to the modern logic of the *function* (Frege) and the unbridgeable difference. *This* time (the beginning of the 19th century) is supposed to be, in my view, the beginning of reflective thought, with Heraclitus, Plato, Descartes and so on preceding reflective thought? Impossible.

But the real value of Saban's statement for us is something else. It shows an additional misreading, namely, that for him "reflective thought" and "the soul's logical life" are synonymous, mean the same thing. They blend into the same. He does not discriminate them. For me the two represent an absolutely crucial difference, the difference between something particular and a universal. And his non-discrimination throws a light on the numerous confusions and problems he has with my view of the history of the soul (as also with Hegel's, or Jung's and Schelling's, for that matter).

The "soul's logical life" has no commencement in history at all. It is not a late product of history. This is part of its definition. History *is* itself the process *of the soul's logical life*. The soul *is* itself logical life. Just as "truth", it is always, as long as there has been soul, as there has been humanness. And everything that takes place in human history, as far as it is of psychological significance, takes place within the soul's logical life. Therefore I comprehended already the most archaic sacrificial slaughterings, prior to any reflective thought in the narrower or explicit sense at all, as the soul's killing *itself* into being, that is to say, as a manifestation of the soul's logical life, and described their complex internal logic. As Jung said, quoting *Faust*, "*'Im Anfang war die Tat'* (in the beginning was the deed). Deeds were never invented, they were done. Thoughts, on the other hand, are a relatively late discovery" (*CW* 18 § 553).

Precisely. Jung understood what Saban blinds himself to. In contrast to "the soul's logical life", which is inescapable (*unhintergehbar*), reflective thought is a particular potential within this logical life from the outset, a potential that only emerges *as such* (explicitly) in the course of the soul's history at a particular point, manifests concretely in a new logical form, and further develops along with history through diverse stages. This means that myth, mythic image, is by no means pre-logical. Just like "deed", "image" is of course a manifestation of the soul's logical life, the apparition of the truth (the truth of a certain stage of cultural, psychological development). But image as well as deed nevertheless precede the status of reflective thought proper, of *logos* in the specific sense ("*logos*" as in the phrase, "from *mythos* to *logos*"), of the *form* of conceptual thought, which emerged, in Western history, only with the earliest Greek thinkers.

And again, the much, much later soul event of "the birth of man" thus in no way amounts to the beginning of reflective thought, let alone to the commencement of the soul's logical life. It is much rather a further, previously unheard-of change, a breakthrough, to be sure, *on* the level of reflection but *to* an utterly new dimension. A change that we can find best *symbolically* expressed in modern man's having been able to leave the earth and to fly to the moon and into outer space, outer space, which in turn, being absolutely hostile to humans, can be considered as the *image* of the logic of that modern radical Otherness hailed by Saban.

Saban's non-discrimination between the logical in the wider sense of the soul's logical life or the existing concept in Hegel's sense, on the one hand, and the logical in the sense of a specific, particular form of reflective conceptual thought, on the other, has the sad effect that for him logos shrinks to the lesser meaning, to explicit reflection, indeed, to the *abstract* formal-logical concept, to the merely rationalistic, stripped of any mystery, depth, and infinity. But this is something Saban has to take the responsibility for. He must not blame others for *his* reductive and abstract sense of the soul's logical life or of the Concept in Hegel's sense.

His utterly abstract sense of logic and thought also comes out succinctly in his difficulty with my distinction between "thought proper" as thought thinking itself and "empirical thought", thought about non-thought. He says he does not "recognize the absolute difference between the two", and points to the fact that "thought is bound up with language, but language is never pure . . . the building bricks of thought can never fully escape their sensible, image-based origins". We see quite clearly that "thought thinking itself (in contrast to thinking about other things)" is immediately understood by him as meaning the stripping of the articulation of thought from all sensible, imaginal, metaphorical traces, which, I agree, would be impossible. A purist abstraction. But my distinction refers to something very different and very simple. What I called empirical thought is thought concerned with trees, animals, houses, mountains and rivers, the stars, our neighbors, events, etc., in other words, with objects in empirical reality. By contrast, thought that thinks itself is concerned, for example, with "identity", "difference", "essence", "being", "cause", i.e., with *concepts* that are exclusively thought's own internal products and property. They exist *only* in the mind and have no referent. Trees (although an image or concept in the mind, too) you can nevertheless in fact see out there. But not "essence" or "being". "Being" does not exist. It is a notion, *only* a notion. And then, also notional, also the mind's internal product and property, there are the figures that we have to deal with as analysts, the philosophical trees, the stone that is not a stone, the slippery mountain of fairytale and dream. They are different from trees, stones, mountains in ordinary parlance in that they, like the logical categories, do not have an external referent. As psychological images they only refer to themselves.

The fact that the language we use is even in the case of thought proper ultimately always in some way image-based is of no relevance whatsoever for the question of the possibility of thought thinking itself. I don't have a problem with imaginal and metaphorical language, or with images in general. I love them. For me they don't threaten thought. But the absence of the psychological difference and of the difference between the semantic and the syntactical in Saban's thinking forces him to work with the totally abstract, literal difference (binary opposition) of the logical or thought, on the one hand, and the sensible or imaginal, on the other, and ipso facto to construe "thought proper" quite literalistically as meaning that our human linguistic expression of thought would have to be absolutely cleansed from everything sensible and imaginal.

This lower-level (personalistic, literalistic) interpretation by Saban of psychological concepts comes out in many other features as well, e.g., in his external literal view of interiority as the "challenge of heroically rising to the level of commitment required", whereby "commitment" is viewed as an existential, if not existentialistic one. He has a totally abstract notion of commitment as if it were something in its own right (sort of: "Commitment for *commitment's* sake", rather than quite practically a person's commitment *to* a particular cause, discipline or approach). The entrance into the standpoint of interiority is seen, in an overblown way, as a "heroic ascent", as an existential "leaving the everyday world behind to enter the abstraction of the psycho-logic". Saban speaks of a "massive labour of transforming one's logical status . . .": Obviously he imagines a *Herculean* task, when in reality it is no more than the task of learning one's trade and practicing it professionally. All this is very far removed from the simple, down-to-earth adoption of a specific *methodological standpoint*, the standpoint of interiority, far removed from any existential commitment. In Saban, everything is interpreted on the semantic and concretistic level because the *distinction* between the semantic and the syntactical (or logical form) is not available to him.

As we have seen, due to his reductive (downwards) blending of the difference between the two senses of "logical", Saban had to misread Hegel's and my view of history as a linear upwards development from Platonic shadow to truth and from clumsy mythic image to the soul's logical life. Conversely, however, on account of this reductive blending, he also incapacitated himself to appreciate the legitimacy of the perception of history as a more or less coherent succession of stages of consciousness. While it is, also for me, indispensable to reject the idea of historical progress in the area of "the truth" and of "the soul's logical life", it would be fool-ish to deny a (very roughly speaking) "linear and one-way" development of history in certain other regards, where, as Saban puts it, "when one stage is completed it can never be returned to, it is left behind forever". He rejects this conception of an at times irreversible development, *has to* reject it, because he cannot, or does not want to, discriminate between the universal and the particular and therefore has not differentiated the higher soul level from the lower practical and phenomenological one. This means concretely that for him the lower level of the phenomenal is not released from the burden of having to immediately carry and express the higher values of the soul.

When we, however, are willing to render unto Caesar the things that are Caesar's (the concrete empirical process of history) and to God the things that are God's (the soul's logical life; truth), when we work with the psychological *difference*, then we can state, quite soberly and relaxed, that once we have iron tools we cannot return to stone axes; that once we have gun powder (let alone explosives and nuclear weapons) we cannot go back to bows and arrows; once we have advanced to industrial modes of production we cannot return to manual spinning and weaving. Once we have gone through puberty we cannot go back to the sexual innocence of childhood; once we have developed a cultivated taste for wine, we cannot go back to a primitive description of wine as either sweet or sour. These are not merely shifts of the prevailing myths, of the stories, changes that could be reduced to semantics. No, they are changes of a different caliber, changes in the logical form of culture or person, in the level of *complexity* and *differentiation*, and as such involve a degree of irreversibility. Now turning to the area of intellectual and religious regards: Once I am in modernity, in the stage of "born man" and of the unbridgeable differ-ence, I cannot go back to classical metaphysics, to Hegel or Schelling, nor to Thomas Aquinas or Plato (although this does in no way preclude the possibility of our learning from them). Let me simply quote Jung: "We cannot turn the wheel backwards; we cannot go back to the symbolism that is gone" (*CW* 18 § 632). Thus, once consciousness has entered the stage of *logos*, of philosophical, critically-reflective thought, of concep-tual thinking (which it did more than 2,500 years ago), it cannot return to *mythos*. Following Jung (*CW* 18 § 632) we can say: It cannot do this because consciousness then knows too much; doubt [i.e., reflection] has killed *mythos*. The innocence, the immediacy, of the former mythic stance to the world is lost.

* * *

After having blamed Hegel and me for favoring a model of a linear and one-way progressive development in history, Saban, surprisingly, believes to detect the opposite theory in my history of consciousness, namely "a powerful mythic story" (that according to him gives to my account its plausibility), namely, "a version of the myth of the fall, whereby a paradisal world . . . is somehow lost. . . ." In other words, first: "From the shadows in Plato's cave upwards to the glory of the notion", now: A myth of the degeneration from a "more perfect age", the Golden Age, to a stage accompanied by a "traumatic sense of loss".

Here we have again the conflation of what in my work comes as a sober phenomenological description of different modes of being-in-the-world with a higher soul value, a secret emotional *pathos*, and a mythic quality. Saban uses a guileful trick. What is in fact part of the obvious *phenomenology* of the 19th century, *its* voicing—through many, many individual voices that capture a generally prevailing *Lebensgefühl* of 19th century man—the loss of meaning, the emergence of nihilism, the death of God, etc., all this *he* tries to twist to make it appear as if it were in truth a hidden "mythical-archetypal" structure in *my* mind, *my* being in the grip of the myth of the fall, a myth that I merely project upon history out there.

But I am not responsible for the phenomenon of the historically *unparalleled* feeling and notion of nihilism, for the emergence in the 19th century of the *absolutely novel*[11] question of and search for the "meaning of life", for Schopenhauer's disillusioned pessimistic philosophy of the *blind* will, for Feuerbach's exposure of metaphysics as illusion, for Marx's declaration of religion as the opium for the people, for Nietzsche's "God is dead", for what is expressed in the writings of Beaudelaire, Edgar Allen Poe, De Quincey, and a host of others. All this is, as it were, part of the "dream *text*" to be interpreted by the psychologist. Saban has not disproved any of this.

---

11 Cf. Jung's "This distinguishes our time from all others" (*CW* 10 §161); "This situation is new. All ages before us . . ." (*GW* 9/I § 50, my transl.).

But "the sense of loss" that is undoubtedly inherent in these phenomena to be interpreted is nonetheless boldly, but illicitly,[12] given out by Saban as not having its place "out there" in the historical phenomena but as stemming from a "powerful mythic story", the myth of the fall, that unwittingly structures the interpreter's (i.e., my) subjective perception from behind. This is a clear mystification, an abuse of archetypal theory. In his paper, Saban at one point himself admitted that "there have been identifiable shifts in consciousness throughout historical time". What I did with my idea of "the birth of man" was nothing else than to (1) *identify* and (2) psychologically *interpret* a historical shift in consciousness. We see: There are for Saban identifiable shifts in history, but when one such shift is identified and discussed, it is for him not a historical shift at all, but merely the projection of a myth upon history. His accepting the idea of historical shifts is without any practical value or consequence. Just talk.[13]

When I speak, with respect to archaic times, of a participation mystique, I mean a particular discernable and concretely describable psychological (not psychic!) condition and not a vague mystified idea of anything "perfect", enchanted, paradisal. I am concerned, quite matter-of-factly and unemotionally, with the logical constitution of the archaic "being-in-the-world", rather than personalistically with people's subjective states.[14] No Golden Age! Nothing desirable. Just as, conversely, there is for me today no need

---

12 The illicit character of his argument comes out quite clearly in his turning an argument I used against Erich Neumann against me, but withholding from the reader that when I charged Neumann with confusing myth with history I could rightly do so because Neumann, while alleging to be providing a *history* of consciousness, exclusively used atemporal mythic material and not once based his *Ursprungsgeschichte* on, or correlated it with, identifiable historical shifts.

13 Just as his initial high praise for the Jungian "mantra" of dream interpretation was just talk.

14 Saban's already quoted, "Surely the relationship between individual and collective cannot really be as dissociated as this? Are the two not entwined to such an extent that they are ultimately indistinguishable . . .?" shows to what extent he is unable to see and hold the psychological difference, the difference between the psychic and the psychological, the semantic and the logical or syntactical, between what goes on in people and the life of the soul. His word "dissociated" points to his psychologistically (or personalistically) reducing the notion of the psychological difference, which is itself a psychological or logical (syntactical) distinction, to an empirical-factual split, the idea of a positively existing duality.

for a "traumatic sense of loss". It is not me who bemoans a loss; for me it is merely a logical change. This whole overlay of "good" and "bad", "golden" and "degenerated", this *his* inflating identifiable phenomenal features or differences with subjective emotional evaluations or ego preferences and overblown mythic ideas is Saban's mystification, for which again he has to take the responsibility. Instead of remaining on the phenomenal level, the level of identifiable shifts (which is, of course, denounced by him as "the literal-historical"), and instead, furthermore, of "sticking to the image" and trying to see to what precise phenomena (psychological states) my descriptions and interpretations refer and what new light my descriptions may possibly be able to throw on the *psychology* of these concrete identifiable phenomena, Saban rather floats away into the height of the disembodied non-committal generality of the mythic and archetypal. Self-blinding.

Equivocation and anti-discrimination

Saban's declared purpose is "to genuinely think mythology as central to psychology". For me, too, mythology is central to psychology. But this idea must not be used to obliterate historical differences. Mythology proper is central to *historical* psychology, not to the psychology of the modern situation.

What we see in Saban is that he has a wishy-washy concept of myth, or not really a *concept* of it at all. He never says what myth is except that it is stories. And he levels out differences, using "myth" equivocally for clearly distinct phenomena. For example, for him myth is

- the stories of gods and culture heroes in archaic, predominantly oral cultures (what I would call myth proper or authentic myth), .
- narratives (such as the "myth of the fall") which unconsciously structure the thinking of a modern theorizing mind, what Hillman might have called archetypal perspectives,
- an *enframing* world-picture,
- modern scientism,
- my idea of "the birth of man",
- even history as such is a myth for him,
- "myth as an individual phenomenon", such as Jung's "my personal myth, the myth by which I do live".

What do so-called "mythic" patterns that unconsciously structure the mind of a modern person have to do with myth proper? The former are only accessible to critical reflection or self-reflection, whereas authentic myth is always publicly known, told, and celebrated by a whole people. It is as much "out in the open" as one's mother-tongue. Myth needs no reflection, is untouched by and precedes reflection *sensu strictiori*, which it also shares with one's language. The unconscious pattern is implicit, veritable myth explicit. The one is mental, "psychological", the other cosmological. The one is only a logical form, whereas the other is concerned with real deities that demand cultic service. How can one use the same term for such different phenomena?

It is inherent in and essential to both history and science (and thus also scientism) that they base themselves on documented or empirical evidence, whereas myth proper precedes all evidential experience. For this reason the results of history and science are by definition a priori open to correction and revision when new findings emerge. Myth, by contrast, is extremely conservative and informs a people of "the a priori", if I may say so: Of the true origins. Myth proper is the soul's free self-articulation. There is no evidence for an Atlas holding up the vault of heaven or for a world ash, Hades, a primordial Chaos.

As to the idea of "my personal myth"—it has never been shown that there is such a thing. And quite apart from the *contradictio in adiecto* of "private myth" (myth proper is fundamentally a social, cultural, public phenomenon)—*if* it is something that needs to be *found*, and this means *sought*, it is the reverse of authentic myth, which, like people's mother-tongue, always already precedes their personal existence and, again like it, is unquestionable. Myth proper is not an *experience*, not a content of experience, not a particular event in life (the way our dreams or visionary experiences are), just as our language is primarily not an experience. It is the *medium in which* early man psychologically lived and experienced.

All these fundamental logical differences are wiped away by Saban as if he were an anti-discrimination official. Myth proper, I insist, is, just as "language" in its own right, but also like "theory" or "(scientific) cognition", one particular, distinct "symbolic form" in Ernst Cassirer's sense. And each symbolic form ought to be *respected* and, in our theorizing, preserved in its intactness. Saban's inflationary use of the term myth makes of it a highly elastic label, a mere word without real substance, without a precise concept. Purely nominalistic.

What is especially objectionable about the particular idea of "my personal myth" is that the higher aura, the sense of "religious" value, of significance and of mystique, that comes with, and is transported in, the old traditional label "myth" is surreptitiously carried over to a subjective experience, feeling, or notion of a modern individual which is thus adorned with borrowed plumes. Modern people may have dreams or inner experiences of an archetypal quality and an impressive depth. But that does not justify using the name myth for them. They are just something that these individuals *experienced*, nothing more. Did, for example, Jung's inner experiences recorded in the *Red Book* represent "the myth *by which I do live*"? They were certainly of great personal importance to him. But did they express that *by which* he lived, or not much rather a particular content of consciousness, a cherished belief, *separate* from his real life in the modern world?

What sets myth proper fundamentally apart from later personal "world-pictures" or "enframing" narratives is that the former was on principle unchallenged and without competition. There had neither been as yet a concept of "superstition" nor did myth co-exist with science, philosophy, various religions, political ideologies, private belief-systems, as in later ages, especially today. There was no market of meanings. Today every so-called "mythic" narrative comes *as* something a priori relativized by all other competing narratives, beliefs, and by our historical and scientific knowledge. This relativity is incompatible with the "symbolic form" called myth.

The wishy-washy nominalistic use of the label myth and the leveling out of specific differences between distinct phenomena through equivocation is my first point in this regard. Now I come to a new issue. It has to do with the elimination of difference as such, not merely with the obliteration of differences between particular distinct phenomena.

Reduction of history to story: Cocoonment in the sphere of ideality

In my response to Saban, in connection with the psychological topic of the radical rupture from "One" to "Two", I had asserted that he believed in the undisrupted continuity of myth. To this he surprisingly responded: "Not so. There are disruptions and violent shifts all the time, as myths are replaced by, and overtake other myths . . .", without realizing that this his answer precisely confirms my diagnosis. He seriously believes that he can fob me off with an answer that obviously follows the logic of "The king is dead, long live the king". The particular incumbents change (sometimes indeed violently, through regicide), but the office of king, i.e., monarchy as such, remains. Disruptions and the violence of shifts occur, in Saban's scheme, only on the semantic or content level (with respect to *which* particular mythic *story* happens to rule), whereas the syntax, the symbolic form of myth itself, inevitably persists. On the psychic, empirical, or experiential level there may be changes (even radical ones), but the logical form of the soul itself is and remains unalterably that of myth. The soul dwells in undisrupted Oneness with itself. The "Two", that is to say: The notion that the soul becomes (or has become) different from itself, that it leaves (has left) the form or stage of myth altogether, that it has pushed off from it through a reflection and critique *of it*, is unthinkable. Of course this *has to* be unthinkable when the psychological difference remains unconscious, unthought, and when consciousness exclusively focuses on what happens on the psychic and semantic level, in the obvious empirical, naturalistic, or personalistic foreground, and when psychology has no rigorous notion of its own root metaphor, soul— although in Saban's very response the difference between the semantic and the syntactical is *implicitly* already in operation.

The king must not die! Even when the king in fact dies! The move from monarchy to republican democracy must not happen! The Two, the emergence of the *difference* as such, namely, the difference, for example, between monarchy and republic, or between *mythos* and *logos* (or, to be more exact: The emergence of logos *as* the difference between *mythos* and *logos*), is absolutely excluded.

But of course, Saban's consciousness *is* a modern one. It is not naive, does not live on the level of the One. It has numerous historical shifts from the One to the Two behind itself, such as that from *mythos* to *logos*, more than 25 centuries ago, that from the pagan cosmos to the Christian "having overcome the world", at the end of antiquity, or more recently, that from the containment in the world of metaphysics to "the birth of man".[15] In fact, his is already the consciousness of "born man". The difference, therefore,

---

15 The shift from One to Two must not be literalized. It was not a one-time event. It, as well as the state of the One itself, are *psychological* concepts, not empirical-factual ones. In empirical reality, or for a naturalistic thinking, once One has turned into Two, there is no One anymore that could possibly divide itself into Two. But *psychologically* this shift happened repeatedly in history and can, and often has to, happen repeatedly because the One restores itself on each new level of consciousness that emerged through the shift from One to Two.

inevitably exists for Saban's consciousness, and for this reason his consciousness must, in order to nevertheless (against *its own* syntactical form) semantically maintain its scheme of the One. It has to resort to a strategy to render the difference (the Two) ineffective, since the Two cannot be disposed of altogether once consciousness has objectively become aware of it.

The difference can be neutralized (so that the one side, i.e., the Two, does not *do* anything anymore to the other) when consciousness succeeds in letting the One subsume or swallow the Two, when the Two is pocketed by the One. If the One can be defined as itself fundamentally ambivalent, as itself being *both* opposites in their mutual exclusiveness, then the One cannot possibly any longer become exposed to a possible *experience* of the Two as happening *to* itself and thus becoming destroyed as Oneness, for now it seems that, as Saban claims, "there never was a time before one became two".[16] By in this way semantically denying that there ever was a time of the One, the One has syntactically achieved absolute immunity. And the Two has become frozen in the permanent oscillation called "ambivalence" within the One.

In Saban this pocketing becomes especially visible in his theory of the equiprimordiality of the Two, namely *mythos* and *logos*, and of myth being always and from the outset both true and false story.[17] We get even an indirect demonstration of the strategic act performed for absorbing the

---

16 Maybe Saban thinks this way because he has a completely mystified idea of the One as something miraculous, a literal state of paradisal bliss? But the One must not be imagined in such a naturalistic or psychologistic way. The distinction between One and Two is a *psychological* one. And in psychological discourse it is not in any way more mysterious as, for example, the distinction in logic or linguistics between language and meta-language. To deny the One would be as reasonable as it would be to deny that there are first-level statements. Meta-language statements are evidence of a higher structural complexity, comparable, in a rather crude sense, to the higher complexity of multicellular over against monocellular organisms. In the phrase "from *mythos* to *logos*" logos *is* "Two" because qua reflection (the reflection *of mythos*) it is in itself the unity of (1) the critique and (2) what it is the critique of. It is a two-tier phenomenon.

17 Saban's equiprimordialization of the Two and of "true" and "false" story is in competition with his other method of explaining logical developments in history away, the one that we discussed earlier: The interpretation of the obsolescence of myth in history as the projection upon history of the myth of the Fall. This is a merely subjective invalidation of the obsolescence diagnosis (the branding of it as a mistake in the observer's consciousness). The theory of equiprimordiality, by contrast, has the advantage of eliminating the difference *in* the object itself, sort of ontologically. (Saban's third strategy of ridding himself of the rupture from One to Two is of course his leveling out of the differences between distinct phenomena by equivocally calling them all "myths.")

difference, so that what actually is a difference that played itself out as a historical succession and as the secondary negation (critique) of a former position was turned into a difference that as equiprimordial and simultaneous is logically subsumed under the One. Saban writes in his paper, ". . . even in the earliest Greek discourse about myth it already has the meaning 'false story'. As Eliade puts it, 'if the word 'myth,' in all European languages denotes 'fiction,' it is because the Greeks declared it to be so twenty-five centuries ago.'" What in Eliade's statement clearly refers to the time of the Greek Enlightenment, to an *act* of the pre-Socratics (their *doing* something to it, denouncing as false the myth which they had inherited from earlier times, in order to push off from it into their own *philosophical*, and as such post-mythological, conceptual thought), Saban twists into a support for his thesis of the equiprimordiality of true and false story in myth as such, even in Homer. What in truth is an earlier/later difference is translated into an *eternal* co-existence and co-dependence.[18] We witness here a withdrawal from history (in the sense of "subsequent moments in a linear/ historical movement of soul") into the higher spheres of atemporality and the generality of principles.

18 Yes, indeed: ". . . even in the earliest Greek discourse about myth" myth does mean "false story." Precisely: Because it is *discourse about* myth, the critical reflections by philosophers about myth. So we are here already in the situation of the Two (1. the meta-level discourse and 2. the phenomenon of myth as what this discourse is about). But the mythic stories themselves do not present themselves as "false stories". They claim to be fundamentally true stories. *Mythos*, we learn from Walter F. Otto, meant linguistically, in contradistinction to other Greek words for "narration" (such as "logos"), "the true word", where truth does not mean dogmatically claimed truth, but something that cannot be questioned at all, *absolutely* true: Freed (absolved) from, or *preceding*, the opposition between truth and falsehood (W.F. Otto, "Der Mythos", in: *Mythos und Welt*, Darmstadt: Wissenschaftliche Buchgesellschaft, 1963, p. 268). I mentioned that *mythos* was unchallenged by critical notions such as "superstition" and by having to compete with science and belief-systems, indeed, that it was similarly unquestionable as one's mother tongue. This similarity underlines once more why the idea of "false story" is totally misplaced. And, conversely, we have to say that the moment when it had become possible to view *mythos* as "false story", *mythos* no longer existed. It had lost that *constitutive* self-evidence and inescapability that it once shared with language, a self-evidence and inescapability that language in contrast to myth was able to retain up to the 20th century (and for most ordinary people [and in everyday contexts anyway] even until today).

In another paper, I had once analyzed the 20th century phenomenon of the experience and idea of disenchantment as one that within itself is the opening up of the opposition of enchantment and disenchantment. Saban quotes this analysis and takes it as a model of or justification for his idea that the "step into logos" (which he unconvincingly locates already in Homer and claims is inherent in myth as such) amounts to "the simultaneous generation of mythos, as a kind of inevitable supplement"—just as if the myths told in Homer had been generated, created by Homer and were not much rather taken from a much older stock of stories and used for his own purposes within his own epics! The real step into logos was, however, taken not any earlier than by the early Greek philosophers. Applying Saban's just mentioned principle to those thinkers, it would mean that their reflection and critical rejection of myth within itself generated that myth in the first place as a supplement, a supplement that they then critiqued. Absurd. They reacted ("re-flection"!) to a given, to stories they had inherited from an ancient tradition, not only poetic-literary tradition (Homer et al.), but also a tradition of popular religious belief and practice. The relation between the mythic stories and their critique by logos is clearly one of "subsequent moments". Again, we see this tendency to hover above history.

This takes me to a third point. Saban states in his second forum post to me that

> . . . for you it does seem to matter whether it [the creation myth which is at the centre of your 'Killings' paper] is 'historically true' or not. . . . For me it requires no further evidence from outside itself to function as an illuminating psychological fable. It already has everything it needs.

I would never speak of "historically true" in the sense of literal history and literal facts, since I am fully aware of the fact that my thesis in the "Killings" paper is *my* version (*my* analysis and interpretation, and in this sense perhaps also my "fable") of the logic of what happens within the phenomenon of archaic sacrificial killings, *my* view of how the soul "killed itself into being". However, I protest against the idea that as a "psychological fable" it has everything it needs within itself. I protest against the abuse of this alchemical insight. What has everything it needs within itself is much rather the prime matter, the dream image, the specific pathology, the myth, the psychological phenomenon, but not our *opus* performed upon it, not our interpretation of it, not the story we tell about it.[19] Only when such stories told by us about it in turn at a later date should perhaps become the prime matter for a new opus, a new psychological interpretation, only then do they already have everything they need. Because *then* (in and for this new psychological reflection) they are no longer stories *we* tell, but a given prime matter.[20]

For me it is indispensable that what I say is about a real matter, is in touch with something outside of me, with a substance—here, in the case of archaic sacrificial slaughterings, with the best knowledge available to

19 This is also why stories *we* tell are never myths, simply on account of their logical form. A myth and, to a lesser degree, a dream, an archetypal vision, are characterized by the fact that it is inherent in their logical constitution that they do not come as our speaking, but come to us as the soul's speaking. We can only listen to them. Jung: "It has a say now, not you." "Say it again, as best you can."

20 If what *we* said can nevertheless for a later opus become a genuine *prima materia*, and if the shift from One to Two has to be understood as happening repeatedly, always as something radically new (rather than an idle repetition), one sees that in psychology a fluidity of thought is needed in contrast to a tough-minded literalism that thinks that it is in the *nature* of a matter per se to be either this or that. In reality it depends only on the methodological perspective. This has momentous consequences. When Jung, for example, said that, "in any psychological discussion we are not making statements *about* the psyche, but the psyche is inevitably expressing itself" (*CW* 9i § 483, transl. modif.), he was already *in psychology* and apperceived those "psychological discussions" from a truly psychological point of view. But the same psychological discussions, even the work of Jung himself, can also be studied as *the human author's theorizing* and thus not as psychological phenomena (that have everything they need within themselves and are self-referential), but much rather as human opinions or statements *about*, e.g., the psyche, statements for which the author has to *personally* stand up. Only in the second case, only when we see each other as *colleagues* and as developing our theories about the soul and thus on the human level, can there be a debate and can the statements, e.g., be criticized as unconvincing or false, whereas when apperceived psychologically, as psychological phenomena (which becomes possible once they have become *historical* for us), those same human statements have to be taken the way they are, just as if they were dreams (in the sense of "What the dream, which is not manufactured by us, says is *just so*" and ". . . the dream itself, which we cannot criticize . . ."). It is not that certain statements are human statements and certain other ones are the soul's speaking about itself. And it will not do either, in order to avoid one's acting out such a tough-minded literalism, to have recourse to the idea of "ambivalence", in which case one's tough-mindedness is not overcome. Pictorially speaking: The trembling in Parkinson's disease is not the opposite of rigidity.

date about early prehistory. How else could it be an interpretation? I am concerned with the soul in the Real—with the *stone* that is not a stone—not with my own self-sufficient fictions or fables.[21] My account has an "about" outside itself. I have and feel a responsibility towards the *given* matter that I am dealing with, towards real phenomena: Real patients, symptoms, dreams, fairy tales, myths, cultural phenomena, historical developments, etc. Psychology is not in the business of creating and inventing "illumining psychological fables". It is in the business of being responsive to a prime matter (whatever this may be in each case), of *reflecting* and *refining* it, of *reconstructing* its inner logical life so as to release it into *its* truth (*its* disclosedness). *Quod Natura relinquit imperfectum ars perficit.* Reflection after the fact, not production.[22] The perfect tense. The owl of Minerva. The psychologist is never self-sufficient. Like the alchemist he is the one half of the "adept-alchemical vessel" *relation.*

With his view that my thesis about sacrifices "already has everything it needs", Saban severs the soul's ties to reality. With it he goes up into the air.

21 This is a fundamental difference between my theory of sacrifices and René Girard's (both of which are for Saban "a fantasy, a myth" in the same sense and on the same level). But Girard indeed offered what was *his own fantasy* of the *origin* of sacrificial rituals, *postulating* mimetic rivalry and a scapegoat mechanism, two factors which are precisely not *in* the *phenomenon* of sacrifices itself. They are his addition to the phenomenon, his postulates or constructs. By contrast, much like Jung said (thereby at the same time incidentally marking the fundamental difference between a naturalistic and the truly psychological approach), "I don't teach how neuroses come about, but what one finds in neuroses" (*Letters 2*, p. 293, to Jolande Jacobi, 13 March 1956, transl. modif.), so I analogously don't try to explain the causal origin of sacrifices at all, but, conversely, describe sacrifice *as* origin (of soul and culture); I don't identify or invent any causal factors that led to sacrifices, but merely reconstruct the internal logic of sacrificial killings on the basis of the main observable features of this phenomenon. I said that my "Killings" paper was my interpretation. Again, let me stress, there is a difference between interpretation and positing a fantasy.

22 When Saban says "For me it requires no further evidence from outside" he turns the real sequence around. There is for me not first a theory or "fable" in the subjective mind that thereafter needs to be bolstered up by evidence from outside. It's the other way around. I begin with the, e.g., historical material as my prime matter. This reversal of the sequence is consistent with and supportive of Saban's denial of the shift "from *mythos* to *logos*" and from the One to Two. For him there is nothing, must not be anything, that precedes philosophical reflection as the reflection's own given prime matter. (But: Reflection is for him, *naturalistically correct*, preceded by "unprethinkable being.")

His psychology's "soul" then hovers in the clouds, in its own bubble. The soul that his psychology advocates is a disembodied soul, uprooted, a soul content with a kind of free-floating, "l'art pour l'art"-type fables. It is *anima alba*.

Saban is very clear about it. He says: "History is, after all, a fable, invented by moderns, and it is just as mythological as any other myth. History doesn't exist outside of the stories we tell . . .". This sounds very advanced, very critical, very post-modern, but it is unacceptable. A perfect self-encasement in a bubble. And in my view also a total missing the point of history in modernity, that is, missing its *psychological significance*. No doubt, Saban is perfectly right to negate the naive positivistic belief in history as literal facts ("how it really was"[23]). Even those alleged facts are, as a matter of course, always already *seen* by us in a certain light, always already part of our accounts. But to say that history does not exist outside of the stories we tell, that history *itself* is a fable and a modern invention is reductive, Saban's not seeing the forest for the trees.

With his negation he only negates *his own* naive standpoint, believing that merely by dissolving history into the stories we tell, into fictionality, he has already escaped the naivety of positivism. But in reality this fictionalism is only the obverse of that naivety, and in no way gets beyond the naive thought structure. What is missing is the negation of that primitive negation of his, that type of negation that Jung, for example, performed when he rejected free association and the stories *we* tell altogether and *thereby* penetrated to the notion of the *objective* soul. Instead of having escaped from the naivety of positivism, Saban in truth merely escaped from the insight into the psychological difference and into the *reality* of the *objective* soul.

"History" and the modern soul's having come down to earth

Within the context of systems theory, Niklas Luhmann made the following illumining point. He said that as soon as in history

> it becomes evident that already during one single life span [. . .] almost everything essential changes, then the difference of past and future (which

---

23 Leopold von Ranke, Preface to *Geschichten der romanischen und germanischen Völker* (1824), third edition, Leipzig: Juncker & Humblot, 1885, p. vii.

of course had also already been known before) enters into the position of a guiding difference for the understanding of time and here replaces the distinction between ever-present eternity and time. The consequence of this is that the present is defined by the difference of past and future, that is, that it turns into a now-point of time (that it previously had only been on the level of the temporality of *events*), a now-point of time that "between" past and future makes possible the constant switching from the one time horizon to the other, but is *not itself time*. [. . .] With this, the present turns itself into the paradoxy of time: into the unity of the difference of past and future, into the third excluded by it, but included within it, into the time in which *one does not have time*.[24]

"History" as such certainly arose in modernity, not earlier.[25] Here I agree with Saban. But it was not *invented* by moderns. History is not just the stories we tell. It exists "outside" them in the objective soul, indeed *as* the *modern* objective soul, namely, as the "difference of past and future",[26] the moment when this difference has become the new *guiding difference* for the understanding of time. The former guiding difference used to determine the understanding of time since time immemorial, from the oldest ritualistic and mythological cultures onwards through the age of Christianity and Metaphysics (in other words: This old vertical difference even survived the shift from *mythos* to *logos*, as well as the later shifts within the age of metaphysics). The world-shaking shift from this old *vertical* guiding difference—the difference of ever-present eternity versus the temporal, the *saeculum*—to the new *horizontal*, that is, *itself temporal* guiding difference along the time-line, occurred during the 19th century and represents one essential aspect of what I called "the birth of man". Because with this strictly temporal, secular

---

24 Niklas Luhmann, *Die Wissenschaft der Gesellschaft*, Frankfurt a. M.: Suhrkamp, 1992 (1st edn. 1990), p. 613 (my italics, my translation).

25 Of course, the Greeks had already numerous historians, and the Hebrew Bible likewise contains historical books. But this was hi*story* as story, as a narration on what Luhmann called "the level of the temporality of events" (*Die Wissenschaft der Gesellschaft*, Frankfurt/Main: Suhrkamp, 1992, p. 613). It did not mean that already then the *guiding difference* for the understanding of time had been the difference of past and future, which is constitutive for history in the modern sense.

26 This is, as it were, the definition of the historical, linear sense of time.

understanding of time, man has logically, psychologically, fully come into the world, the *saeculum*. He has really come down to earth.[27]

This shift is not just a fable. And its result, history (history in the sense of the "forest", not the "trees" = the historical events or our stories about the events), is a psychological *reality*, our psychological reality, part of the objective soul. It is a power, and it exists outside the specific historical stories we tell, which are always up for revision. It is the reason why we tell, have to tell, historical stories. We all are keenly familiar with that time in which one does not have time, the time experienced as *stress*. We inevitably think in terms of past and future. We cannot help it. We have to think historically. And we cannot really (as, during 18 centuries before, people certainly were able to) think anymore in terms of the Bible Stories about God's creation and salvation work as ever-present origin, on the one hand, and merely-temporal events here on earth, on the other. Not even fundamentalist creationists can *really* do this without some kind of self-induced brainwashing. We think in terms of Darwinian evolution and see ourselves and the human organism as a result of evolution. We explain our psychic conditions in terms of our personal childhood history. We have archeology, museums, the concept of the world's cultural heritage that needs to be conserved. We restore old historical buildings (rather than using their stones as building bricks for our own construction of new buildings). In certain types of psychotherapy we look back to Greek myths for meaning.

Darwinian evolution is of course a *story* or, if you wish, "fable". But regardless of the entire question whether this story is factually correct or not and whether it is an "illumining fable" or not, the historical point of view and the dependence of it on evidence is in any case a psychological truth, a reality of the modern soul, a "factor" in Jung's sense.

---

27 Here one can see that my metaphor of the birth of man has a concrete descriptive quality, rather than telling a new "story", a "myth of lost oneness, of having fallen into twoness". I psychologically interpret a specific identifiable historical *phenomenon*. This fundamental shift is also a good example for the succession of stages of consciousness. The new guiding difference is not *added* to the old (the way Saban likes to view things), but, as Luhmann says, *replaces* it, thus irreversibly rendering the former one obsolete.

What Saban aims for with his thesis of history as nothing more than our stories is ultimately the dissolution of historical time into space (spatial extendedness, juxtaposition). It is, as it were, the story-book idea of history: All kinds of different "myths" spatially side by side on the same level. In the imagination, all stories and images are simultaneous. And as such this theory is the undoing of historical time as successive sequence of moments and as development altogether.

But the *psychological* function and meaning of history is precisely that through the *ritual* of our historical *dating* of the events we talk about and our thereby *positioning* also ourselves at some specific place on the time-line, the soul localizes and firmly moors itself in the *temporal* world as such, in the *saeculum*, that is, down here on the real earth, and ipso facto cuts its ties that used to connect it with ever-present eternity. Each time we try to give an account of some historical event we logically *attach* ourselves anew to something empirically real (in the psychological sense of empirically real), and thus *root* ourselves in the Real. As finite and "civilian man", *unborn* man too had as a matter of course his place down here in earthly reality. *Psychologically*, however, he, that is, his soul, lived in the *illud tempus* of myth, in *that* heavenly, metaphysical time that "never was, but always is" (Sallustios, modified), in ever-present eternity, which as ever-present was Time *as* atemporal space. The soul of modern born man can no longer be content with *psychologically* living in that ever-present eternity. It insists on also psychologically or "metaphysically" coming down to earth and grounding itself in temporality.

To that space of the metaphysical Time that never was, but always is, Saban cannot, and probably even does not want to, return. It lies irretrievably behind us. But, so it seems, he tries to establish his psychology (and thus also himself *as* psychologist) in an emaciated abstract modern version of it. By rejecting the idea of history as directional process in favor of mere replacements of stories, he dissolves history into a *fundamentally homogenized* sphere. No successive stages. For stories fundamentally co-exist in the same spatial and atemporal sphere of the imagination. Saban still *calls* the stories myths, but they are now in reality nothing but "(more or less) illumining fables", self-contained and self-sufficient two-dimensional *narratives*. Qua narratives they exist high above the Real in the free-floating bubble of their own timelessness and fictionality.[28] What makes *these* narratives two-dimensional and fictional and turns them, in contrast to myth proper, into *mere* narratives without soul dignity is that, to be sure, they are, much like myth, about "what never was", but (a) precisely neither tell us anymore "what always *is*", nor do they (b), following the modern soul's need, aim at and tie themselves to what is "historically true".

But the soul's move into temporality involves more than our necessity to think historically, to base our stories on historical evidence[29] and to revise them whenever new evidence comes to light or a new assessment of the old evidence becomes necessary. What it in addition means is that "what always *is*", the mythic-imaginal and metaphysical *substance* itself (in short: The "archetypal" objective soul) has come down to earth into the sphere of the historical. The religious or metaphysical treasures that the soul of former ages possessed have ceased being for the soul of modernity an immediate *present reality*, ceased being *ever-present* eternity (accessible, above all, through initiations or personal faith). These treasures are now a *historical*

28 The theoretical withdrawal from the temporal world into the sphere of fictionality might perhaps also explain the strange fact that Saban had to construe the word "commitment" abstractly as absolute (he speaks, for example, of his "stubborn inability (unwillingness) to 'commit'") and to give to it an existential(ist) meaning. Since he is, as a *theoretician* (I am not speaking about him as person), in this atemporal sphere, the word commitment seems to have instinctively suggested to him the imposition to have to give up his position in the heights of the realm of stories and to come down into the temporal world. As a fundamental plunge from one theoretical *level* to another, "commitment" does not refer to an object. It means "commitment per se", simply having to give himself (as theoretical consciousness) over to the *saeculum*, the historical world, and thus it does have an existential aspect. By contrast, for a theorizing consciousness that from the outset has its place in temporal-historical reality and therefore is concerned with the real phenomena presenting themselves to it, the word "commitment" would immediately suggest a practical and perfectly unspectacular commitment *to this or that*. Similarly, Saban's absolute construal and hypostatization of "the dialectic" is one that is pictorially imagined from high above and outside, whereas for a theorizing consciousness that dwells with the phenomena in the sphere of the secular world, "the dialectic" is as a matter of course always the specific dialectic *of* and *in* this or that. Also "the other" is absolutized in his discourse. It is an abstraction and functions as the fiction of "the other per se", "the remnant per se", "alterity as such". For me such an abstract other does not exist. There are only concrete, specific others in the plural and in their eachness, as well as "my own other", "this reality's other", "the soul's other". "*Tout autre est tout autre*" (Derrida)!

29 That is, let them be *interpretations of* something real.

presence, a presence in Mnemosyne, presence mediated through the ample treasury of what is already given to us in the a priori *distanced* and *reflected* form of *texts* or cultural *works* by our *historical* tradition ("historical" in contrast to the mythological, religious, or metaphysical traditions, which were precisely the traditions *of* the ever-present eternity as present reality[30]). "Texts and works" means: Something to be studied in the spirit of critical scholarship, such as the ancient myths, symbols, and fairy tales, the gospel of John, the letters of Paul, the precious works of art, the texts of Homer, Sophocles, Dante, Cervantes, Shakespeare, as well as Heraclitus, Plato, Aristotle, Meister Eckhart, Descartes, Hegel, Nietzsche, to arbitrarily select a few names from an endless list.

The modern soul does not want an *immediate* presence, an immediate reality of this presence, a *direct* access to eternity. It demands of us to *acquire*, as fully *conscious, enlightened mind*, a presence of the eternal or infinite, to *make* it present, through our own conscious laborious learning and study of texts, through our devoted penetration—with all the power of thought and the depth of passionate commitment available to us—into the inner infinity and truth accessible in the (*historically* present) treasures of the past. *Opus.* Soul-*making*.

Jung was fully aware of the soul's move down from the heights of heaven and ever-present eternity. He realized full well that the spirit "has descended from its fiery heights" (*CW* 9/I § 32) and become heavy, that we live in "an age in which the spirit [is] no longer up above but down below, no longer fire, but water" (*CW* 9/I § 50). He understood that "the stars have fallen from heaven" (*CW* 9/I § 50). However, intruding into his insights with his subjective desire, he nevertheless kept insisting on immediacy. He wanted the individual's *Urerfahrung*, primordial experience, as a new present reality. "I must have a situation in which that thing becomes true once more" (*CW* 18 § 632). And so he came up with a compromise formation, with something that, on the one hand, was an ever-present eternity, one which, however, on the other hand, was no longer above but below: As the collective unconscious. The archetypes of the collective unconscious, *they* are nothing else but those same former stars that have fallen from heaven, that

---

30 The difference can easily be illustrated with an example: The Bible as Holy Scripture, as the Word of God, on the one hand, versus the Bible as a historical record, a psychological document, on the other.

allegedly, however, even after this fall nevertheless still "hold[-] sway", even if now "as a secret life" "in the unconscious"—as "spirit that has become *nature*" (*CW* 9/I § 50, my italics).

Nature, living water, immediate primordial experience. This is what Jung was committed to. He would have laughed at the now fashionable idea of narratives, "the stories we tell".

However, what Jung was not ready to allow was that the fall of the stars was, instead of a change from spirit to nature, precisely a move from directly experienced spirit to *historical* heritage, to text and letter, to what is not a priori alive, but what can come alive only through our studying, the *work* of our reading, thinking, and understanding. Over against the spirit that has become nature, over against the living water holding sway in the collective unconscious, over against *experience* and "revelations" coming from the unconscious, Jung slighted the historical cultural heritage:

> In the end we dig up the wisdom of all ages and peoples, only to find that everything most dear and precious to us has already been said in the most superb language. Like greedy children we stretch out our hands and think that, if only we could grasp it, we would possess it too. But what we possess is no longer valid, and our hands grow weary from the grasping . . .
>
> (*CW* 9i § 31)

The problem with this last idea is of course that to Jung only a (metaphorically) literal "grasping with the hands" seemed to be conceivable (which is due to his insistence on immediacy). But there is also a very different kind of grasping. And this is why I say: It is precisely to the *dead letters* of the texts and art works of our historical heritage that we have to bring to bear Faust's insight: "The spirit world is not barred shut; / Your mind is closed, your heart is dead! / Up, adept, bathe without reserve / Your earthly breast in aurora's blush." The texts have everything they need within themselves.

History as a psychological reality must be distinguished from all the specific historical stories we tell about particular events or developments. I mentioned the difference between the forest and the trees. History conceived as nothing more than the stories we tell (or, more naively, the events about which these stories go) has nominalistically been reduced to the visible semantics of it, the empirically existing historical accounts. History as such, however, the *logic* or *syntax* of history, that is, the importance *for the modern soul* of "historicism" as the *commitment* and obedience to the (I admitted) "fiction" of historical truth and thus to documented evidence, has then been excised—and along with it the soul's logically, psychologically irrevocably rooting itself in the world as the Temporal.

The fact that all our historical accounts are incomplete, that they always are *our* interpretations, *our* stories, even our "fables", rather than "the literal truth", the fact, furthermore, that "historical truth" is only an idea or ideal and never a fact,[31] is *psychologically* neither here nor there. It belongs to the empirical foreground, to the sphere of "the ego", so to speak. It does not detract in any way from the reality and significance of *history itself* as a soul need and a modern psychological acquisition. Psychological reality is absolute, that is, absolved (freed) from the opposition of fact and idea/ideal. History is a modern acquisition, not because the moderns allegedly invented it, but because in modernity "the soul" definitively descended from the heavenly height of the mythological and metaphysical spheres of the *illud tempus* and ever-present eternity and began to feel the need to immerse itself in the Temporal.

Brute, unassimilable alterity

The first thing to turn to under this new heading is the idea of "unprethinkable being". And although this phrase is taken from Schelling, we have to keep in mind that we are speaking as psychologists and not as philosophers. What the term may mean in Schelling and what its philosophical legitimacy, as well as the legitimacy of Schelling's arguments against Hegel, may or may not be within his own philosophy is of no concern for us. Saban shows himself impressed by this phrase, but he does not in any way show that his discourse is on the level of philosophical thought, of real *thinking*. He merely expresses his own views and argues for them. Schelling, by contrast, truly *thought*. He was one of the great thinkers, and he deserves to be respected as such, which means that we must not bring phrases taken from his works down to our commonplace level discourse. The same applies to Hegel. This is also why I never considered or presented myself as a Hegelian, all the less so since I think it is impossible today to return to

---

31 Cf. Jung's statement that "The goal is important only as an idea; the essential thing is the *opus* which leads to the goal . . ." (*CW* 16 § 400).

Hegel's (or Schelling's) philosophy. It lies irretrievably behind us moderns, which, however, does not mean, that we cannot learn a lot from Hegel and that *studying* his philosophy could not be indispensable for anybody who wants to make sense of our present reality. I have gratefully learned a few things from Hegel, but I have always only spoken as a psychologist and on my own responsibility.

Psychology must not base itself on a philosophy, i.e., on some other, but autonomously on nothing but its own concept: Psychology as the logos of the soul.

Having said this it is clear that I will take issue with "unprethinkable being" *only* insofar as it is an idea that comes up in Saban's psychological text. Then I can say that it does not make sense to me. As pointed out earlier, "being" is a word, a concept, the mind's own property. The notion of "being" is a product of reflective thought and itself an expression of reflective thought. There is no place anywhere in the empirical world where you could find "being". The concept "being" does not have a referent in outer reality. It is a category, not itself a being or entity. So how can it be unprethinkable? How can it be "outside logos"? As a product of the mind and as its own category it is itself a manifestation of logos. When Saban presents a paper, when he writes his texts, he is practicing reflection. How does he get, inside his reflections, to something outside of reflection *when* what he is referring to is not given to us from outside, by the senses and empirical experience, but is reflection's own product? With this idea Saban *thinks* himself outside of thought. Thought does have the capacity to think itself outside of itself. But it nevertheless is still thought.

Furthermore, can there, *for psychology*, be anything "outside logos"? Logos here does obviously not have the narrow meaning of the word (explicit reflection, philosophical, conceptual thought) that is used when we speak of "from *mythos* to *logos*". In that narrow sense, *mythos*, e.g., would of course (by definition) precede *logos* and in this sense be outside of it. What is meant here, however, is much rather logos in the comprehensive sense, the world of shared meanings, the mind as such, the soul's logical life. Since the only topic and object of psychology is the soul or mind (and not the physical organism, nature, positive facts), since it is human experience, human ideas, images, feelings, thought (all of which have inevitably logos-nature), the question arises: How can there possibly be something outside logos for psychology? It would be a contradiction in terms.

For psychology the question of the concept of the "unprethinkable" is a methodological and not an ontological one (not one of "fact"). It is constitutive for psychology that it apperceives the phenomena that become its subject matter exclusively as the soul's speaking about itself, as motifs, statements, ideas, meanings, existing beliefs, and documents of the soul, while systematically and on principle leaving out of consideration the naturalistic question of whatever efficient causes that may have produced, and whatever possible substrates that may be the underlying carriers of, the *psychological* phenomena (i.e., phenomena apperceived in the mode just described). I quoted Jung's, "I don't teach how neuroses come about, but what one finds in neuroses" (*Letters 2*, p. 293, to Jolande Jacobi, 13 March 1956, transl. modif.). This means that neurosis itself as the thought (*arrangement*, *mise-en-scène*) that it is—i.e., neurosis as a self—is what psychology has to take into its purview, not what lies outside of or precedes this thought or is the natural(istically imagined), positive-factual precondition of its possibility. About a religious idea Jung said, "*I am concerned with the statement only*, and I am interested in its structure and behaviour" (*Letters 2*, p. 570, to Robert C. Smith, 29 June 1960), that is, concerned with the statement as a self and interested in its internal logic and functioning.

What is really outside logos is outside of human experience and ipso facto beyond (external to) psychology. What we don't experience, what we don't know, feel, sense, have an idea, image, or hunch of, simply does not exist for us. But the moment something does exist for us, it is ipso facto irrevocably already thought, captured in linguistic, logical form, even if it may be utterly vague, nebulous, and puzzling. The faintest odor, the slightest hunch, the most vague impression that "there was something", even the idea that there was *nothing*, all happen in logos, where else? Here we may also remember Jung's statement that "We are in truth so wrapped about by psychic images that we cannot penetrate at all to the essence of things external to ourselves" (*CW* 8 § 680). Our envelopment in psychic images, and this means in logos, is inescapable. No exit—as long as we exist as soul and mind. Even the very fiction *of* something outside of logos is a logos fiction, and what is allegedly "unassimilable" has ipso facto already been assimilated, namely *as* something unassimilable (which is a logos concept and not an empirical fact or external referent), because if it had *not been assimilated at all* there would simply be a blank, that is to say, not even the awareness of something unassimilable, not even the feeling of anything having been missed.

An example might be the bacteria that caused the plague. It is to be assumed that naturalistically speaking these bacteria caused this illness even during the Middle Ages when they were not known. But this is our perspective. For medieval man, however, the bacteria simply did not exist at all because he had not even the vaguest concept of such a thing as bacteria. There was no "remnant", nothing unassimilable. The very possibility of suspecting something like bacteria or viruses as the actual pathogen did not exist, was simply absent (and can only be called "absent" from our modern perspective). Medieval man therefore looked for the cause of the plague on a completely different (a "macro") level, for example, the religious and moral level of God's punishment for people's sin, or on a social level as the evil doings of Jews, etc., and in this or some other way *assimilated* the frightening appearance of the plague.

On the other hand, what is this constant harping on about "the other", about "brute, unassimilable alterity", "the remainder", and "the ungraspable", polemicizing against? And what does it have to offer in its own right? The enemy seems to be the mind's fantasy of a theory that purports to present an absolutely watertight totalitarian rationalistic account of everything, an account that altogether excludes surprise, mystery, unsolved questions, infinity, etc. But such a fantasy is just as childish as it is absurd. And because it is so absurd, I also find it silly to feel the need to object to it, as Saban does by insisting on brute alterity. Anyone working as a psychotherapist finds himself time and again confronted with surprising phenomena, with puzzling dream images, patients' symptoms, and life situations. Does a therapist's dialectically trained mind eliminate all question? Are for it the dreams or myths to be worked with "sublated into sameness" "without remainder"? And as to Hegel, although he is really *not* our topic here—did he claim to be able to deduce "Klug's writing quill"? Did he get rid of surprises, the accidental? Did he dissolve mystery and infinity into thin air (or, worse, into dry rational formulas)?

It is a triviality that for us, for the finite mind, much remains unknown, uncomprehended, and that we bump into surprises. So why this whole fuss about "the other" and "the remainder"? What's new with those ideas (apart from this fuss and the fetishization of them)?

But all I have said so far about this is only a rejoinder on the level of external reflections. Much more central is the fact that the process of real thought leading to the uncovering of the dialectic of things is *in itself* full of surprises, a real adventure. Was it not surprising what emerged when above, rather than reducing it to a sealed mantra, we read *thinkingly* Jung's dream interpretation maxim about not letting anything in that does not belong? The false dichotomy between Saban's "alternative" leading to surprises and the dialectical approach obviously viewed by him as a mechanical routine that only leads to foreseen results bears witness to a mind that never let himself in for real thought and never experienced the excitement brought by the discoveries possible on the path of veritable *thinking*.

The devotion with which Saban speaks about, and permanently insists on, "unassimilable alterity" sounds as if he considered our all too often manifested human incapability to assimilate or grasp something particular a virtue, and "the remainder" a precious treasure, and "the gap between" an "infinite Other" and an "assimilable same" as something that at all cost needs to be cultivated. Pascal wrote, "Man is obviously created for thinking. This is his entire dignity and all his merit; and it is his whole duty to think correctly".[32] For Jung, too, "man has the gift of thought that can apply itself to the highest things". And he wondered, for example, "whether it is not much more dangerous for the Christian symbols to be made inaccessible to conceptual thought and to be banished to a sphere of unreachable unintelligibility" (*CW* 11 § 170, transl. modif.). Saban's highest goal is precisely to make a certain region (or whatever it may be) *by definition* inaccessible to conceptual thought, to banish it to a sphere of unreachable unintelligibility.

In the light of the fact that Saban disapproves of our "picking and choosing the bits of Jung we like and rejecting the bits we don't like" and wants "to read him as a whole", it is utterly astounding that he does not see that his own insistence on brute alterity is absolutely counter to the main line of Jung's thinking and his deepest concern. Jung is anything but a thinker of the totally unassimilable, of the fundamental gap mentioned, of brute alterity. Here I insert just a few key phrases and ideas of his as a mere list:

- *Mysterium coniunctionis.*

- "The connection between 'humans and gods.'"

- The Relation Between the Ego and the Unconscious.

- Jung's story of the Pueblo Indians who help their *father*, the sun, to travel across the sky.

---

32 Blaise Pascal, *Pensées*, ed. Léon Brunschvicg, Paris: Librairie Hachette, 1904, #146, my transl., cf. #365.

- The conception of the other not as brute Other, but precisely as "the Self"! The soul's *own* other.

- Jung's bank employee who shows his friend "*his* bank" (which in an illumining way contrasts with the exclusive otherness that exists, in the Marxists' scheme, between the proletariat and the capitalists).

- Jung's "spectrum" metaphor used to highlight the unbroken connection between instinct/affect/emotion, on the one hand, and image/thought, on the other.

- God as "one of the most natural products of our mental life [1. product, 2. our mental life!], as the birds sing, as the wind whistles, like the thunder of the surf". (*Letters 2*, p. 253, to Snowdon, 7 May 1955)

- "That was the primal stuff which compelled me to work upon it, and my works are a more or less successful endeavor to incorporate this incandescent matter into the contemporary picture of the world" (*MDR* p. 199): Incorporation, integration, assimilation into logos. (As a deterrent to the idea of the brute unassimilability we might here also keep in mind that trauma, such as one caused by torture, is due to "the unassimilability" of the experience by the person to whom had it had happened.)

No, no bridge leads from a Lévinas-inspired Other back to Jung. Jung was not one of the so-called post-moderns, by no stretch of the imagination. Jung was committed to the preservation, or recovery, of the *metaphysical* mode of being-in-the-world, the logic of the copula, the logic of the alchemical ligamentum or vinculum. He circumambulated the center.[33] No, there is in Jung no artificial "forcing together" of "the apparently exclusive and contradictory ideas of myth on the one hand and individual experience on the other". Jung does not need such a *violence* in the joining together (*coniunctio*), because for him in the depth of the soul the bond between the opposites has not been broken at all. There is not for him the "disruptive

---

33 The center psychologically remains a full-fledged center even if for Jung it is not a literal one but merely an idea. For the soul an image, thought, idea, or ideal to which the soul happens to be seriously committed (cf. "is it *my* fable, *my* truth") is just as real as something factual.

relation" hailed by Saban, however much *empirically* at first the relation between the ego and the unconscious may be neurotically dissociated.[34]

The idea of a "brute, unassimilable alterity" can have a place only in a brutish, not really "human" (humanized), psychology.

My refusal to accept the idea of a "disruptive relation" for Jung does not mean that I exclude surprise and overwhelming experiences and the experience of a counter-will from his scheme. Not at all. My point is only that all this did not represent a fundamentally disruptive Other in his view, but on the contrary was conceived as what needed our "work upon it" in order to *integrate* it into consciousness.[35]

* * *

If we now ask what the psychological function of the fantasy of the radical Other and of "brute, unassimilable alterity" within the economy of Saban's scheme is we can say that it is the reification of consciousness's *stance* of aloofness itself, the semantic image into which the abstract *logic* of exteriority congealed. As such it functions also as the guardian and guarantor of this standpoint, of the principle of a fundamental difference, the unbridgeable gap as such. It is the literalization and fixation of the first negation, the negation as ontologized. If you have this radical Other in your theoretical scheme, it logically cements the ordinarily existing *naturalistic* position (based on the opposition of consciousness: subject–object) and protects you

---

34 It is interesting to note that concerning the opposites Saban insists on their objective, static *relation's* being disruptive, whereas he does his best to deny any *historical-temporal* discontinuities or ruptures, which play a crucial role in Jung's and my thinking. It was Jung who repeatedly emphasized the psychological importance of the idea contained in Nietzsche's "Then, suddenly, friend! One turned into Two / And Zarathustra passed me by. . . ."—of course, we must also remember that there is at times in Jung some sense of brute otherness, such as when he talks about a "collision of duties" or in the way how he imagined the immediate encounter with God as an overwhelming will. But these are semantic details in Jung's thinking merely referring to the *psychic, experiential* level that do not undo the basic psychological logic of his thinking about the *coniunctio oppositorum*. Much more serious in Jung is, however, the problem of a radical otherness and dissociation on the syntactical or structural level of the fundamental logic of his psychology, which, however, is not our topic here. It has to do with his concept of "*the* unconscious" and the split between the semantics and the syntactical form.

35 One way of integrating and assimilating for Jung is practical: Religion, the symbolic life ("Have you got a corner somewhere in your house where you perform the rites . . .?" *CW* 18 § 626; ". . . to serve a god is full of meaning and promise . . ." *CW* 13 § 55).

from the necessity to have to give yourself over to the phenomena at hand and to go under in what you study or work upon, in the prime matter in the hermetic vessel—to go under in that spirit that is expressed in Faust's already cited alchemical exhortation to himself (which *we* as moderns and psychologists should neither take literally, nor metaphysically, and also not existentially, but only *methodologically*): "The spirit world is not barred shut; / Your mind is closed, your heart is dead! / Up, adept, bathe without reserve / Your earthly breast in aurora's blush." Alchemy's immersion in the bath. Letting oneself *thinkingly* in for what manifests. This is my response to brute alterity.

The unassimilable Other is what remains (just think of "the remainder"!) of the Real when—at a time when the soul insists on uncompromisingly rooting itself in the temporal world, the *saeculum,* and when ipso facto the Real is *defined* as the temporal world—consciousness refuses to moor itself in the temporal by letting itself be bound by historical evidence, and when it instead prefers in its psychological scheme to stay in the higher sphere of so-called myth, of stories, self-sufficient narratives, that is, in the homogenized space of the imagination. The radical Other represents, as it were, the (residual) Real the way it appears from that psychological position that refused to get committedly involved in it, from out of that bubble into the aloofness of which the said mind withdrew. It is the utterly abstract, emaciated remainder of the Real, its zero-stage, completely non-descript—just "other" (whatever that may be), in other words, the ghost of the Real.

But qua ghost it is also mystified and overblown with significance ("fathomless alterity", "the endless excitement . . .", Saban's celebration of "the ungraspable", "the call of the other"). The "call of the other", which, as an *ethics,* is addressed to "civilian man", to the ego-personality, is, it seems to me, the mirror reflection, in the sphere of the ego-personality, of the unconscious memory of the fact that the soul's real move into its *real* other (the temporal world down here) has not simply been followed suit, not been accompanied, by consciousness. As such it is the return of the repressed. The *refusal* reappears as the fantasy of the *bruteness* of alterity,[36] the avoided

---

36 The notion of "brute alterity" reflects, and is in turn reflected in, the tough-mindedness of Saban's understanding referred to above: his tough-minded abstract understanding, for example, of Jung's dictum about the image that has everything it needs within itself, of Hegel, of the shift from One to Two, and of "the dialectics."

psychological entrance into the temporal world as the fantasy of an unending *ethical* call (an ought!), and the missed *phenomenal simpleness* and concreteness of the manifold phenomena of the historical world as the fantasy of the oversized, inflated, but abstract and vacuous "Other".

And finally, the fetishization or idolization of the Other that we sense in the emphatic feeling-tone of Saban's speaking about it shows that *psychologically* it is a God-term, God incognito, the rescued, but *nihilistic*, remnant or substitute of what once used to be God (*deus absconditus*). For Saban the brute, unassimilable alterity is absolutely unnegotiable. It is a supreme value. Through it the sacred, the untouchable, the absolute taboo enters through the back door. This new God is nihilistic, God's zero-stage, because nothing can be said about Him but that He is "other". Former gods had a specific story and concrete attributes: Creator, almighty, savior, our Father, the highest good, Spirit, Love, etc. This God is reduced to the naked, abstract concept of alterity and unassimilability.

Joseph Campbell spoke of "The Masks *of* God". "The Other" *is* God, but God as *nothing but* a mask. The ghost of God as a theoretical construct.

The wrong patron saint

The "alternative approach" that Saban wanted to offer was announced by him as one "informed by Schelling's philosophy of mythology". I already pointed out that I find it problematic to use certain phrases or ideas pulled out from the living *thought* and spirit of Schelling's philosophy and to make use of them in a very different, (a) no longer philosophical (*thinking*) discourse and (b) a discourse not really informed by the metaphysic of Schelling but by a decidedly anti-metaphysical post-modern thinking. There is in Saban's writing some obvious misrepresentation of Schelling's ideas.

In his attempt to defend "Jung's idea of the personal myth", Saban says that Jung discovered that "soul is to be found in the mythic conflict at the heart of the modern individual" and adds:

Here he is following Schelling who suggests that the modern individual is called to structure from this evolving (mythological) world, a world of which his own age can reveal to him only a part. I repeat: from this world he is to structure into a whole that particular part revealed to him, and to create from the content and substance of that world his mythology.

But when we look at this passage in the early Schelling's *Philosophy of Art* we find that the sentence subject of Schelling's statement was by no means "the modern individual" (neither "modern" in our sense,[37] nor "individual"[38]), but the "great poets". His examples are Dante, Shakespeare, Cervantes, and Goethe. And as befits a philosophy of art, he is not talking at all about the "soul" "to be found in the mythic conflict *at the heart of the modern individual*" but about works of art by great poets, in other words, about something essentially of public cultural significance. And Schelling is speaking about this in the context of a reflection about an envisioned distant future "when the *Weltgeist* itself will have completed the great Poem that it plans". For Schelling, "Jung's question, what is my myth, the myth by which I do live?" would not make any sense, nor would Saban's idea of a "shift from myth as collective phenomenon to myth as individual phenomenon". Schelling is precisely very much aware that the present is not a fulfilled present (which Jung's "by which I do live" implies), and he puts his hope on his vision of the *future*, a future fulfillment determined by the *Weltgeist* and precisely not the individual.

By the same token, the late Schelling's Positive Philosophy is a philosophy of religion whose system unfolds as historical succession of (1) natural (= mythology), (2) revealed (= Christianity), and (3) future philosophical (i.e., comprehended) religion. In Schelling we therefore find that very linear, one-way scheme of history that is so despised by Saban.[39] We find a history of subsequent stages of which the later ones overcome the earlier one(s). And on top of it there is in Schelling, with his hope for a final *comprehended* religion, the idea of a full *assimilation*, albeit only in the future, of religion (mythology and [Christian] revelation) into *logos*. In this regard, Schelling and Hegel are much closer together than suggested. The also existing disagreement between them has to be understood differently from the way that is intimated by Saban, namely in strictly philosophical terms. The same applies to Schelling's insistence on "unprethinkable being", which

---

37 See his examples; Dante is not exactly what *we* mean by "modern".

38 Explicitly and decidedly not (see, e.g., a few pages earlier the very beginning of the same § 42 of his *Philosophy of Art* from which Saban's Schelling-quote was taken).

39 Cf. also the passage from early Schelling's *Philosophy of Art* (*SW* vol. V, p. 424, my transl.): "Never has it been possible for the course of the old history to break off in such a way [and] to begin a truly new world, which with Christianity *has* in fact begun, without an apostasy permeating, as it were, the entire human race."

has to be seen in the light of his (to my mind: Titanic[40]) attempt to truly think philosophically "the real process [*Hergang*], a *free world creation*"![41]

Another problem I have concerns Saban's understanding of Schelling's "tautegorical" myth interpretation and his viewing *my* myth interpretation as "allegorical" because, so he claims, my interpretation conceives mythic images as expressive of "the notion" or "the dialectic".[42] But by these standards, Schelling's myth interpretation too would, even much more so than mine, have to be seen as *allegorical*, inasmuch as for Schelling "tautegoria" is the speaking about the same in different mythological systems! Schelling sees, for example, numerous diverse figures as actually representing Dionysos rather than themselves (cf. his famous dictum: "everything is Dionysos"[43]), and he viewed Dionysos, and along with him the stage of mythology as such, as a foreshadowing of Christ. Dionysos is in truth the Logos, who comes into his own through Dionysos's transformation into Christ. Mythology is for Schelling Dionysiology and ultimately the workings of

---

40 Cf. also his raising and wanting to answer the question, "Why is there something in the first place? Why is there not nothing?" (F.W.J. Schelling, *Sämtliche Werke*, Stuttgart-Augsburg: Cotta, 1856–61, vol. XIII, p. 7, my transl.).

41 F.W.J. Schelling, *Sämtliche Werke*, Stuttgart-Augsburg: Cotta, 1856–61, vol. XIII, p. 132, my emphasis, my transl.

42 He asks, "Is Giegerich really suggesting that all myths of all time from all cultures are nothing but imaginal representation of the dialectic? I do think this is not only an implausible idea but perhaps more importantly a depressingly dull one." A silly (dull) misconception. "*The* dialectic"? What is that supposed to be? Here we have again one of Saban's utter formal-logical abstractions. He reifies "the dialectic" as if it were a kind of entity, something in its own right, and always the same thing. But we are not hunting for "*the* dialectic" as our object of desire. We are trying to understand, e.g., *the myths* psychologically and in depth, each one on its own terms. His comment is as insightful as if a person would say that all the numerous biographies that exist are depressingly dull because they all are nothing but the representation of "the life". But they are of course the representation of the very different lives *of* all the different persons. I made it very clear in my writings that for me all the different myths are portrayals each of a different archetypal or soul truth, a different notion, a different moment within the whole spectrum of the soul's life. And each myth, as the imaginal portrayal of that particular soul truth that it is about, reveals itself *to a psychological in-depth understanding* as the narrative unfolding of the (again particular, concrete) inner dialectic *of* this one soul truth.

43 F.W.J. Schelling, *Sämtliche Werke*, Stuttgart-Augsburg: Cotta, 1856–61, p. 463f., my transl.

the Christian God incognito.[44] For Schelling, without the freedom reached through the transformation of Dionysos into Christ, man *remains entangled in the web of mythology and does not reach his goal* (which lies beyond mythology). Is Saban's pleading for "mythology-as-central-to-psychology" really "informed by Schelling's philosophy of mythology"?

But in both cases such interpretations have really nothing to do with allegorizing. Saban confuses here, I submit, a non-literal, seeing-through-type reading (be it philosophical or psychological), in Schelling's case a reading along the lines of "the masks of God", with an allegorical one. Saban could only view such readings as allegorical *if* "tautegorical" has shrunk for him into meaning the flatness of a literal, abstract formal-logical self-identity without internal depth and difference. Schelling's term "tautegorical" aimed at the rejection of, for example, the euhemerist-type of allegorical myth interpretations, of interpretations that reduce the mythic gods to something empirical or positive-factual, something other than the divine (such as stars, nature's growth and withering cycles, prehistoric great kings or heroes, etc.).

Schelling would have shuddered at Saban's ahistorical and wishy-washy concept of myth and his insistence on unassimilability, that is, unintelligibility. His whole work throughout his life was to make intelligible. He was firmly rooted in the stance of Christian metaphysics (although he certainly went to its utmost borders). And merely on account of a certain formal similarity to retroject a "post-modern" stance of unassimilable alterity unto him and into his ideas of "unprethinkable being" and "*Abgrund*" is doing him a great injustice.

To these my few points about Schelling let me here append a brief comment about Hölderlin's idea of an "eccentric path", because it shows again that it will not do to pick out individual phrases from a body of thought and insert them, without regard to the context and spirit of the whole work of the respective thinker, into one's own different thought. Žižek's description of the phrase (quoted by Saban in his paper) as implying a "permanent oscillation between the loss of the Center and the repeated failed attempts to regain the immediacy of the Center . . ." is un-Hölderlinian. Hölderlin's word *Bahn*, first of all, suggests from the outset a unidirectional path. An oscillation is out of the question. The word *Bahn* in German is used, for

---

44   F.W.J. Schelling, *Sämtliche Werke*, Stuttgart-Augsburg: Cotta, 1856–61, p. 333.

example, for the "orbit" of planets, for "railroad", *Autobahn*, for "trajectory", "racetrack", etc. Hölderlin describes the *exzentrische Bahn* as the only "way [. . .] from childhood to completion", from a "state of highest innocence [*Einfalt*]" to a "state of highest *Bildung* [cultural refinement]",[45] both in a historical (cultural) and a biographical (personal) sense. And it has been shown (Michael Franz[46]) that the course of this path follows a mathematical, geometric figure and that Hölderlin's whole conception of the "eccentric path" is inspired by complicated Platonic mathematical ideas (accessible to Hölderlin through the *Timaeus*, as well as through Proclus' commentaries to Euclid and Plato).[47] This is of course not the place to go into this in detail. May it suffice to point out that it is a spiral and in no way center-less.

* * *

After this lengthy exposition we are now ready to answer the question raised in the title of this paper. Saban's alternative is certainly an alternative, first, in an external, comparative sense, because it represents a fundamentally different scheme incompatible with a psychology as the discipline of interiority, and, secondly, in a definitional sense and thus doubly so because in itself, through what it is committed to, it is a scheme *of* brute alterity.

But it is not an alternative *to* psychology as the discipline of interiority, in the intrinsic sense of being a new option *for* it, or of being in competition *with* it, because in order to be that it would have to share a common ground on which to engage with it.

---

45 Friedrich Hölderlin, "Fragment von Hyperion", in: *Sämtliche Werke und Briefe*, ed. by Michael Knaupp, Darmstadt: Wissenschaftliche Buchgesellschaft, 1998, vol. 1, p. 489.
46 Michael Franz, "Hölderlins Platonismus. Das Weltbild der 'exzentrischen Bahn' in den Hyperion-Vorreden", in: *Allgemeine Zeitschrift für Philosophie* 22(2): 167–188 (1997).
47 "Eccentric" in Hölderlin's phrase harks back to the Greek expression for "radius": "The line (drawn) away from the center (*hê **ek toy kentroy** grammê*)."

Chapter 7

Two Jungs[1]

Apropos a paper by Mark Saban

An example of the "personal equation"

Mark Saban's paper "Another serious misunderstanding: Jung, Giegerich and a premature requiem" has the exclusive purpose of showing that my notion of psychology as the discipline of interiority and my view of soul as speaking about itself "finds no source in Jung's psychology, implicit or explicit".[2] I could counter that easily with (explicit!) quotes from Jung demonstrating the opposite, such as:

> In myths and fairytales, as in dreams, the soul speaks about itself, and the archetypes reveal themselves in their natural interplay, as "formation, transformation / the eternal Mind's eternal recreation".
>
> (*CW* 9i § 400, transl. modif.)

But throwing quotes at each other is a rather stupid game. Instead of asking who is right, who wrong, it may prove psychologically more profitable to follow Jung's example. In response to the early debates between Freud, Adler and Jung, Jung raised the problem of the clash of their divergent views about the same to a fundamentally higher level by introducing into psychology the idea of the "personal equation". The naive *intentio recta*, one's attempt to prove that a given statement about reality is objectively true or false, is replaced by a self-reflective interest in the role of the subject in the constitution of the object, and this not only in a

---

1 Written in 2012.
2 Mark Saban, "Another serious misunderstanding: Jung, Giegerich and a premature requiem", *Journal of Analytical Psychology*, Feb. 2015, 60, 94–113, p. 94.

DOI: 10.4324/9781003611417-7

transcendental-philosophical sense concerning consciousness-at-large, but in the specifically psychological sense of the question how the *individual personality* is reflected or expresses itself in a person's statements about the object. According to the notion of the personal equation, what Freud, Adler, or Jung say about psychic reality amounts to their respective "confessions", that is to say, it tells us at least as much, if not more, about those psychologists as about psychic reality. Already in 1797 Fichte had proposed, in connection with the analogous conflict prevalent at that time in philosophy between "dogmatism", on the one hand, and (Kantian) "criticism" or (transcendental) "idealism", on the other hand, that

> What type of philosophy one chooses depends on what kind of person one is: for a philosophical system is not a dead household good that one could put down or accept as we please, but it is animated by the soul of the person who has it.
>
> (My transl.)[3]

This may sound as if one choice were as good as the other. But with respect to "dogmatism" and "idealism" Fichte had pointed out (right after the passage cited) that these two do not lie side by side on the same level as simple alternatives. There is a difference in rank: Certain types of persons "will never *rise* to idealism", just as Schelling had stated a year or two earlier in a similar context that what system we choose depends on "the freedom of spirit that we have *gained* for ourselves" (italics mine). "Dogmatism", Fichte goes on to say, "is completely incapable of explaining what it needs to explain".[4] It is deficient because other than "idealism" it lacks the capability of reflecting the subject's involvement in its assertions about the world.

Be that as it may, Jung's insight about the personal equation means that the psychology we believe in and teach is reflective of the psychology we *have*, or better still: The psychology that we *are*, as which we exist.

3 Johann Gottlieb Fichte, *Erste Einleitung in die Wissenschaftslehre* (1797), Einleitung, section 5, in: *Johann Gottlieb Fichtes sämmtliche Werke*. Band 1, Berlin 1845/1846, p. 433.

4 Johann Gottlieb Fichte, *Erste Einleitung in die Wissenschaftslehre* (1797), Einleitung, section 5, in: *Johann Gottlieb Fichtes sämmtliche Werke*. Band 1, Berlin 1845/1846, p. 434.

It follows that in the way I read Jung I betray who I am or, as we say in German, *wes Geistes Kind* I am ("whose spirit's child" I am). And Saban's presentation of his interpretation of Jung is by the same token his self-display. His and my personal being determine in each case how much of, and how deeply, Jung can be understood. Like is only seen by like. Saban has *his* Jung, I have mine.

By way of a single example I now want to contrast Saban's and my reading of one and the same dictum of Jung's, namely, his quote from the Talmud that "the dream is its own interpretation" (Jung, e.g., *Letters 2*, p. 294, to Jolande Jacobi, 13 March 1956). I could also say that in this way I want to contrast his Jung and my Jung. Saban vehemently rejects my insistence that my interpretation of this Talmudic adage as meaning what it says (in the sense of the dream's self-referential nature and the soul's speaking about itself) derives from Jung. He lists four references to where the phrase "the dream is its own interpretation" occurs in Jung and points out that in three of them it is used "in the context of a comparison between his [Jung's] approach and that of Freud":

> Freud sees the meaning of the dream as disguised, and its interpretation as the uncovering of a latent meaning which not only hides behind, but is often radically different from (and not infrequently opposite to) the apparent meaning of the image. For Jung, on the other hand, interpretation is not an unveiling of what is hidden, but rather, as he puts it, a translation from one language into another, from the language of the unconscious to that of the conscious mind (Jung, 1935 § 172). The dream interpreter, according to Jung, needs therefore to "adopt the method of the philologist".[5]

This is Saban's Jung, a Jung, we should note, speaking at the Tavistock Clinic (Institute of *Medical* Psychology) to an audience of British clinicians, which means that he is both literally and psychologically on foreign soil. What turns this into Saban's Jung is the fact that for Saban Jung stops here. According to him, the Talmudic saying means *nothing but* Jung's rejection of free associations and his pleading instead for the method of the philologist who wants to decipher a difficult Sanskrit or cuneiform inscription.

---

5 Mark Saban, "Another serious misunderstanding: Jung, Giegerich and a premature requiem", *Journal of Analytical Psychology*, Feb. 2015, 60, 94–113, p. 97.

This Jung, and Saban with him, does not see any conflict between the idea of "translation *from* one language *into another*", on the one hand, and the idea expressed by the Talmudic adage about the dream interpreting *itself*, on the other. Inscriptions certainly do not interpret themselves. In this passage and context, the "wise word of the Talmud" sticks out like a sore thumb. It transcends and points beyond the horizon of the thinking otherwise prevalent in this passage.

I too am familiar with that Jung of the Tavistock Lectures, that Jung who tries to explain and defend his own psychological theory in front of common-sensical scientifically minded practitioners. But *my* Jung is characterized by the fact that he does not stop here. He goes beyond this and has more to say on the subject. To learn about this "more", let us turn to another one of the four Jung passages that Saban consulted to gain insight about Jung's understanding of the Talmudic dictum. This passage written many years later (13 March 1956) comes from *Letters* 2, p. 293f., and this time Jung is speaking (or writing) to an insider, one of his disciples, Jolande Jacobi. To be sure, here too the text begins with a rejection of the Freudian technique of dream interpretation. "I don't use free association at all . . .", Jung states categorically. So far Saban is right. But Jung goes on and ends his comments about this topic in this letter with a brief and very different hint about his way of working with dreams:

> In dream analysis I proceed on principle by circumambulating it, having regard to the wise Talmudic saying that the dream is its own interpretation.
>
> (Transl. modif.)

The *CW* translation's phrase, "in a circumambulatory fashion", is of course not wrong, but by rendering a German verb (participle), *zirkumambulierend*, by means of a noun phrase, an adjective subordinated to a substantive, the active sense of the word and the suggestion of the human subject's entering into a living motion gets more or less lost. Jung, according to this sentence, does not use a method of circumambulation. He circumambulates!

Circumambulation in dream work

As brief as the quoted statement is, it can tell us a lot. The first thing to be noted is that "circumambulate" is not a word of ordinary language and not part of the ordinary modern world. Nor do I think that it has ever been

used by philologists deciphering inscriptions for describing their own doing. Rather, the word is reminiscent of ancient religious, ritual practices.
Applied to the psychologist's work with dreams it suggests—instead of a
fixed, mechanically-to-be-applied hermeneutic technique—a whole attitude, the attitude of the whole man (*homo totus*) involving especially also
his deep feeling (rather than merely the philologist's intellect). Similarly,
the word "wise" indicates that the whole sphere of a discussion of technical
methods has been left behind. Amplification might perhaps be said to be a
better or more adequate method than free association, but it could not be
referred to as "wise". "Wisdom" suggests depth, some "deeper" or "higher"
awareness than that gained from empirical "worldly" experience or that
merely refers to practical hermeneutic methods.

In Jung's passage the religious and "higher" connotations of both "circumambulation" and "wise" should of course not be taken literally, as if it
were really a question here of religion and wisdom *sensu strictiori*. The two
words have been transplanted (*metapherein*) from their own native fields
into Jung's *psychological* practice, but they have been chosen precisely because of the special atmosphere clinging to them so that they might all the
better signal to the reader that a shift from one type of *discourse* to another
discourse has been performed. The technical-practical and formalistic discourse about the right technique (amplification versus free association) has
been transcended. We all of a sudden are now on a different level and in a
different sphere or dimension beyond the practical mind of clinicians who
"apply" methods: We are even beyond "philology".

Now turning from the appreciation of the linguistic tone or style of the
sentence in question to the meaning it expresses we have to think through
what the *concept* of "circumambulation" means and involves, that is to say,
what exactly "circumambulating" *does* and what result it achieves. The
first obvious point to be made is that it draws a circle around the dream.
But not abstractly and once and for all, e.g., by "drawing" a graphic line
around it, but by a live "act", namely by the psychologist's own continuous movement. He himself has, as it were, to *be* this "circle" around the
dream through his performing this movement. In alchemistical terms we
could say: He has to *be* the containing glass wall of the alchemical retort
(which in psychology is not a subsisting thing, but consists and exists only
in the psychologist's own performance of this mental, methodological en-
circling movement). Circumambulation entails also that he does not merely
mechanically perform a circular movement in the purely formal sense of

geometry. Rather, in order for this movement to truly *be* circumambulation at all, a certain dedication is required of the person performing it, a
self-abandon to that which is encircled: Thus establishing an inner connection on the feeling level with it as its center. It is this dedication that
first establishes the dream as a center in the full sense of the word.[6] For the
duration of his working with the dream, *all* the psychologist's attention and
devotion go to the dream.

The dream's firm enclosure in this magic circle and the described total con"centration" upon the dream on the part of the circumambulating
psychologist establish *interiority*, the logic of interiority: What lies outside
is totally "forgotten", nonexistent (for the time of one's working with the
dream). To be more precise, they establish *absolute* interiority, that is, one
that does not border on any outside or refer to anything external. Practically,
this means that the moment any external matters or considerations are allowed to still play a role, the circular movement would simply cease to be
circumambulation. On the other hand, precisely because interiority has become absolute and is thus no longer defined in opposition to the external, it
must no longer pedantically be taken in a narrow literal sense, as something
that needs to be defensively guarded and immunized against any actual
knowledge that the psychologist already has when he enters into his work
with the dream. Its absoluteness makes this interiority free—and along with
it him too. The point is that in the case of a real circumambulation such
memories appear within, and from within, his wholehearted concentration
on and dedication to the dream at hand as sole center.

Jung did not use the word "circumambulating" nonchalantly. The word
was loaded for him and had a central place in his psychological thinking.
Above all, it was deeply connected with his idea of the individuation process and "becoming self". "There is no linear evolution; there is only a

---

6 We could of course also turn this around and say that the apperception of the dream as
  one's center in the full psychological sense of the word is what first makes circumambulation in the true sense possible. Without a real true center any circling movement would be
  a pointless formality. At any rate, circumambulating motion and center, just as alchemical vessel and prime matter, constitute each other. They are equiprimordial. Only for an
  alchemical retort can a matter (any matter) be a true *prima materia*. And only for a *prima
  materia* can there be an alchemical vessel or circumambulating movement. Without their
  intrinsic logical connection the one would be a dead fact and the other a mere technical
  utensil or operation. Abstractions instead of psychological reality.

circumambulation of the self" (*MDR* p. 196) and "Mandalas and the circumambulation of the center" (*MDR* p. 197) are central statements or phrases we read in *Memories, Dreams, Reflections*. And Erich Neumann, too, gave to a series of volumes with his collected essays the series title, *Umkreisung der Mitte*.

Saban's scheme, taken from Jung's Tavistock lectures, showed the simple situation of a separation of two clear-cut compartments, conscious mind here and the unconscious over there. This is the situation of a fundamental dissociation, with "translation" from the one to the other serving as the defense mechanism that *keeps* the opposites neatly apart and thus maintains and stabilizes this condition of dissociation. For the translating ego as the third, "translation" in this context means *logically* staying aloof in between and vis-à-vis the two, as a neutral mediator, neither fish nor fowl, and playing, much like in the case of one's juggling with two balls, the one against the other. It is the stance of external reflection.

In the new situation of our "circumambulating Jung" all this is gone. No compartments and no duality. By himself describing the circle around the dream through his own continuous movement, he *is* the living periphery of the circle, just as the center *qua* center exists only through his circling movement. Periphery and center, though clearly different, are nevertheless the Same; they are the one reality called "circle": Identity of identity and difference. Therefore, no need for translation here either, translation from the original language of the dream into a fundamentally other, alien language (especially since this "other language" has simply been left behind the moment that the circumambulation established the center and along with it interiority; the human subject is now *in* psychology).

The fact that the need for translation is altogether gone is also why Jung could write to Herbert Read on 2 September 1960:

> We have simply [!] got to listen to what the psyche spontaneously says to us. What the dream, which is not manufactured by us, says is *just so*. Say it again as well as you can.
>
> (*Letters* 2, p. 591)

Listening, simply listening, and "saying again", not translation, that is what the circumambulating psychologist does. He tunes, so we might say, into the dream and what it says, and repeats it—in its, the dream's or soul's language. The dream's language is—somehow—also his own. Only somehow—for despite this fundamental sameness there is of course also an inevitable distance between periphery and center, and so this "saying again" will be a repetition only "as well as you can". By emphasizing the phrase, "is *just so*", Jung makes it very clear that he insists here on a logic of identity and center.

But how can the dream's language be—somehow—also his own language? Only because the psychologist does the circumambulating not as the ordinary person that he is, not as civil man, as ego-personality, but as soul. If he wanted to do the circumambulating as ordinary ego-consciousness, his movement would be a merely technical circling behavior and an idle, pointless acting out. He would never become and *be* the center's own periphery. The circumambulation can only be done by him who has logically already elevated himself from the level of civil man to the level of soul. This may sound like mysticism or miracles, but it has nothing to do with that. It is merely a methodological shift of standpoint. However, the decision to perform the "ritual" of circumambulation and to take this new standpoint could never be made by the ego. If it were the ego, there could not be any circumambulation in the first place. This decision, if and when it indeed occurs, is already "the soul" (the standpoint of psychology) stirring in the person of its own accord. At that point it is, to be sure, as yet no more than the first immediacy of "soul". Only the continued process of circumambulation is the process of the methodical full realization of this elevation of himself from the level of civil man to the level of soul or psychology.[7]

After what has been discussed we understand why Jung at the end of our passage cites the Talmudic statement that the dream is its own interpretation and, furthermore, that this adage not only means much more but also something totally different from Saban's reducing it to the meaning of nothing

7 The full realization of this elevation should again not psychologistically be misconstrued in terms of self-development as a permanent change of the person to a status of "higher man" (an almost ontological change) or mystified as a breakthrough to something like Zen *satori*. It is very soberly just the *event* of a real dawning of a psychological understanding, the real entrance into psychology, and it is real only for as long as this particular act of circumambulation around this particular dream lasts. The person stays the same (except that now he has had the *experience* of one real moment of psychological insight; the difference between before and after is not greater than that between people who have had the experience of falling in love or having gone through the bereavement of a beloved parent or spouse and those who have not).

but Jung's rejection of free association. The dream is[8] not at all in need of interpretation here in the sense of translation. It is not we who have to interpret it, it does its interpreting all by itself and within itself, and, furthermore, it IS (that is to say, it always already comes as) its own interpretation. This is what makes a dream psychological (in the emphatic sense) instead of its being a merely psychic event, a fact. More accurately, I should, of course, say that only *if* we *view* the dream in this way is it apperceived psychologically, as a manifestation of soul. The dream is in itself circular, uroboric (for *my* Jung and for psychology proper), because it is not merely a statement, but both a statement and its, the statement's, own interpretation. What we have here is the logic of self-relation and self-reference. The fact that this fundamentally different logic from our everyday type logic prevails here is also the reason why the Talmudic statement could deservedly be called "wise" by Jung.

Whereas Saban merely scanned the four Jung passages that include the Talmudic saying for a single simple and clear-cut message to be abstracted from them, I have, one could perhaps say, myself circumambulated this one sentence from Jung's letter to Jacobi in order to allow it to unfold its own inner richness and deeper meaning. Now that I have presented my discussion of this sentence, I think I can rightly claim that I have been able to demonstrate that at least in this one instance my view about soul, interiority, and dream does find a source in Jung's psychology. But of course, it finds this source only in *my* Jung's psychology, not in the psychology of Saban's Jung, as I am quite willing to concede.

Difference of rank

At the beginning I mentioned that for Fichte the two competing philosophical systems he was talking about were for him not alternatives on the same level and of equal right. One was higher than the other, because it presupposes one's own having elevated oneself to that higher level or (as Schelling had put it) to a self-gained freedom of spirit. Comparing what the saying, "the dream is its own interpretation" means for Saban with what it

---

8 This "is" does not indicate an ontological assertion. In psychology something *is* what it is through the psychologist's (or patient's) particular perspective or methodological act with which it is approached.

means according to me, we can similarly discern a difference of rank between them. I do not say this on the basis of a subjective value judgement, but of an objective difference intrinsic to their own internal structures. What I called *my* understanding of the Talmudic adage has, according to Saban's express statement, "no source in Jung". This means that in terms of his conception he cannot account for *my* Jung's view; more than that, he adamantly excludes it, indeed, has to be blind to it. For him, my Jung simply does not exist. His Jung is, in the context of a discussion of the Talmudic saying, exclusively concerned with plain practical-technical questions. By contrast, what Saban described as *his* Jung's simple view is fully accessible and familiar to me; nor do I in any way deny it. This makes "my Jung" more comprehensive and in this sense logically more complex, more differentiated.

But "not denying" this everyday side of Jung does not mean adopting it as the valid stance of psychology. The Jung who talks about dream work on a flat commonsensical technical level (free association versus amplification) and the Jung for whom, as Saban happily quotes, psyche means "the totality of all psychic processes, conscious as well as unconscious" (*CW* 6 § 197), presents trite, often rehashed textbook ideas from the early days of depth-psychology—so to speak, psychological "elementary school" stuff that one who has gone through psychological "high school" and "university education" should have outgrown. This whole thing about translating the dream from the language of the unconscious to the other language of the conscious mind (and about these two separate compartments in the first place) is part of a naive childlike psychology, or a psychology for pedestrians or first beginners. No need here for an elevation of the mind, for one's having conquered for oneself a freedom of spirit.

It goes without saying that Jung was not a systematic thinker. He was not in the habit of expressly correcting or revoking his earlier views in the light of his later, more refined insights in order to always bring his theory as a whole consistently up to date. Also, he never tried to resolve the conflicts between the numerous theoretical theses he advanced at different times in the course of his life, for example, about archetypes. And on top of it there are the differences between early and late, alchemy-inspired Jung, and between the strictly scientifically minded and the more intuitive soul-oriented Jung, as well as that between Jung the psychological scholar and the Jung who indulged in theosophical speculation, etc. For the biographer and historian, and perhaps for Jung fans, all these diverse theses, interests, and views as well as all the stages of development of his psychology are of equal interest and significance. But not so for the analytical psychologist. For him not everything Jung said is of equal value and relevance. From all the wealth of ideas and statements Jung presented us with, the present-day analytical *psychologist* must select that which is appropriate to and essential for a psychology that deserves its name, and in turn leave everything else aside or, respectively, push off from it. That's what his *métier* demands. The psychologist needs to have a rigorous notion of psychology. For him the "total" Jung is neither here nor there.

It is much rather incumbent upon us who come after Jung to "discern the spirits", that is, to search out those individual instances and places scattered over his lifework as a whole where Jung managed to rise to the apex of his psychological theorizing and then to turn what for him were so many *pinnacles* (his most advanced, deepest and most subtle insights) into our *starting-point* and general *basis* on which to ground our own psychologizing. We have to take them as individual "symbolizations" or "concretizations" of a general spirit in terms of which psychology as a whole needs to be *reconstituted*.[9] In this way we stay truly faithful to Jung even while in some regards doing violence to a literal, orthodox reading of his texts.

Ultimately, it may be far less my particular statements and their content that make Saban want to object to them than my emphasis on "spirit" and the spirit prevailing in my work (or even *that* there is a spirit prevailing in it). When Jung was asked by Vera von der Heydt about certain controversial views (on the role of active imagination and individuation) among British Jungians, he objected to "this conceptual hair-splitting" for which, as he said, certain concepts become "either much too narrow or much too broad" and wrote

> Your question evidently emanates from an atmosphere in which many words are buzzing about. . . . From such discussions we see what awaits me once I have become posthumous. Then everything that once was fire and wind will be bottled in spirit and reduced to dead nostrums. Thus are the gods interred in gold and marble and ordinary mortals like me in paper.
> (*Letters* 2, 469, 22 December 1958)

"Fire and wind" versus "paper" and "buzzing words". But no doubt, even Jung himself has also a "paper" side. He himself also contributed to the

---

9 Cf. Hillman's early, in some regards similar idea and project of "Re-Visioning Psychology".

bottling of dead nostrums. The Jung talking in Saban's Tavistock quote could perhaps be seen as an example of the "paper" Jung, as was that Jung who tried in *Psychological Types* to bottle key psychological notions in fixed "definitions", which themselves inevitably are at one and the same time "much too narrow" and "much too broad", for which reason the "fire and wind" Jung did not stick to definitions, even if it was he himself who had once established them. As a free mind he did not give a damn about definitions and the use of words as fixed technical terms. He did not think on the plain level of words, sentences, fixed *dicta*, on that whole "paper" level, but was concerned with and operated on the level of the living idea, experience, or psychic reality itself in each case, to which the words used were merely pointers. Criticizing (in the same letter to Jolande Jacobi cited above) the use she made in a book of the phrase the "idea of wholeness", Jung wrote: "The 'idea of wholeness' is a word I perchance use. . . . Concepts [to wit, technical terms] play no role whatever with me . . ." (Transl. modif.). Jung's relation to words and technical terms can be described as his *ad hoc*, perchance use of them!

As we see, for Jung there existed a creative tension between the "paper" and the "fire and wind" dimensions, and not as simple alternatives, but as a *dynamic*, a kind of vector from the one to the other. As readers of Jung we are therefore confronted with a choice: Do we accept the challenge of the dynamic inherent in his psychological thought—or do we content ourselves with the "paper" aspect of his psychology, with his psychology as a fixed doctrine, with his definitions, simple schematic separations (such as "the relations between the ego and the unconscious"), with the literalness of his many, at times conflicting *sentences*? Maybe what incenses Saban the most is that I do *not* operate on the level of sentences as manageable objects, do *not* juxtapose in front of myself "the many" as fixed dicta in their diversity or possibly even blunt unresolved antinomy,[10] but circumambulate each *one* that happens to be the topic at hand in order to penetrate to, and partake of, the inner life that animates it—its own internal "fire and wind", its soul.

---

10 Saban expressly favors "the antinomial approach" and "The antinomial Jung", i.e., what in psychology we call *dissociation*. See his "The dis/enchantment of C.G. Jung", in: *International Journal of Jungian Studies*, Vol. 4, No. 1, March 2012, 21–33.

Chapter 8

"Katako" and the Japanese psyche[1]

Reflections after reading an article by Megumi Yama

Megumi Yama's article, "Ego consciousness in the Japanese psyche: culture, myth and disaster" appeared in 2013 in the *Journal of Analytical Psychology* but came to my attention only in spring 2021.[2] It is a very informative paper. It makes Westerners without intimate familiarity with Japanese life and culture aware of essential Japanese attitudes and forms of behavior, which is quite interesting. The article is well-written, consistently argued, and easy to follow. The author begins her discussion of the differences between the Western and Eastern psyche with the report of a personal experience, the instant deep and physically manifesting culture shock, when at age 13 she was exposed to the US due to her father's work. This report shows her as a person of a fine psychological sensitivity; the brief case example of her work with a Japanese patient likewise reveals her as a therapist open, and with authentic access, to the depth of soul in a genuinely Jungian spirit. While on account of all those features Yama's paper is at first captivating, at second thought the main thesis that she propounds in this article creates discomfort. It does not convince me. I see a discrepancy between the phenomenology of the Japanese psyche she herself describes, on the one hand, and the theoretical interpretation of this phenomenology given by her, on the other hand. In the following I will explore my misgivings.

It would, of course, be a ridiculous presumption on my part as a Westerner, and on top of it one who is neither a Japanologist nor even capable of speaking Japanese, if I claimed to know the Japanese psyche better than

---

1 Written in 2021.
2 All references to Yama in this chapter come from the following publication: Megumi Yama, "Ego consciousness in the Japanese psyche: culture, myth and disaster", *Journal of Analytical Psychology* 58, 52–72.

DOI: 10.4324/9781003611417-8

Yama and to be able to give a better interpretation of it. So let me point out right at the beginning that in this paper I am not giving my interpretation *of the Japanese psyche* itself, that I am not venturing to propound a theory of my own, and on my own responsibility, about the psychology of the Japanese. My topic is something else. It is an immanent, article-internal critique of Yama's conception. I read it a little bit like a dream in which one can compare and contrast what the soul offers to the dream-I and what the dream-I's attitude and reaction is to the tasks, conditions, or events presented to it by the soul. For the present paper this means that I am only working with what Megumi Yama's own article *describes* as the way of life of the Japanese and I compare and contrast these described phenomena with her psychological view about this material. Therefore, how the Japanese psyche *in reality is* and how this real psyche should be psychologically understood lies entirely outside the purview of my comments. I am only working with and within a *text*.

It is interesting that the article is written in a decisively Western style, but that *what* it discusses in this style is what it presents as that style's own other, the peculiarly Japanese psyche. This means that the latter does not express itself directly in the descriptions given in this article. It does not display *itself* in its own terms, innocently, in genuinely Japanese style. Rather, it is presented in already reflected form, observed and described not only from outside, namely, from the point of view of the "Western ego" and its rational, scientific approach, but, as we will see, also *conceptually* with the categories and expectations belonging to and only appropriate for the one of the two things to be compared, the Western psyche.

Critique of substantiating thinking in psychology

Yama's thinking about the matters to be discussed is informed by the model of the difference between the structure of the Japanese psyche and that of Westerners presented in 1976 by Hayao Kawai (p. 58, Figure 1). The drawings display the psyche (in each case) as a circle the center of which is called "Self" and the major area of which is "Unconscious"; only a small, demarcated area at the top of the circle is "Conscious". Whereas the demarcating boundary line in the Western case is solid, it is a broken line in the model of the Japanese psyche; and whereas in the very center of the conscious area of the Western model the word Ego[3] is written, with rays going out from this center in all directions to the borders (circumference) of this area, the word Ego in the center of this conscious area in the other drawing is missing and the corresponding rays in the Japanese case start out from the Self in the unconscious area instead, and they go only upwards towards and then all the way through the conscious area. Yama explains:

> The ego is the centre of the conscious personality and the Self is the unifying centre of the total psyche in Western Jungian thought. According to Kawai, in the Japanese psyche, the boundary between consciousness and unconsciousness is much more vague than the Westerner's. He adds that in Japanese psyche, "as the structure of the consciousness is formed with the Self as the center, which is in the unconscious, it is even doubtful whether it really has the center" (Kawai 1976). In other words, the ego is buried in the unconscious depth of psyche.
>
> (p. 58 f.)

One problem here is that such pictorial models seduce the mind of the psychologist to a reifying thinking about the psychological reality after the model of things. The psyche or the personality is presented as a structure with parts or regions (consciousness, the unconscious) and fixed structural components (ego, self). The model behind this way of thinking is that of the body. It has a definite structure and permanently existing structural elements, the body organs. Or the model may even be that of an apparatus (the phrase "the psychic apparatus" was a frequent expression in early psychoanalysis). But for psychology, above all a psychology with soul, such a style of thinking is misguided.

---

3 "Ego" is the established psychological term in English. This Latin-origin word is deliberately used because it sounds scientific, but has psychologically the serious disadvantage that it no longer expresses the first-person singular pronoun, but rather a noun, turning the I into a third-person It. Freud and Jung used the German ordinary-language word "*das Ich*" instead. Following them, I generally use "the I" in my English writings and reserve "ego" and "the ego" for a special different meaning. For a more detailed discussion of this question see, for example, my *The Historical Emergence of the I*, London; Ontario: Dusk Owl Books, 2020. Here, however, in order not to complicate matters, I will stay with Yama's word "ego". For the same reason I mostly retain here the term "psyche", rather than consistently sticking to the terminological distinction between "psyche" and "soul".

Before I come to this aspect, I must dismiss the one concept included in these schemes, that of the "Self" (capitalized!) as center of the psyche. The idea of such a Self is fictitious, although no less a man than Jung was its inventor. There is no phenomenological or empirical basis for it. For those certain imaginal experiences, e.g. mandalas, that Jung claimed were images of the Self in the psyche he never showed why they rightly deserved to be qualified precisely as "self", nor did he make it plausible that those "images of the Self", apart from being psychic *images*, i.e., fantasy material, were also the reflection or depiction of a really existing unifying as well as organizing center of the total personality, in other words, that they had a referent in the reality of people's psyche. Mandalas represent the idea of center, of a centered world. But the *idea of* a center does not prove the existence of such a center in the structure of people's psyche. Ideas come and go. But Erich Neumann even invented and believed in a so-called "ego-self *axis*".

So we have to forget the substantiating (reifying) concept of the Self and stick to the use of "self" as reflexive pronoun: myself, himself, herself, i.e., to the notion of self-relation and self-reference (which is a logical act, not an existing entity or psychic organ).

Also, despite the fact that there is ample phenomenological evidence for "the Western ego", its nature (what it is and how it needs to be conceived) is misconstrued if it is considered to be the center of consciousness, although this idea, too, was advanced by the early Jung. There is no such thing as a center of consciousness. What the nature of the ego is will concern us later in more detail. For now I want to return to my critique of reifying thinking in psychology, of any thinking in terms of existing layers, regions, organs or centers, and exemplify my critique by the concept of consciousness.

Consciousness is not a persistent structural element of the personality, in the psyche of people, not a region or layer. Rather, it is a state or condition. I do not *have* a consciousness. I can only *be* conscious (and if I happen to be conscious, then I can speak of the existence of consciousness). But this my consciousness (my being conscious) disappears altogether without leaving a trace when I fall asleep, when I faint, or fall into a coma. On the other hand, when I dream in my sleep, a kind of consciousness, not identical with the waking consciousness, comes into being within my sleep state. When while awake and conscious I get drowsy, enter into a state of reveries, or get into a trance, etc., each time the ordinary full-fledged waking consciousness is *replaced* by a different degree and condition of consciousness. The only thing that persists for human beings all the time is the fundamental predisposition for being conscious, but not consciousness as a realm or part of their psyche. With consciousness it is like with emotional states or with types of weather. One time I am happy, another time I am sad, depressed, and each time it is the total me that is happy or whatever. Happiness and sadness are not permanent structural components of my personality. They come and go. When I am depressed or bored or angry (I as total me), happiness has totally disappeared. Rain and storms, heat and icy temperature are temporal processes, not constant "parts" of weather the way brain, heart, liver are permanent structural "parts" of the healthy body. Earlier it was raining, a little later it simply *stopped* raining. In an analogous way I can, for whatever reason, stop being conscious, or become semi-conscious or enter states of extraordinary consciousness.

When I am conscious, my consciousness is always a specific (and thus essentially limited) consciousness *of this or that*, and it *is* only consciousness through whatever particular contents that it happens to be conscious of. It is not something general like a permanent vessel.

By the same token, there is also not an existing "unconscious" bordering on my consciousness (regardless whether bordering with solid or broken boundary line). It does not make sense to conceive in a substantiating way of "the unconscious" as an entity or realm. When I stop being conscious I do not enter "*the* unconscious" as a given (and constantly present) part of the psyche surrounding consciousness or located underneath it, but I am simply no longer conscious and am only in this concrete (and adjectival) sense "unconscious". What and "where" I psychologically am when I am no longer conscious, is a useless question. This is why Jung, when at his best, said that the unconscious is simply what is unknown. We cannot say anything about it. Not even that there is such a thing.

So far I have shown why and in what sense structural models of the psyche are in themselves misguided. They try to conceive and present psychological reality with categories that are appropriate only for the physical world. The world of psyche or soul is essentially spiritual (*geistig*) and as such processual or performative. Now I come to a second critique that pertains only to the described model of the structure of the *Japanese* psyche, namely, that I think that this model does not correspond to the phenomenology of the Japanese psyche described by Megumi Yama at various points in her article.

The wrong model for the Japanese psyche

Yama explains that

> the Japanese, who have adopted the modern Western ego superficially, are inclined to horizontal splits which collectively are enacted in a double-layer society. . . . When Japanese people think intellectually and try to insist on their opinion, they do it according to the Western rational way, but they actually "live" their lives in traditional Japanese style, unconsciously.
>
> (p. 54)

I will concentrate in the following only on the *traditional* Japanese psyche and ignore the modern (we could say: "Imported") superficial upper layer of the described horizontally split double-layer Japanese society. What do we learn about the traditional Japanese style from her article?

Right at the beginning Yama tells us how she behaved when as a teenager, after 15 months in the US, she returned to her native country, Japan.

> I was careful not to express myself clearly and directly, as this would run counter to the Japanese style of communication where we are expected to express ourselves in an implicit way and guess the intention of the other from a given context. I kept quiet so as not to stand out . . .
>
> (p. 53)

Later we hear more generally: "In relationship, Japanese are hesitant to say 'no' or make definitive decisions; there is a pull toward ambiguity and vagueness." (p. 60). "Japanese people are surprisingly strong when they share a sense of unity with the fantasy of being connected with each other in a big protected container . . ." (p. 61). About the individual members of society we hear:

> And he/she knows that it would be almost impossible to continue to live there if he/she broke the uniformity. . . . Japanese are good at burying themselves in the mass as a whole and hide their individuality in the undifferentiated collective; they are motivated not to stand out so as to protect themselves.
>
> (p. 61)

Lastly, "In the Japanese language, 'who the subject is' nor 'one's will or intention' are rarely expressed" (p. 67), "it is usually surmised from the relational context and surround" (p. 68).

If this is an adequate description about the (traditional) Japanese mode of being-in-the-world we are forced to realize that the previously discussed model of the Japanese psyche that tried to depict the structure of the individual personality is completely off the mark. It succumbed to the naturalistic fallacy which made it take the obvious fact that *physically* the Japanese each exist as individuals as also relevant for psychology. *Biologically*, the Japanese each have their own individual body, their own personal character traits, their own particular gifts, weaknesses, desires, emotions, etc. But what we learn from the just cited description Yama has given is that the *psychology* of the Japanese is a fundamentally communal one. They all share together only one and the same psyche. They are *psychologically* not individuals. They are psychologically "buried in the mass as a whole", that is, logically sublated elements in the communal psyche, in the unity and harmony of the group.

The above model of the structure of the Japanese psyche placed the Self in the center of the individual personality. I critiqued the notion of "the Self", but if we were to nevertheless make use of it at the present point of our discussion, we would have to say that traditionally the Japanese, all of the members of a social group, have together their one single self outside themselves, namely in the community as a whole.

Phenomenologically this shows itself in a further detail presented by Yama. It is "the hollow centre structure", which was also discussed by Hayao Kawai. According to this description, leaders in (traditional) Japan were not active decision-makers, managers, bosses. A "leader is the one who is in the centre but does 'nothing' and as such keeps the proper balance among the members. . . . The ultimate leader for the Japanese might be the one who is just there doing nothing but maintaining the harmony of the universe/all things" (p. 62). The empirical person of the leader does nothing, must not, is not allowed to, do anything, because he is not there as the real person that he is, but as nothing else than the visible symbolic representation of the fundamentally invisible unity and harmony of the whole or as the group self. The whole mentioned ideally extends far beyond the immediate social community into the harmony with nature and the universe. We could also say that the center is essentially empty or hollow because it has to represent the felt *presence* of the entire circumference (which is an *abstract idea*), rather than to be an empirically real and literal center (like the hub of a wheel).

If, according to Kawai, "the boundary in the Japanese psyche between consciousness and unconsciousness" is much more vague than that of Westerners', we may now see that the observed phenomenon that is supposed to be described with this formulation needs a different description. It does not seem to be a question of consciousness and the unconscious and the border between them at all. The psyche of Japanese individuals (in the traditional situation) is much rather, to use Yama's term, "buried" in the unity of the whole. She also uses the image of a "big protected container". But more adequate than "buried" or "contained" (which suggest the idea of solids) might be to say that individuals are—*psychologically* (of course not empirically!)—*immersed* and *floating* in the unity and harmony of the whole all around them, as in the medium in which they live and from which they draw their inner support. This might also help to understand the (from a Western point of view) astonishingly easy access, with deep feeling, to dreams and sandplay images on a nonverbal or pre-verbal level as well as to the "Nothingness" Yama refers to (esp. p. 57), namely, for example in analogy to the direct contact and fluctuating interrelation between crystals and the solution in which they float. In her case description Yama herself once refers to the alchemical operation of "solutio" (although, I assume, on the basis of the conventional model of the psyche she introduced in Figure 1).

The methodical mistake in the comparative model of the different structures of the Japanese and the Western psyche shown in Yama's Figure 1 is that this model of the Japanese psyche simply starts out from and takes over the model of the Western psyche and accounts for differences merely by minor internal modifications (broken instead of solid boundary line, absence instead of presence of the Ego). In this way the real difference is from the outset obfuscated, namely the difference between a psyche that is psychologically a priori defined as individual psyche (the psyche of full-fledged individuals in the sense of "man for himself") and a psyche that is irrevocably communal, psychologically containing the existing physical individuals merely as *moments* within itself.

It would therefore need two radically different, even incompatible diagrams next to each other to adequately illustrate the difference between the two structures. For the Japanese psyche one might think, e.g., of a drawing of a multitude of small circles (representing the Japanese *people* of a community) gathered around another small circle representing the empty center as their unifying organizing principle. The (traditional) Japanese soul is not inside people. It is out there all around them and enveloping them. The very point of the structure of the (traditional) Japanese psyche is that there cannot be an ego and therefore *psychologically* also no diagram of the individual psyche, because all individuality has to be submerged and "buried" in the external encompassing whole in order to guarantee the ideal of unity and harmony within the communal soul that, after all, consists of those empirically real and factually divergent individuals, and in addition in order to guarantee also the unity of the communal soul with nature and the universe.

This methodological mistake may be due to the fact that the "psychological difference", the difference between the "psychic" and the "psychological", between people and soul, is not paid heed to. People exist of course as "the existing physical individuals" I just mentioned. And *this* their physical or external individuality is immediately visible, an impressive fact that strikes one's eye. As individuals in *this* sense they each also have their own *psychic* make-up, their own emotions, drives, character traits, degree of intelligence, etc. All this belongs to the "psyche" of the human animal and as such is in the last analysis part of the biology of the body, the nature of the organism. But whether individuality, to mention only it, is also part of their *psychological* definition, of the logical constitution of their consciousness and their social and cultural mode of being-in-the-world, is an entirely different question, but *it* is in our context the psychologically only relevant one. The psychologist must not allow himself to be misled by the picture that the obvious foreground of physical reality and external facts presents. His job is to "see through" to the hinterland of the soul. True psychology cannot be conceived as *personalistic* psychology (psychology of what is going on inside people). It has to deal with the background processes of the *objective psyche*, that is, the (invisible) soul.

The difference between the two structures of the psyche is not that the Western psyche, in addition to what the Japanese psyche has, also has an ego and not that this addition simply makes small modifications necessary in the general scheme valid for both. For one thing, Westerners do not *have* an ego. The ego is nothing that can be "had". Ego, you can only *be*. The Western ego is not something *in* me, in people's psyche, but it is the constitution or logical form of the whole me. And so here is the place to discuss how this Western-style ego, this *being* ego, became possible.

It became possible because in a situation of a communal soul (not identical with, but similar to the Japanese communal soul), the real individuals all of a sudden dared to take *themselves* more seriously than the unity of the whole. To the extent that one prioritizes *oneself* over against the unity of the whole, one has become ego. This is a *revolutionary* act. Imaginally speaking we could say that it is the individual's seizure, appropriation, and interiorization into *himself* of what in the Japanese scheme is out there as "the empty center" or the group self. The logical interiorization of the before communal center into the individual means that the latter, all by himself, established *himself* as his own center. The Western ego is not a structural element, a psychic organ or entity, not a (or the) center of consciousness. It is each I's setting itself up as its own center *for itself*, as the ultimate center (for itself) of the experience of the whole world (rather than an internal center of the I's consciousness).

The Western ego is essentially a *result*. It is produced. It is the result of a doing, the result of the logical "impertinence" of the real individual's emancipation from the communal soul through their own *self-assertion*, self-affirmation, vis-à-vis or over against the communal whole. And as a result of this act of self-assertion, the ego exists only *to the extent that*, and lasts only *for as long as*, this self-assertion, self-establishment as center for everything is actively maintained by a given individual. The "Western ego" is not a permanent possession.

In this way the incompatibility of the structure of the traditional Japanese psyche and that of the Western ego once more leap to the eye. But it becomes clear at the same time that the notion of a "structure" is misleading. Just as I showed that the Western ego is the result of a doing (and ongoing doing), so we learned earlier from the phenomenological material about the Japanese psyche laid out before us in Yama's paper that the Japanese soul's communal unity and harmony, too, is also the *result* of a doing: Of the individuals' hiding their individuality, their burying themselves in the whole. Both are thus performative.

Here it is necessary to correct the false impression that my way of speaking about the production of the ego may have created. These active doings are not empirical behaviors by actual people, nor by their consciousness, but logical, psychological acts performed by the objective soul and in the recesses of the objective soul. They "happen" to consciousness, if and when they occur. The consciousness of real people, real individuals, finds itself in them and informed by them, once the interiorization of the communal self into the *concept* of the individual has in fact taken place. There is no room here for ego or personalistic psychology, nor any room for moral evaluations or judgments (which are ipso facto egoic), just as Megumi Yama likewise pointed out that the Japanese "way of communicating is neither good nor bad, but it is valuable to be conscious about what is going on in the undercurrent of the society and deep within oneself" (p. 54).

The Japanese soul's own interpretation of itself

To become more conscious of what is going on in the *undercurrent* of the traditional Japanese *objective* psyche I now turn to one more item of the phenomenology of the Japanese soul presented by Yama (pp. 54 and 69), because since it is an old fairy tale it is an authentic document of the soul itself, that is, an innocent piece of the soul's own speaking about itself, rather than an already reflected external description by the modern psychological mind as "scientific" observer. This document of the soul is the tale of "Katako" (Half-Child). It can give us the *inside* view of what is psychologically behind, and going on in, the Japanese's need to "bury themselves in the whole". The story, briefly summarized, goes as follows.

> An oni (a Japanese ogre) asked a woodcutter if he liked rice-cakes and was told that the man loved them so much that he could give his wife for them. He was given lots of rice-cakes by the oni, but when he came home his wife was gone. He went on a search for her and after ten years came to the island of the oni. There he found a 10-years old boy, Katako, who was half oni (on the right side) and half human (on the left side), the son of that oni who had given him the rice-cakes and of the man's wife. The woodcutter, his wife and Katako with great difficulties escaped from the oni to Japan, which was possible only thanks to Katako's help. Because of his being half oni, Katako is not accepted in Japan. He therefore ultimately commits suicide, after advising the parents what to do with the oni-half of his corpse so that it might serve for them as a magical protection from the attacks of the oni.

Megumi Yama introduced this story in connection with her own suffering during her childhood from her readjustment difficulties in Japan after her return from the US. When reading the story of the "Half-Child" and

Hayao Kawai's commentary on it, she was deeply affected. "I was honestly shocked because the story and Kawai's discussion reflected my suffering and at the same time revealed the Japanese tendency to eliminate what is foreign and heterogeneous" (p. 54). Now, we have to realize that this reaction is based on a "sociological", not a psychological, reading of the tale, a reading of the fairy tale as if it were a kind of report about some *people's* behavior and fate, a human-interest story.[4] And the implied critique of the Japanese tendency to exclude what is foreign as a Japanese character fault in addition introduces a moralizing perspective. This becomes even more apparent when the conclusion drawn by Kawai from this story is that to become more open to what is foreign is a task for the Japanese of today.

If, by contrast, we give a psychological reading to this tale things look completely different. Jung stated that "In myths and fairytales, as in dreams, the soul speaks about itself . . ." (*CW* 9i § 400, transl. modified), i.e., our fairy tale does not speak about people, what *they* do and what happens to them. In speaking about *itself*, the soul merely uses in such tales images from the human world as well as from the world of natural processes and events as "symbolic" means of expression for the representation of its own inner logical life, but it is not *about* these diverse characters, behaviors, and events in the narrative. Furthermore, as, e.g., Plotinus clearly realized, what is actually *simultaneous* moments within the logic or internal constitution of the one particular soul truth to be portrayed in a given tale is forced down by the imaginal and narrative mode of presentation into the empirical and experiential medium of time and space. It then appears as if the figures in the story were separate, independent people interacting with, and reacting to, each other as well as to the events that are narrated. But nothing is happening in the Katako fairy tale, there is no action, no process or development. All apparent "figures" and "happenings" are symbolic depictions

---

4 If, as a soul story, a fairy tale can invent an island of the oni, an ordinary woodcutter who is capable just like that of going to the island of the oni, and a Katako that is half oni and half human and so on, it can also invent how the Japanese behave towards Katako after the woodcutter family returns to Japan. It is free to make the *fairy-tale* Japanese reject Katako, or accept him without much ado, or even hail him as something special. We cannot, within our attempts at understanding a given fairy tale, take some elements as fantasy inventions and concerning others take recourse in empirical facts such as in sociological observations that *the Japanese* (in reality, outside the fairy tale) tend to exclude what is foreign. The rejection is invented for the tale's own purposes.

of the complex "blueprint" of one timeless (Jung might have said "arche-typal") *possibility*. Anything like the ideas of individual subjects, cause and effect, change from initial to final situation must be rigorously kept away *if* the story is to be seen as the soul's self-expression in one single one of all the possible diverse moments that it can be in.

Thus, for a psychological approach our tale is not a sob story. It does not present a disaster. There is nothing shocking or deeply moving about the boy's suicide, just as stories like the ones about the dismemberment of Osiris or Dionysos-Zagreus, of the flaying of Marsyas, of an eagle's time and again hacking and eating the (nightly growing-again) liver of bound Prometheus are not meant to elicit pity or compassion or horror. All human emotions and sentimentality are here totally out of place. Such stories are utterly sober, matter-of-fact-like; they do not play in the sphere of the human-all-too-human, but are the imaginal, symbolic portrayal of purely objective soul necessities, the abstract logical relations that reveal the internal logic or pattern of a specific *possible* soul situation or soul truth. (Whether and when and where this logic is actually materialized in real empirical events or in real modes of being-in-the-world is a totally different issue.) At any rate, Katako's suicide in our tale is not an unfortunate, deplorable outcome, but the very point of the story, the aim or purpose for which it exists.

After this clarification, let us see what the particular "archetypal" situation or soul truth is in which the soul displays itself in the Katako story.

The soul presents itself in this timeless instance of its logical life in *the symbolic guise* of a ten-year old boy.

That the boy is ten years old is not haphazard. This age must be chosen on purpose in the fairy tale, because it must be the reason why the woodcutter's journey in search for his wife had to take ten long years, which is, considered by itself, not so plausible, especially after his disdainful remark about his wife in the beginning. The tale could just as well have made the woodcutter arrive on the island of the oni, say, after ten months or one year, two years. Why would it have to be a search for ten years if not so that at the time of his arrival on the island the boy could have reached this age?

The age of ten years is at the threshold of teenage, puberty, and adolescence. As such it is a time of crucial transition. We could also say it is a kind of border that separates the innocence of childhood from the beginning self-consciousness of the adolescent. "Innocence of childhood" means: Existence in *(psycho-)logically* unbroken (*not* empirically-practically unbroken) unity, in harmonious containment in the fold of the parental home. For the adolescent this unity breaks apart. The *participation mystique* with the parents is dissolved. A state of *reflection* (the a priori reflectedness of whatever is experienced) takes the place of the original *immediacy* of just being and experiencing. A psychological separation from the parents occurs; they become dethroned; their authority is all of a sudden questioned or even completely denied. The adolescent's own views, own judgment rank higher than what the parents say. He makes himself psychologically independent and develops a sense of his own *selfhood*.

A geographical border is a harmless line that marks a static, uncomplicated separation between two regions. As a *psychological* border the "crucial transition" is more complicated, more dynamic. The moment that the psyche's development has transported the psyche to the beginning of the transition phase, the transition has already happened, the psyche has at once already irrevocably arrived on the other side, across the border. The innocence of childhood is definitively over. The complication mentioned arises because the psychological crossing is a double crossing: in addition to the objective *psychic* event of having been transported across the divide, a *psychological* decision about how the soul relates to this its transportation needs, on this other side, to be made by the soul. And depending on what its decision is, it may or may not get itself into a dialectic contradiction. The inevitably ongoing forward journey on the new, other side of the "border" can continue in two fundamentally different ways. The soul can either decide, while factually moving forward, to keep looking backwards in its innermost essential orientation and to continue to uphold its loyalty to the (in fact irrevocably left) original state. Or it can move forward with a likewise forward looking orientation.

All the mentioned features about the transition are aspects of one and the same new situation, at the very entrance to which the soul depicts itself in this fairy tale. But they are symbolic features. The story is not really about a boy's growing up, about his parents, about his loss of childhood innocence, etc. In these images the soul speaks much rather about its own transitional stance between its own "childhood" innocence (its own childish naivety) and its potential of negating and overcoming this its innocence and entering the state of self-reflection, self-consciousness, and thus ultimately its own "manhood". But in discussing this soul situation further, we will work with the tale on the level of its own imaginal, narrative presentation.

The dissolution of the *participation mystique* with the parents entails that the father image divides itself into two. This shows itself in the well-known mythological idea of dual fathership. It is the idea that the empirical father, with whom one grew up, is in reality not at all "one's true father". In truth, so this imagination goes, one is, on the contrary, the son of an unknown, higher (spiritual, "archetypal", or divine) father. This archetypal idea of one's own two fathers is ultimately behind the mentioned devaluation of the empirical father and also legitimizes psychologically his loss of authority in the eyes of the adolescent, a loss precisely due to the fundamentally higher authority of the spiritual father. The "spiritual father" is nothing but the first immediacy—in still imaginal, mythological representation—of what we nowadays would call reason, rationality, self-responsibility, the realm of principles, whereas the "empirical" or biological father belongs to the sphere of the natural, earthly, merely factual reality.

The idea of two fathers does not place them side by side on the same plane, the way modern children after the divorce of their parents may get a new father in the new husband of the mother, while also still spending some time with their actual father. No, the imaginal two-fathers motif means a horizontal divide between upper and lower, between masculine Spirit and feminine nature, between the realm of principles and that of positive facts and thus the intrusion of the dimension of verticality. In other words, along with the psychological division, for the youngster growing up, of the notion of father into two, he also becomes dimly aware of the "paradoxicality of humanness", the double nature of man, the fact that we each exist *as (internal) opposites*, namely as human animals, on the one hand, and as soul, spirit, or mind, on the other. Jung expressed this truth of the double nature in a mythologizing fashion, for example, in the words, inspired by Christian thinking, that we are "more than autochthonous *animalia* sprung from the earth", and that as "twice-born" we have our "roots in the divinity itself" (*MDR* p. 333). Another time, critiquing Freud's reductive thinking about the soul exclusively in terms of the "inexorable circle of biological events" and the "family romance", he pointed into another direction by quoting a statement taken from a drama by Ernst Barlach: "The strange thing is that man will not learn that God is his father" (*CW* 4 § 780).

By depicting itself as "Half Child", as half oni and half human, the soul shows that it is the essential point of this particular "archetypal" moment of its logical life portrayed in the fairy tale that it is the instance in which it has become aware of the "paradoxicality of humanness". Katako is the symbolic embodiment of the divide that goes right through human existence. The vertical split (right side oni, left side human) must probably be understood as the pictorial (and thus imperfect) representation of an idea that Martin Luther, in his very different theological contexts, expressed conceptually in the sentence: *sunt duo toti homines* ("there are two 'whole persons'", the wholeness of man exists twice, in two fundamentally different, if not opposite forms), which, applied to Katako, would mean that he is simultaneously *wholly* oni AND *wholly* human. As one and the same whole person he has two different natures.

In addition to the two "halves" in him or rather the two "natures" of him, the fundamental divide is also displayed in the fact that he has two fathers in the story. Of course, the fairy tale does not explicitly say (nor even hint) that the woodcutter is Katako's natural father. But according to the logic of the story he is. He is the husband of Katako's mother, and Katako returns with the married couple to Japan, deserting his oni father. Above all, the three contests fought out in the story between the woodcutter and the oni show that implicitly woodcutter and oni represent each other's counterpart. It is the fight between, as it were, the "earthly" and the "heavenly" father for the son. But already the appearance of the oni to the woodcutter right at the beginning of the story and the woodcutter's indirectly (unconsciously) "selling" his wife to the oni for a mass of rice-cakes indicates the transference of the principle of true fatherhood from the human person to the oni. The wife or mother is here logically no more than a pawn that can be shoved from the one to the other or also back again. What counts is alone which paternal principle has the upper hand.

In the light of what I explained about the devaluation of the empirical father in the name of the higher father and the adolescent's newly discovered awareness of the higher sphere of reason and principles, we could surmise that the fact that the woodcutter is not explicitly said to be his father is due to the fact that this story portrays the soul in this one particular instance of its logical life in which it has newly discovered the higher father principle as its true origin and therefore is so "disillusioned" by the natural father that the latter simply has no longer the status of father for it. Katako's belief in the oni as the true father, the one and only true father, absolutely outshines the empirically real father, who is not recognized as his father at all.

I mentioned that the moment that the psyche has transported itself into the transition phase, it has at once already arrived on the other side. I think this is why in our story Katako is not shown to be *born* in Japan and then *transported* to the "island of the oni", but as having his very origin on that island. "Katako" is the tale of the transition phase and thus consistently and appropriately *begins with Katako on the other side,* as being born there. A *psychological* transition is not a gradual movement in time from here to there in analogy to physical journeys or to the body's growth, but *when* the transition appears it *is* only as its always already *having* happened.

We heard that the fairy tale was said to reveal the Japanese tendency to eliminate what is foreign and heterogeneous. But this interpretation does not do justice to the oni. He is, of course, not a foreigner at all, the way Koreans, Chinese, Filipinos, or Westerners indeed are "foreigners" for the Japanese. The notion of "foreigner" holds the contrast between the Japanese (including the woodcutter) and the oni reductively down on the horizontal level, so to speak on the flat surface of the earth, in empirical, geographical reality. At the same time, Katako's problem in Japan is banalized as a problem of human interrelation, his experience as one of the common non-acceptance of what is foreign. But the oni is not merely an empirical other, not just a stranger from another country. He is absolutely different, absolutely "strange", because he is not human, not even part of natural, empirical reality. He belongs to an altogether different *order* of being, that of spiritual beings. The difference is a *vertical* one. Or: The oni is not only different (like foreigners), but has the character of being the very opposite of the ordinary and familiar human-all-too-human world. As such he represents in our story the higher father principle, the (in a psychological sense) "paternal" principle of reflection, spirit, and selfhood in contrast to nature and to material reality (the rice cakes so loved by the woodcutter!).

Of course, we might wonder why this *higher* principle appears in the form of an oni, rather than (as, for example, in Jung's dictum) in the splendid ideal form as "the divinity itself" or as Barlach's "God". An oni is, after all, a decisively lower spiritual being, an ogre, demon, troll, or, originally, the spirit (ghost) of the deceased. An oni has usually negative connotations. In addition, he is generally depicted as a rather ugly creature. The discrepancy between his having the function in this tale of representing the *higher spiritual principle,* on the one hand, and the embodiment of this higher principle *in the lowly form of an oni,* on the other, could be explained in terms of the continuation of the story, Katako's betrayal and rejection of his oni father, of the higher father principle.

Here we have to keep in mind the mentioned fact that the story does not show consecutive events, but is the (to be sure, narrative and thus consecutive) *portrayal* of the *simultaneous* aspects of one soul truth or soul moment. The end of the story, although *told* at the end, is true from the outset, just as the beginning situation is still true at the end. They are reflections of each other. The end defines already the way the beginning appears. For, this tale is the peculiar story of the *initial appearance* in consciousness of the principle of reflection AND the with-this-appearance-*coincidental rejection* of that principle. The appearance does not come first, the rejection afterwards. Both are equiprimordial in the Katako story. It is, we could say, the story of the a priori *rejected appearance*. The simultaneity of beginning and "outcome" makes the relation circular: Seen in the light of the rejection, the "higher" father principle can of course not appear in splendid ideal form, but can only be apperceived in the contemptible form of, e.g., an oni. And the contemptible form of oni in its turn provides the justification for the rejection.

The crucial fact and theme of this story is in this sense that Katako, now again narratively speaking, makes his choice. (This is the *psychological* decision that in addition to the objective *psychic* event of having been transported across the divide [here, in Katako's case: to "the island of the oni"] needs to be made to complete a psychological border crossing, as I pointed out above.) Utterly unexpectedly and surprisingly, Katako turns against his oni-father and sides with the woodcutter, even helping him *against the oni* (what a betrayal of his oni-father!), thus (indirectly) now choosing the former, the empirical, human father, as his only father and opting for the ordinary human world of Japan as his future home, while once and for all abandoning the yonder of the "island of the oni". The contest fought in the story between the woodcutter and the oni shows that the central issue, both of this tale and for Katako, is the competition between the two father principles for the purpose of a one-sided decision. By contrast, the woman, Katako's mother, or more generally the feminine or maternal aspect, is only of secondary importance in this story; rice cakes, as we see right at the beginning, are here of higher value and esteem than the whole wife! What is really and only at stake here is the internal vertical difference and tension *within the masculine or father world* of the soul or, in the sense of my earlier remarks, the "human paradox".

This paradox can either be viewed and related to as an inherent dialectic, or it can be seen as something that needs to be decided unilaterally in favor either of the one or the other aspect. Our tale is about a clear-cut decision for the one and the elimination of the other. That Katako decides for the woodcutter, means that along with the lower empirical father he opts for life in the ordinary natural and traditional social world, in the innocence and immediacy of existence as it was prior to the intrusion of reflection. He categorically turns his back on the "island of the oni", which implicitly represents in our story the higher paternal realm of reflection, selfhood, and rational principles, although explicitly it is treated derogatorily.

However, Katako *is* already touched, affected, and once and for all "spoiled" by the experience of the higher paternal principle, carrying its stamp indelibly in his very nature. He *is* half oni. The experience of the higher principle cannot be undone, just as in puberty one cannot go back behind the experience of sexual desire, back behind one's *knowing* about the dimension of sexuality, to the innocence of children. This means that a literal return to "Japan", to childhood innocence, to the harmony of and with nature unwounded by reflection, is from the outset impossible.

The only way how the contradiction between the impossibility of a return to the *status quo ante*, on the one hand, and the literal, factual return, the move to Japan (psychologically: Consciousness's wholehearted rejection of the higher father principle), on the other hand, can be resolved is by suicide, Katako's killing *himself*. Suicide is in itself dialectical. It presupposes the level of reflection and self, nay, it even is an affirmation and active confirmation of selfhood, AND it is the elimination of oneself. One can only kill oneself by making use of a *self* that has already become conscious of itself (and this includes that, psychologically, consciousness stands above and vis-à-vis oneself so that it can freely decide about one's existence); that is, suicide is possible only after the rupture of the innocent, unwounded wholeness and the containment in the natural process. So we can say here that it is the oni half of Katako, the higher father principle in him, that brought him the consciousness of selfhood and ipso facto also the basis for the ability to commit suicide.

Of course, what narratively is displayed as *his* suicide (the killing of himself as person or human being) or as his self-sacrifice is, psychologically understood, the *killing of selfhood*, the sacrifice of the very principle of selfhood altogether that Katako through his oni half represents. What is sacrificed is the possibility to take himself *more seriously* than the people in Japan who scorn him, in other words, the possibility to ruthlessly *assert himself* over against them. In this story it is not the Japanese who eliminate what is foreign and heterogeneous, but it is Katako who eliminates the possibility of self-assertion and along with it the possibility of "impertinently" wresting the sense of "center" from the social group, of ipso facto establishing *himself as center* over against the communal whole and thus as ego and individual *in his own right*.

I have chosen the word sacrifice intentionally. Because Katako does by no means kill himself for purely personal subjective reasons, not, for example, out of desperation and as an escape from being mobbed. His suicide is not a late tragic result of his "unbearably" suffering from not being accepted in Japan. No, he commits suicide as a means for making the "return to Japan", to the *status quo ante*, finally successful, a return which on account of the actual impossibility of such a return could otherwise not be realized. The suicide is not a new event after his arrival in Japan. Rather, it must be understood as being from the outset inherent in, indeed identical with, his decision to desert his oni father. It is nothing but the explicit spelling out of the inner meaning of his choice. His decision is one for the participation mystique. The latter is absolutely incompatible with the principle of selfhood and requires its elimination. And so Katako sacrifices himself *for the social whole*, for the undisturbed harmony and unity of the community of the Japanese. His real (completed) return to Japan is possible "only over his dead body", as the saying goes. We see this clearly from the fact that his killing himself is from the outset conceived as serving a higher purpose that far transcends him personally: He tells his parents to dismember the oni half of his corpse and to use the pieces, put on stakes and fixed to the front door, as a lasting magical defense of the harmony of the social whole against the permanently existing threat of the intrusion of the oni, i.e., against the invasion of the higher father principle, the divisive principle of selfhood and reflection.

Katako's rejection of and fight against his oni father is not what we normally mean by "father-son conflict". In the latter kind of conflict two persons fight with each other. But the relation between the oni and Katako is only narratively a father-son relation. Psychologically it is a totally different one. The oni represents the higher father principle *as abstract ideal principle, as "archetypal" possibility*, whereas Katako as half oni, half human is this same principle *as real*, as something that in addition to being a *psychological* principle has also become a *psychic* possibility, an empirical factor in real life. It is the oni-half of Katako that through its suicide as this real psychic possibility excludes the "ideal" higher father principle from reality, from becoming real in psychic life. Katako, as the possible *psychic reality* of the principle of selfhood, *exists only for* his self-sacrifice. Without his suicide, the soul would not have needed to invent Katako in the first place.[5] He *needs* to exist, because without his actual existence this principle could not *really—in practical reality*—be excluded. But to be successfully excluded, he needs to have killed himself.[6] Both simultaneously! Earlier I said in the same spirit that this story is a priori conceived as the tale of the *rejected appearance* of the higher father principle. So we see again that what this fairy tale is concerned with is possibilities, tensions, and relations within the masculine, paternal, spirit side of the soul and concerning the real fate of the spirit. By contrast, all ideas of the "matriarchal" qualities of the Japanese and the dominant role of the mother in Japanese society need to be kept away from it.

There are many fairy tales and myths in Japan, and in all of them the soul speaks about itself, each time about itself in a different moment or possibility of itself. The question I need to answer is why I singled out this one story of Katako in the context of our general discussion, occasioned by Yama's article, about the ego and the Japanese soul (apart from the more superficial reason that this tale happens to be the only one referred to in Yama's paper as pertinent for this topic).

The reason is the singular relevance of this fairy tale to the question of the ego in the Japanese psyche. Its particular topic is how the sense of I, how self-consciousness and selfhood can be integrated into the conventional Japanese mode of being-in-the-world (= "taken from the island of the oni to Japan", or brought from the land of soul into the empirical reality of Japan) *without revolutionizing* the logical constitution of this conventional mode. No "harm" must be done to the latter. As we have seen, the Katako story revealed itself as a tale about the soul's crucial transition phase, about the *krísis* between psychological innocence and reflection. It is a story in

---

5 A happy ending of the fairy tale with the whole woodcutter family peacefully living together in Japan ever after would psychologically be ridiculous. Pure ego; wishful thinking.

6 A simple *repression* of this principle would not do. It would be a fake solution, a neurotic one. But what is presented here is an honest solution. The full price for the reward has been paid. Furthermore, a repression would be the *psychic* achievement of individuals. It would be their empirical doing. But what the tale portrays is the objective soul's own solution, the solution on the level of the *logic* of traditional Japanese being-in-the-world, a logic by which all individuals are informed, carried and supported.

which the psychological decision pertains to whether the basic further orientation will be one for or against selfhood and ego individuality. And if we recall to memory all the features of the phenomenology of the traditional Japanese psyche described in Megumi Yama's article, we can see now that the tale of Katako with the particular decision made in it fits perfectly to this phenomenology. We can say this fairy tale presents admirably nothing less than the unfolding, in imaginal and narrative form, of the very logic of the described structure of the Japanese psyche, the complex internal logical *life* of it. This story can be considered as the picture of this psyche seen *from within*, and a picture authentically portrayed by the objective soul itself as its innocent self-expression, no longer only a description from outside by modern scientifically trained consciousness. The *self*-sacrifice of Katako for the purpose of preserving the unity of the whole logically undisturbed by the intrusion of reflection and for the protection against people's turning into self-assertive ego-personalities is not merely an ancient story. It is what sight unseen is actually happening constantly, still today, in every Japanese individual partaking of the traditional Japanese mode of being-in-the-world. The higher father principle, the principle of selfhood and reflection, needs constantly to be sacrificed on the altar of the hollow center. The unity of the whole needs to be, and in fact once and for all *is*, magically protected by this (logical) sacrifice from the threatening intrusion of "the oni".

Of course, it would be a grave mistake to think that this sacrifice takes place as people's literal empirical behavior. What I described is a background process, is the automatically prevailing, and largely unconscious, logical *form* of being for the individuals. The decision has been made, once and for all, by the objective soul on the level of its historical opus magnum. The individuals with their personal feelings, decisions, and behavior—their opus parvum—find themselves *within* the choice that the soul has always already taken for them. *They* do not have to give their personal answer to the great question. The answer is already, once and for all, provided: As the inescapable framework within which, and in inevitable *fundamental conformance with* which, they live their personal lives.

The fact that it is the soul that took this decision also means that nobody is to be blamed for it. This decision is not "wrong", not an avoidance, does not amount to a lack. It expresses the Japanese soul's goal, its *telos* and distinction.

But what we learn from this tale is also that this logically undisturbed unity of the whole in Japan is by no means the innocent and self-sustaining primordial unity, but a unity that is *secondarily* restored *after* the already happened incursion of "the oni", the principle of selfhood and reflection. The harmony *of* the social whole and *with* nature is logically (not empirically) *artfully playacted*. The practice of maintaining this harmony *apparently* "undisturbed" is culture, not nature. The true, natural unity, the innocence of being in the world, has in principle already irrevocably *been* disturbed, indeed, ruptured, the "Half-Child" (the psychic reality of the higher spirit principle) has already come into being. This is why his self-sacrifice, his (i.e., this principle's) self-elimination, is indispensable. The (logical) suicide is the price of the preservation of the unity of the whole, *once* the rupture, the transportation to the island of the oni and consciousness's being affected by the oni, has already taken place. *Small children* live in the logical unity with their parents quite naturally. They do not need to eliminate their selfhood. They have not yet been to the island of the oni.

The idea of the harmony with nature as a secondarily, in "artful playacting", produced work of culture rather than a work of (psychological) nature may spontaneously call to mind the decisive role of *the aesthetic* in the traditional Japanese world as well as the typically Japanese "aesthetic solution to conflicts" (James Hillman, Hayao Kawai). With the "oni" (the dynamic paternal Spirit principle, the active principle of reflection) being once and for all excluded, and without the active presence of the emphatic sense of "I", the energy of the cultural soul could not invest itself in the "syntax" or logical constitution ("the spirit") of the substantial core of Japanese culture, bringing about a further development *of* this "syntax" in the course of history. It could only apply itself to the *external form* of the culture's semantic *contents*, continually making it and them more subtle, more refined, more exquisite (this is the traditional Japanese soul's particular *telos* and the task assigned to Japanese culture). *The whole depth of the soul went into the aesthetic form.* The particular representative works of certain types of art in Japan, bonsai, ikebana, some aspects of the typically Japanese garden, and in poetry haikus,[7] might even serve as direct visible/audible illustrations of their having Katako's suicide within themselves as their soul, the logical determinant of their beautiful form. Are they, psychologically seen, not perhaps the beautiful veil over the soul truth of "Katako" and the Japanese soul's ever new *cultic celebration* of this truth? Or: Are they not perhaps Katako's self-negation condensed and transfixed into

---

7 One could also think here of Zen kōans.

single objects, lasting sensually visible or audible realities to be deeply revered and meditated?

It is not enough to see that bonsai and the Japanese garden present a fundamentally *reflected* nature. Even more significant is that *reflection* itself is aestheticized. To be sure, nature is subdued to reflection, but reflection in turn is subdued to nature, disguised as *as-if natural*. It is forced to speak the language of nature. We see this most clearly by contrasting the Japanese garden with the French garden. In the latter, nature is not only subjected under reflection, but also to a reflection that speaks reflection's own (no longer natural, but abstract, intellectual) language, in this case the still rather primitive and simple language of geometry. Whereas the French garden in this way makes the blatant oppositional character of nature and spirit/reflection expressly visible, the Japanese garden naturalizes reflection so that the opposition is reduced to that kind of soft intranatural tension that is felt to be "beautiful" in the sense of Japanese aesthetics.

In the fundamental transition phase that is the particular soul truth depicted in the Katako fairy tale, that is, at that point in the soul's development when the double nature of humanness has become conscious and needs to be dealt with, a negation is unavoidable. In fact, this phase is nothing else but the entrance of the explicit awareness of the logical principle of negation into psychic life and the confrontation with its inescapability. Above, I pointed out that it is the oni half of Katako that by bringing him the consciousness of selfhood was as such also the basis for his ability to commit suicide. But now I have to add that it was exactly the ordinary human half of Katako, the half of him in whose favor he had rejected the oni father, that *executed* the suicide as his form of the negation. Suicide is a literalization of the negation, the physical acting-out of it, and what *is* negated by it is again the physical, bodily existence of Katako's whole being. This concretistic negation needs to be contrasted with a completely different possibility not chosen in our fairy tale: a negation in the sense of a conscious taking over into his own responsibility of the *internal* differentiation (*différance*, distancing, distension) into the two halves into which Katako has factually already been divided and along with it the (logical) downgrading of and pushing off from the ordinary human part and the (logical) rise to the higher spirit level. It is, of course, quite fitting that—in open contrast to the possibility of a rise to a higher logical level or status—the particular *form* of suicide chosen by Katako was to throw himself down from the tip of a high tree into the depths.

Just as our fairy tale ends with Katakos's suicide, which is the literalization of negation, but which, precisely in its painfulness, is at the same time felt by the Japanese reader as "beautiful", so we also find in numerous other Japanese fairy tales that they end *negatively* with a loss or the inexplicable disappearance of the beloved, that is, with a *semanticized* negation (or a semantic nothing, a semantic lack or emptiness), which again evokes the feeling of "beauty". It might be better than speaking of an "aesthetic *solution* of conflicts" to speak of the aestheticization of reflection and logical negation through their naturalization, literalization or semanticization. Nothing is solved. Reflection is simply *stillgestellt* (immobilized, frozen, so that logical *acts* now appear as semantic contents) and disappears in the narrated event of the loss, disappearance of the hero or heroine. This loss or disappearance creates a felt emptiness or nothingness that works dynamically like a "black hole" absorbing all feeling into its depth. And this absorption into the emptiness *is* precisely the aesthetic quality, the experience of "beauty".

By the same token, I mentioned before that the paradoxicality of humanness can be answered either dialectically or by aiming for a unilateral victory of the one father principle and the elimination or exclusion of the other, the paternal spirit principle altogether. Whereas Japan seems to have held on to the original unity of the whole by paying the price of undialectially negating the "oni" principle, the West, we might say, acknowledged the "oni father" to whom the soul's own process had transported it. It stayed, so to speak, on the "island of the oni"—and paid for it the price of the loss of, pictorially speaking, the higher numinous aura of the empirical father that is given with the original participation mystique, and of the loss of the primordial harmony of the whole, letting the empirical father return without son to the land of origin and stay there as a now completely "secularized" father, that is, as just another human being who merely once upon a time *used to* be one's father. This is the dialectical solution of the transition phase. There is no choice for the one and against the other, but the acknowledgment of the new psychological reality as the new truth *together with* the concomitant reduction of the original reality to one's old, former, i.e., now obsolete truth (but still a truth!) and thus to a *sublated moment* within the new. Sublated: Preserved and negated and superseded.

The search for an equivalent in the Japanese psyche to the Western ego

If, as I suggested, the fairy tale of Katako presents the internal logic of the communal structure of the Japanese psyche and if the logical "suicide" of the principle of selfhood is at the core of it, then this confirms the absence of the ego, more than that, the impossibility of the ego, in traditional Japan. Its becoming possible is deliberately prevented. Megumi Yama, while acknowledging the fact of the absence of the ego in the structure of the Japanese psyche, nevertheless advances the thesis that "the establishment of a subject in the Japanese psyche (has) evolved differently and (has) roots that go far back into a rich cultural history" (p. 68) and she speaks of "the Japanese ego", saying that "the Japanese ego tends to be an ego buried in 'the wholeness'" (p. 62). "I attempt to explore the way that the ego emerges in the Japanese psyche by returning to the narrative embedded in the oldest layer of Japanese culture . . ., in order to present another possible way that the ego may develop, different from its evolution in the West" (p. 53).

There are several problems with this thesis.

1. The ego in its strict psychological sense is, wherever it appears, always the same. There are not different types of ego. It can have different degrees or intensities of realization, but it is always based on the self-assertion of the individual, the latter's logically setting himself up as *the* center in contrast to the social whole. Just as in physics there is not a special "Japanese gravity", in mathematics not a "Japanese zero" different from a "Western one", so it does not make sense to introduce the idea of a "Japanese ego" in contradistinction to the "Western ego". "Western" in "Western ego" does not indicate a special variety, but merely the place where the ego happened to have first manifested itself in reality.

2. An ego *buried* in "the wholeness" is a contradiction in terms. If "it" is buried, it is not ego. Being buried would be the result of "Katako's suicide". The same applies to the idea of "subjects" when these subjects are said to be "part of an emerging whole" (p. 67). Then this whole is the real "subject".

3. Yama's discussion of the beginning of the *Kojiki* and especially of the word and notion of "*naru*" ("becoming") is very interesting and reveals something important and quite peculiar about the Japanese culture and mentality. The very slow progress during the age of the Gods over seven generations from the invisible, intangible, and abstract until at long last finally something visible, tangible, and concrete emerged is certainly impressive and quite particular. But although clearly based on real phenomenological evidence (on the *Kojiki* as a definite document of the soul), it is not relevant concerning the topic of the emergence of a Japanese "ego" or "subject". The *Kojiki* itself talks only of the First Parents Izanagi-no-kami (Man-Who-Invites-Deity) and Izanami-no-kami (Woman-Who-Invites-Deity) as the end product of this long line of

development and not of ego-consciousness or anything similar. The mere first emergence of something visible and concrete does not imply "ego" or "subject".

Besides, the appearance of "something" or "somebody" in a tale considered as a document of the soul, that is, a merely *semantic* appearance in it, would psychologically not suffice to imply the realization of "the ego", because, even if in the story this "something" or "somebody" were explicitly *called* "ego", it would, as something or somebody, still remain an object of consciousness, a third-person "It" or "He"/"She". It is essential to realize that it is inherent in the concept and special nature of the ego (the "I") that it can only manifest in a document of the soul on the syntactical level: Only if it is an *ego form or style of consciousness* in which the tale is told, or an *ego standpoint from which* what is narrated or reported is conceived. Because only then is "ego" present as what *per definitionem* it is: Subject and not only object *talked about*.

Moreover, it is obvious that the notion of an ego is downright incompatible with the idea that it "becomes", "emerges", or takes place spontaneously and naturally in the special Japanese sense of "becoming" (*naru*) that is characteristic of the mentioned process. An ego comes about only abruptly through its own active setting *itself* up, through this revolutionary, "impertinent" act. By contrast, what in the beginning of the *Kojiki* is described, from a psychological point of view, may indeed be, or may not be, the very first, most primitive manifestations of emerging consciousness. If this *Kojiki* creation story should be about the slow manifestation of consciousness it would nevertheless certainly not be the "emergence" of "ego consciousness in the Japanese psyche", as Yama suggests (so already the title of her paper). It would at most be comparable to how a vague consciousness very slowly develops initially in babies. It does not make any sense to claim that this story shows "another possible way that *the ego* may develop, different from *its* evolution in the West" (p. 53, my italics). There is not a hint of "the ego" in this story.

4. But Yama uses her terms relating to this question of ego indiscriminately. When she is talking about "the Japanese ego" she speaks of "the ego", "ego consciousness", and plain "consciousness" (e.g., "this gradual emergence of consciousness", p. 52, Abstract) without clear distinctions. That the Japanese have consciousness, that they "are capable of differentiation and decision making" (p. 68), that they can think and be inventive, that

among them certain individuals may have strong, impressive personalities, all that goes without saying. Nobody questioned that. But all this has nothing to do with "the ego" or a pronounced sense of "subject". Consciousness and the aptitude for speech (language) and a degree of intelligence are anthropological constants, inherent in the biological make-up of the human animal. Even higher animals have a limited consciousness. The strength or weakness of personality is likewise a *psychic* (largely biologically based) property of individual human beings. "The ego" in the pronounced psychological sense, by contrast, is an altogether different matter, a special product of culture, a late new acquisition in the long history of the soul.

5. When Yama states, as quoted, that the ego may develop differently "from its evolution in the West" and again that "ego consciousness and the establishment of a subject in the Japanese psyche have evolved differently and have roots that go far back into a rich cultural history" (p. 68) one gets the impression that the motivation behind such statements is the feeling that if "ego" and "subject" were missing from the Japanese psyche this would amount to a serious shortcoming, a deficiency, so that proof has to be supplied that the Japanese psyche does have an "ego" and "subject" after all, only one that is different in kind from "the Western ego", but equally dignified. But why, then, is there a Japanese "inclination to eschew standing out or taking an individual position", why is this way of relating even "built into the language itself", in which "the subject is often missing and rarely clarified in Japanese sentences", usually being "surmised from the relational context and surround" (p. 68)? Is this linguistic as well as behavioral evidence not the Japanese soul's real and spontaneous, unreflected self-expression and as such a telltale sign that it regards the subject as on principle negligible? Jung once stated, "We have simply got to listen to what the psyche spontaneously says to us" (*Letters 2*, p. 591, to Read, 2 September 1960). Not our claims and interpretations, not what names *we* give to phenomena, not what we want them to be, but what the phenomena themselves betray about themselves is what counts.

What would be important to know in this connection is whether in the cultural history of Japan "ego" (in its Japanese form), "subject", "subjectivity", and "the individual" were topics of serious interest and concern, i.e., were explicitly discussed. One would expect that if there is an ego in the (traditional) Japanese psyche, an explicit theory about it would necessarily have been developed and would have become a lively theme for discussion.

Did traditional Japan develop words, distinct concepts for these ideas that were of real cultural significance, did it produce explanatory theories about them? If so, it would be legitimate to speak of the Japanese ego. Yama's article does not include any information about these questions.

But they are crucial questions. For we are speaking here in the realm of psychology. Ego, subject, and individual are *psychological* realities, not *natural* facts like trees, rivers, the moon, the heart, or the brain. Natural facts, for example, bacteria and viruses, existed and did their thing even in prehistoric times when they were completely unknown. But psychological realities, like "ego" or "subject", do not exist without representation in language and cultural productions. They are created by the soul and come only into existence in and through language, thought, images. Such a thing as "melancholy", for example, is a cultural invention, not a fact of nature. It did not exist before it was, above all during the Renaissance, conceptually described and named and presented in imaginal or theoretical works. In high cultures, what is psychologically of importance becomes also an explicit topic for the great minds, and, conversely, new psychological possibilities that made their first appearance in (we could even say: Were first "invented" by) philosophers, poets, and artists, slowly, over decades or centuries, sink imperceptibly down into the psyche of ordinary people as their *then* real attitudes, feelings, self-understanding, and style of world relation.

Thus, if it should turn out that there are no concepts of cultural significance for "the Japanese ego", for "subject" and "the individual", this might well indicate that such a thing as "the Japanese ego" (by which we mean something that is fundamentally *more than* the ordinary psychic capability of people to refer to themselves as "I") did not have enough weight and importance to express itself and thus to come into actual psychological existence. The Western ego, at any rate, did not only show itself in the practice of people's behavior, in their outlook and inner self-definition as well as objectively in the whole scientific and intellectual relation to the world, but also explicitly in numerous works by thinkers devoted to the concept of it, to its foundation and logical justification, its capacity as well as limitation. These works are themselves "documents of the soul" showing that the ego was and is very much alive in the Western soul (although now its high time seems to be already over).

Could it be that the labored and not really convincing attempt to prove that there was a special "Japanese ego" is motivated by an unconscious dominance over the author's consciousness of the form of the Western psyche, just as in the discussed diagram of the structure of the Japanese psyche the basic structure of the Western psyche was taken as standard model merely in need of minor retouching to also fit to the Japanese psyche? If so, it would not only prevent one's clearly and in bold outline seeing the real difference between both forms of cultural psyche, but also damage the insight that the form of the traditional Japanese mode of being-in-the-world is psychologically *perfect in itself* the way it is, even, nay precisely, without ego.

Just for the record: Observations about "Eranos"[1]

In response to Christa Robinson's paper in *Spring*, vol. 86

In Christa Robinson's report the impression is created that "Eranos" ("Eranos conferences in Ascona") refers to one and the same continuous reality.[2] But the word "Eranos" is an equivocation for three distinct realities. What we normally mean in Jungian circles when speaking of Eranos is

• the original Eranos, that Eranos tradition inspired by Rudolf Otto and molded, in psychological regards, above all by C.G. Jung, Erich Neumann, and James Hillman, and in other regards by numerous other scholars: Mircea Eliade, Karl Kerényi, Henry Corbin, Gilbert Durand, David Miller, and Erik Hornung, to mention only a very few.

This Eranos was ended by Rudolf Ritsema in 1988. It was a brutal ending.

What came after this rupture, but was still *called* Eranos, was something different and new, and, most importantly, it appeared as *two* separate inimical offshoots:

• on the one hand the Eranos Conferences ("Amici di Eranos") organized first by Erik Hornung and Tilo Schabert, later ("Verein zur Förderung der wissenschaftlichen Tagungen von ERANOS") by Erik Hornung and Andreas Schweizer, a project that tries to keep alive, in slightly altered form, the high tradition of the original Eranos while being deprived of the original Eranos locality (including the famous "Round Table"); and

---

1 Written in 2011.
2 All references to Robinson in the Appendix come from the following publication: Christa Robinson, "Eranos: A Place, an Encounter, a Story", *Spring* 86 (2011): 165–182.

- on the other hand that Eranos that still took place on the original Eranos location but was turned into events circling around Rudolf Ritsema's personal pet project, the *I Ching*.

So there are three Eranos, not one. And when the Editor's note to her article introduces Christa Robinson as a "former President of the Eranos Foundation", one has to know that this has nothing to do with the original Eranos, but refers only to the third-mentioned Eranos, the "I Ching Eranos" (as we might call it) *after* the fundamental break with the old Eranos tradition. Robinson herself hides from the reader the fact that this break gave rise to *two* secondary Eranos.

To make Ritsema's killing blow to the old Eranos more palatable, Robinson fabricates legends. She says that it was in 1987, i.e., one year ahead of the last traditional conference, that he announced his intention to end the Eranos Conferences. But what incensed everybody so much was that he announced it only at the very end of the last (1988) conference. This made it so brutal. It may of course be that he had announced it in 1987 to his wife or to Christa Robinson and two or three others. But for the speakers and the audience this announcement came in 1988 as an absolute surprise and shock. It was as if in the final ceremony of some Olympic Games the president of the Olympic Games committee announced, "Oh, by the way, these were the last Games".

To end the Eranos Conferences had been Ritsema's solitary decision and been his absolute secret. Robinson reports that he "consulted the *I Ching*" (!) (p. 178), when he should have consulted all those people who for many years had during the greater part of each year invested much of their research, thought, and enthusiasm in the preparation of their lectures, and for whom the ten days at Eranos each year were really dear to their heart. All this, and, on top of it, the fact that Eranos was supposed to be ended for no other purpose than that it could be utilized for Ritsema's personal project, "let loose", as Robinson puts it, "storms of fury" (p. 178). But they were perfectly in place. Even if there may have been an excess of fury or a "betrayal" in the case of the one or the other of those who fought his decision (about which I have no knowledge), we must not forget that, if it indeed occurred, it was a reaction secondary to Ritsema's initial betrayal of the Eranos tradition.

Another part of Robinson's report that must be relegated to the realm of legends is the intimation that during the last years of the original Eranos the conferences had degenerated. Her first point in that vein, though, can hardly be evaluated as addressing a degeneration: The lectures, she says, "became increasingly intellectual" (p. 176). First of all, what would be wrong with that? That was what the speakers, after all *scholars*, were invited for. And secondly, why "increasingly"? Had Jung's, Martin Buber's, Max Knoll's, Hugo Rahner's, Max Pulver's, Shmuel Sambursky's, Gershom Scholem's lectures been any less intellectual? And was there an inappropriate intellectuality in the later lectures, those of James Hillman, Ulrich Mann, Erik Hornung, David Miller, to name only them? And finally, even if Ritsema had felt that the lectures were becoming too intellectual, he could have invited other speakers, since he alone made the decision about who was invited or not invited.

Her next point is a corruption: "For some participants, a tendency grew to market the event and to exploit it for personal gain" (p. 177). I ask, what possible personal gain can be gotten from being a participant at Eranos? Of course, Robinson claims that

> By this time, to present a lecture at Eranos held a reward of enviable status, and sometimes even a salary increase at home. Yet Olga herself had attracted distinguished scholars to Eranos with little more tha[n] the offer of room, board, and rich conversation. As the desire for prestige gained ground, her founding values began, it seemed to me, to slip into the background.
>
> (p. 177)

I find this slanderous and absurd. First, she herself quotes from an article by a well-known philosophy professor about Eranos in which Eranos is denounced as "a strange bastard [arising from the parentage of] science, culture, and life help" (p. 178). This is representative of what in wide circles of the academe was thought about Eranos, if note was taken of it at all. Prestige? A reward of enviable status? Ridiculous. And as to salary increases, James Hillman and I as analysts were not salaried in the first place. Ulrich Mann, A. Hilary Armstrong, and probably a number of the later speakers were emeriti professors. Did David Miller, Jean Brun, Erik Hornung, Herbert Pietschmann, Jean Servier, Hayao Kawai, etc., depend on Eranos for a salary increase? Did all these people have a need to *market* the event? Were they not all well-known enough and much sought-after speakers? Did they *exploit* Eranos for personal gain, put personal prestige above the founding values of Eranos? All this is a preposterous insinuation. But even if it had been so, it had been Ritsema himself who selected the speakers. Furthermore, were these participants of the later conferences not, exactly as the ones at Olga's time, "distinguished scholars" to whom "little more that [sic!]" "room, board, and rich conversation" were offered (p. 177)?

Now, concerning these rich discussions about the conference topics "at Olga's old round table" (p. 176), Robinson is right to state that they became less frequent, which was deplorable. But Robinson forgets to mention why this was so, why it had to be so. It was not the participants' fault. Such conversations were (I don't know if intentionally, but certainly) systematically made impossible by Mrs. Ritsema, who *insisted* (1) on herself assigning everybody a specific place for each meal, with the effect that two or three speakers who happened to have been in an engaged conversation were separated and hindered from continuing it at the table "while the iron was hot". And (2) she insisted on always alternating a speaker and a spouse (of another speaker) at the table, which meant that each speaker had spouses as neighbors on either side and usually had to engage in polite small talk with them because with a few remarkable exceptions they were not interested in pursuing an intellectual discussion arising from the impulses which were generated by the lectures. Everyone would have been happy if Mrs. Ritsema would have given up her rigid regime and allowed a free flow of conversation among the speakers.

All those things mentioned by Robinson cannot serve as an excuse or justification for Ritsema's suddenly breaking off the old Eranos tradition, nor do they support Robinson's mystifying interpretation in terms of a "Hestian pathology" (p. 177) and "Hestian energies" (p. 178). Especially the cryptically hinted-at problems that emerged later during her own time, but also the decision of 1988, were due to very human, all-too-human traits and passions, at least in part to too much ego. It is *people* who have to accept responsibility for them. Responsibility cannot be shifted away from the human persons involved onto anonymous powers, archetypal "energies".

One real reason for the necessity of the end of Eranos seems to have been the financial situation. But this was also no excuse for discontinuing the old Eranos tradition. The tight financial situation had been known for some time, and a number of solutions had been at hand, a fact about which Robinson keeps silent. For example, our Jungian colleague, Robert Bosnak, who had known the Ritsemas on a personal friendly basis for a long time and was a native Dutchman like Rudolf Ritsema himself, had offered to organize the necessary funds (they were available!). He was also ready to take over Ritsema's place when it would become time for the latter to retire. Bosnak would have been an excellent head of Eranos. There had also been other concrete options. But Ritsema refused them all, preferring, with his eyes wide open, rather to let the old Eranos slowly run into the ground than to give up his sole control. Considering what he afterwards did with the rump-Eranos, namely, let it center around his hobby-horse, one may even wonder whether he had not been looking forward all along to the demise of the real Eranos.

Index

absolute negativity 6, 23, 24, 27, 31, 58, 62, 89, 91, 96, 97, 155
absolute-negative interiorization 63, 64, 68, 81, 86, 99, 129, 161; of a given phenomenon into itself 85, 86
Adler, Alfred 4
Alberti, Leon Battista 114
Albertus Magnus 65
alchemy: explicitly negates image ("the stone that is *not* a stone") 96; its inner logic is beyond the imaginal. It is conceptual 94
alterity, literal, unassimilable 150, 158, 159, 184, 190, 191, 193–195, 198, 199; *see also* Other, the, *also* otherness
"angels in words" 40, 42
anima alba 60, 62, 97, 180
Annunciation to Virgin Mary 42
anxiety 106–110, 112, 125, 128; as explicit *archê* and principle of a psychologist's writing 106; leads to ego-centeredness 110; possibility of overcoming one's anxiety not seen 107; to stay with the anxiety is seen as an ethical obligation 110
apocalyptic threat: to give urgency to the call for repentance 123
Apollo 59, 60; Delphic Apollo 68; was still ignorant of "the logical", still in the *anima alba* 60

archetypes: as forms, types vs. as ever-present agents, "factors" 28; "the tyranny of unconscious presuppositions" not caused by archetypes 30; theory of, incompatible with Jung's awareness of *Geistigkeit* 28
Aristotle 185
ashes, *caput mortuum* 57, 64, 65, 67, 82–85, 87, 95
assimilation to consciousness: does not mean dissolution, disappearance of what is assimilated 55; means our initiation into, and being taught by, the phenomenon 56
aurum nostrum vs. *aurum vulgi* 72, 79, 94, 129, 156
authorship, question of 44
Axis Mundi 127

Barcellos, Gustavo 32
Beaudelaire, Charles 169
"behind the impressions of the daily life another picture looms up" 127, 129, 157, 158
"Beware of the physical in the matter" 43, 79, 162
birth of man, born man 164, 165, 168, 170, 171, 174, 181, 182, 183
black sun, image of the 54–71, 87, 97–101, 103; appears to a consciousness that is still in the status

linear upwards movement vs. a metamorphosis of truth 163; a linear irreversible development, but not one
from pre-truth to final truth 168
logic: modern, of the "unbridgeable difference" 90, 115, 116, 159, 164, 168
"logical light", Marlan's idea of 69, 70,
87, 100; lies outside the horizon of
the black sun image 59
logical, the sphere of the: comes into
being through the demise of the my-
thol./imaginal mode 58; is the real
dark seeing as deconstruction of the
imaginal mode 69; seen by Marlan
as the poisonous state of splendid
solar isolation 68
Luhmann, Niklas 180, 182
Luther, Martin: *sunt duo toti homines*
227

Mann, Ulrich 244
Marlan, Stan 52–96, 98–104; challenge
to his theoretical stance interpreted
by him as one to his narcissism 71;
cites "light of darkness itself" but
neglects to *see* in this light 98; ego
sentiments substituted for the actually demanded psychological "going
under" 71; ends up with an unassimilable enigma or abstract "wonder"
98; fails to painstakingly try to *think*
Hegel's thought 73; has not *entered*
psychology in Jung's understanding
75; his euthanized dog Curtis 67,
70, 71, 73, 79; insists as psychologist on this commonsensical reality
79; no concern for the needs of
psychology as a discipline in its
own right 81; predilection for ashes
and the *caput mortuum* 67, 82, 85;
professes his resistance to thought,
is sold on the imaginal mode 92;
religious ardor of his speaking 102;
"there always remains a dark remnant in the retort ..." 82

meaning *see also* synchronicity: objective meaning structure vs. providing
Meaning to us 8
mediation: through ontic intermediate
realm or through *performance* of
mediation 16
Meister Eckhart 185
Melanchthon, Philipp 38
Mersenne, Marin 38
metaphysics 120; conclusion of Western metaphysics 121, 164
method, methodological 38, 53, 64, 65,
71, 72, 76, 78, 80, 82, 98–100, 102,
124, 129, 153, 156, 167, 178, 189,
194, 204, 207, 208, 220
Miller, David L. 14, 242, 244
mirror: speculative mirrors show the
true Other 65
Mogenson, Greg 14, 37, 68, 70, 103
moralism 122, 125
music, piece of: needs re-creative hearing to *become* a work of art 21
mysterium coniunctionis 16, 89, 95
myth 190; central to historical psychology 171; Jung's idea of the personal
myth 195; meaning fiction since
Greek Enlightenment 176; "the
myth of the fall, whereby a paradisal
world ... is somehow lost" 169; term
"myth" is equivocally used 171; the
appearance of the truth, not a moment on the long way to truth 163;
the *illud tempus* of myth, ever-present
eternity 183, 187; undisrupted continuity of myth or its obsolescence
173
mythology: innocence vis-à-vis "the
logical" 60

narrative mode of presentation: makes
the *moments* of one soul truth appear as separate people or event 223
"Nature rejoices in nature. Nature
subdues nature..." 118
natural world: as *explicatio dei* 115

For Product Safety Concerns and Information please contact our EU
representative GPSR@taylorandfrancis.com
Taylor & Francis Verlag GmbH, Kaufingerstraße 24, 80331 München, Germany

www.ingramcontent.com/pod-product-compliance
Lightning Source LLC
Chambersburg PA
CBHW050345270326
41926CB00016B/3605